Ellen Redling,
Christian Schneider (Eds.)

Gothic Transgressions

Gothic Transgressions

Extension and Commercialization
of a Cultural Mode

edited by

Ellen Redling and Christian Schneider

LIT

Cover image: © Corinna Assmann

This book is printed on acid-free paper.

Bibliographic information published by the Deutsche Nationalbibliothek
The Deutsche Nationalbibliothek lists this publication in the Deutsche
Nationalbibliografie; detailed bibliographic data are available in the Internet at
http://dnb.d-nb.de.

ISBN 978-3-643-90364-8

A catalogue record for this book is available from the British Library

© LIT VERLAG GmbH & Co. KG Wien,
Zweigniederlassung Zürich 2015
Klosbachstr. 107
CH-8032 Zürich
Tel. +41 (0) 44-251 75 05   Fax +41 (0) 44-251 75 06
E-Mail: zuerich@lit-verlag.ch   http://www.lit-verlag.ch
Distribution:
In the UK: Global Book Marketing, e-mail: mo@centralbooks.com
In North America: International Specialized Book Services, e-mail: orders@isbs.com
In Germany: LIT Verlag Fresnostr. 2, D-48159 Münster
Tel. +49 (0) 2 51-620 32 22, Fax +49 (0) 2 51-922 60 99, E-mail: vertrieb@lit-verlag.de
In Austria: Medienlogistik Pichler-ÖBZ, e-mail: mlo@medien-logistik.at
e-books are available at www.litwebshop.de

Acknowledgements

We would first of all like to thank the International Gothic Association (IGA) for putting their trust in us and letting us convene and develop a theme for the 2011 IGA Conference *Gothic Limits / Gothic Ltd* at the English Department of the University of Heidelberg in Germany, which brought together almost two hundred scholars from around the world. This conference inspired fascinating discussions on the transgressive nature and current commercialization of the Gothic, which in turn gave rise to this present collection of articles on *Gothic Transgressions*. We would very much like to use this opportunity to thank all of the contributors to this volume. Many thanks are also due to Prof. Peter Paul Schnierer, Dr Oliver Plaschka and Dr Andreas Schardt, who convened and coordinated the conference together with us, and to Lisa Haubeck, Eva Leschinski, Julia Peter, Nadja Rehberger as well as Kathrin Pfister and the many other helpers and colleagues whose support proved to be invaluable at this huge event. Finally, we would particularly like to thank Corinna Assmann, who drew the cover image of this volume, and Jan Bauer, Dr Plaschka, Dr Schardt as well as Adriana Lopez, Tim Sommer and Katja Utz for their much appreciated help in proof-reading and formatting this collection of articles.

Ellen Redling and Christian Schneider

Contents

Part III: Intermodal Gothic: Sinister Idylls

Part IV: Intermedial Gothic: Woodcuts, Comics and Films

Part V: Gothic Ltd: The Current Commercialization of the Gothic

Ellen Redling and Christian Schneider

Introduction: Gothic Limits / Gothic Ltd

The Gothic is transgressive in seemingly endless ways – not only in terms of its contents, forms, aesthetics or effects, but also regarding the very boundaries of the phenomenon itself. As David Punter points out, "in studying Gothic fiction almost nothing can be assumed, not even the limits of the field" (*Literature of Terror* 20). When does the Gothic begin or – potentially – end? Is it a genre or a mode? Does it originally 'belong' to a certain medium and national context? Is it literary or cultural? Is it traditional or commercial? Time and experience have shown the Gothic to be an enormously adaptable concept, but this also means it is a very "slippery phenomenon" (Wellington 171), begging the question: if there are no boundaries, how is one able to use the term 'Gothic' at all? The difficulty in defining or delimiting the limitless Gothic was the key theme of the 2011 International Gothic Association conference on 'Gothic Limits / Gothic Ltd' in Heidelberg, Germany, which we organized and at which nearly two hundred international scholars gathered. This conference in turn gave rise to the articles presented in this volume, which discuss a variety of aspects regarding the both widespread and diverse extension of the Gothic and its current commercialization.

The Gothic is frequently said to begin in the year 1764 – with the publication of Horace Walpole's hugely popular novel *The Castle of Otranto* in England. Other crucial Gothic works of this era include the novels by Ann Radcliffe as well as Matthew Lewis' *The Monk* and Charles Maturin's *Melmoth the Wanderer*. As Fred Botting writes, eighteenth-century Gothic typically features: "Spectres, monsters, demons, corpses, skeletons, evil aristocrats, monks and nuns, fainting heroines and bandits" (*Gothic* 2), and the action takes place in haunted castles, dark monasteries or labyrinthine vaults. Form and structure of these novels fit the contents in that they are often themselves labyrinthine and "[t]orturous, fragmented" (Botting, *Gothic* 2). Excesses of this kind may not necessarily impress twenty-first-century readers accustomed to post-modern fragmentation and all sorts of horrors presented on TV, in movies and computer games, but at the time they had the ability to evoke fear. This was because they transgressed Enlightenment and neoclassical notions of the primacy of reason, simplicity, realism, probability, clarity, symmetry and of a unifying meaning (Botting, *Gothic* 3). They thus brought with them scary visions that potentially shook up any belief in certainty and security.

The very term 'Gothic' is crucial in this respect since it signals a connection of the eighteenth-century phenomenon that deals with transgressions of e.g. aesthetic, social and political boundaries to the freedom-loving Goths of the Middle Ages – a time which was often disparagingly referred to as the 'Dark Ages' by Enlightenment thinkers. 'Gothic' thus suggests that there is something past, primal or even atavistic about the fears it evokes – a notion which opposed eighteenth-century and, even more so, nineteenth-century ideas of constant evolution and progress. Through its link to the eponymous 'Northern' medieval tribes, the Gothic referred to a "«Northern» tradition that runs counter to the neo-classical «Southern» tradition that was so prominent in the art forms of the eighteenth century, and since the Renaissance [...] has represented a conventional way of legitimating specific literary, architectural and artistic traditions" (Martin 196). The evocation of a dark, medieval past is also important in that the Gothic tradition is not only indebted to the eighteenth-century development of the genre of the novel, but also to medieval romance and its supernatural occurrences.[1]

At the same time, however, nineteenth-century Gothic often incorporates advanced scientific technology and thereby reaches out to the future. For instance, Mary Shelley's *Frankenstein* from 1818 has become a classic example of questioning what humans may be able to achieve and what harm they can do in the face of ground-breaking scientific developments. The novel thereby also discusses the notion of a monster located *within* the self, not just without. Other novelties also influenced and transformed the Gothic. For instance, the rapid growth of the cities during the Victorian age inspired many writers to change the typical Gothic scenery of haunted castles and abbeys to that of a scary and dark metropolis,

---

[1] Victor Sage writes regarding the Gothic novels: "Set in the medieval past, such novels were thought of at the time as subversive or childish 'romances', according to one's point of view, and they inserted themselves, at the extreme end, into the critical debate between Novel and Romance which ran from the mid eighteenth-century to well on in the nineteenth century" ("Gothic Novel" 83).

thereby creating the so-called 'Modern Gothic'.[2] This can, for example, be seen in the late Victorian work *Dracula* by Bram Stoker, which famously depicts a frantic search for the vampire Count Dracula in London and thus combines primal, mythical fears with modern ones. The 'Modern Gothic' can also be perceived in *The Strange Tale of Dr Jekyll and Mr Hyde* by Robert Louis Stevenson, which at the time directly reflected anxieties caused by the actual unidentified serial killer Jack the Ripper, who brutally murdered at least five people in and around the Whitechapel district of London in 1888. The 'Modern Gothic' implies that gruesome happenings 'now' lurk right around the corner – not just in some faraway place. Furthermore, sexual and queer readings of Stoker's and Stevenson's works suggest that the 'Modern Gothic' also transgresses Victorian domestic and sexual norms of propriety and 'straightness'. The Gothic therefore further and further invades the most private locations and innermost feelings of the human being.

The Gothic is thus enormously flexible and adaptable to a large variety of contexts: it looks to the past, present and future as well as into the distance and proximity, which enables it to transcend boundaries of time and space. In fact, the Gothic was by no means limited to England or the British Isles, but soon became a wider phenomenon – with Gothic works being written e.g. in France, Germany and the United States by authors such as the Vicomte d'Arlincourt, E. T. A. Hoffmann and Edgar Allan Poe. Neither was the Gothic ever completely tied down to a specific genre. Already in the eighteenth century Horace Walpole and Matthew Lewis wrote not only Gothic novels but also Gothic plays. The Gothic presented itself as landscape gardening as well as in the form of architecture during the various phases of the Gothic revival from approximately the 1750s onwards (Sage, "Gothic Revival" 90-103), and the German artist Caspar David Friedrich, who lived at the end of the eighteenth and beginning of the nineteenth century, portrayed Gothic scenes in his famous paintings. Furthermore, the Gothic was not always out to shock; through extreme exaggerations it could also provoke "ridicule and laughter" (Botting, *Gothic* 9). One can conclude from this

---

[2] Confer Dryden's work on the 'Modern Gothic'. See also Botting: "In the eighteenth century [the Gothic landscapes] were wild and mountainous locations. Later the modern city combined the natural and architectural components of Gothic grandeur and wildness, its dark, labyrinthine streets suggesting the violence and menace of Gothic castle and forest" (*Gothic* 2).

that the Gothic is also able to combine different modes – e.g. the 'serious' dark one with grotesque or comical ones.

These border crossings suggest that both the existence and appeal of Gothic works go beyond any boundaries pertaining to time, nation, genre, medium or mode. On the other hand, the *rise* of the Gothic is closely linked to (Dark) Romanticism (Martin 196), which featured prominently in the arts and cultures of the countries mentioned above. In a similar vein, references to new developments in science and figures like Jack the Ripper make clear that anxieties raised by the Gothic are only in part timeless and imaginary; they can also be regarded as topical reactions to actual fears – be they religious, scientific, social, economic, domestic or sexual. While long-standing religious traditions were of course not suddenly extinguished, the increasing secularization during the eighteenth century led to a situation of both freedom and crisis. The individual being, whose sense of self had been cultivated by many thinkers since the late Middle Ages and Early Modernism,[3] now frequently found himself or herself lacking any fixed theological framework. On the one hand, this meant the possibility of an increase in individual freedom. On the other hand, this development could imply a sense of loss. The individual is all alone in the world, with nothing else to fall back upon but himself or herself.

Both notions – freedom and fear of loss – can be found in nineteenth-century Gothic, especially so in the works by Lord Byron. He created the dark, solitary and defiant figure of the Byronic hero (Gray 49). But he also evoked a dissolution of individualism in his famous poem "Darkness" from 1816, in which the anonymous last men on earth face the complete extinction of the earth and humankind.[4] One could say that Byron employed methods of both terror, which entails the idea of an "expansion of one's sense of self" (Botting, *Gothic* 10), and horror, which "describes the movement of contraction and recoil" (Botting, *Gothic* 10). On the whole, however, it is traditionally the freedom-seeking individual rather than an unidentified mass of people that is foregrounded in the Gothic – since this is a figure who radically

---

[3] For a general overview of the rise of modern autonomous individualism, see for instance van Dülmen or Waage.

[4] Confer Eva Horn's observation that "Darkness" is a poem 'without a tragic hero' (63).

transgresses social, moral, domestic and sexual norms and who therefore suited the times of the fights for *liberté* during the French Revolution, when the Gothic novel reached its heyday.[5]

Secularization was helped along by growing scientific research and the concomitant increase in the belief that a human being is part of nature and of a natural process of growth and decay, rather than part of a larger religious plan that includes either eternal salvation or damnation. In eighteenth and early nineteenth-century Gothic, nature played an enormous role and in part took the place of traditional religion. Especially the concept of looking at a sublime nature – that is scenes of nature that evoke both awe and terror – became a type of substitute for an ecstatic religious experience of God's grandeur.[6] One prominent example of the use of the sublime in Gothic literature are the scenes that depict Frankenstein's monster in the Alps and in the Arctic in Mary Shelley's *Frankenstein*. A magnificent spectacle such as the Alps often evoked wonder and fear in an eighteenth- and early nineteenth-century reader, especially so since at the time "climbing the Alps was a largely imaginary enterprise" (Chandler 74).

The natural world of the eighteenth and nineteenth centuries also offered its share of *sudden* fearful happenings. The terrible 1755 Lisbon earthquake, which of all days happened on the 1st of November, All Saints' Day, and killed many people while they were attending church services, appeared to cancel out any belief in either God as such or in a

---

[5] As Victor Sage writes, "the Marquis de Sade['s] […] judgement in 1800 that these [Gothic] novels were 'the necessary fruits of the revolutionary tremors felt by the whole of Europe' has proved highly influential in later critical debate, marking a tradition of linking the Gothic novel with the French Revolution" (83).

[6] In his famous *Philosophical Enquiry into the Origin of our Ideas of the Sublime and Beautiful* from 1757 Edmund Burke describes the feeling of the sublime as a sensation of both "terror" and "curiosity" (191) in the face of something of "terrific grandeur" that takes you on the "pathway between Time and Eternity" (190). This is a feeling which no rational explanation, no book or "school-master" (192) can completely evoke or clarify. His work was to some extent indebted to a long tradition dating back to Lucretius and Longinus, but on the other hand a novelty in that it focused much more extensively than its precursors on the feelings of the viewer of a sublime spectacle. This emotional theory thus provided a fertile ground for the growth of the emotional or even sensational Gothic.

well-meaning God. It promoted both Voltaire's ideas of scepticism and Immanuel Kant's work on the sublime. Similarly, the eruption of the volcano Tambora on the island of Sumbawa in what was then the Dutch East Indies (now Indonesia) in April 1815, which due to its large emission of ashes caused a dark summer all over Europe in 1816 and led to Byron's writing of his poem "Darkness", seemed to give a foretaste of the end of the world (Horn 73). Other apocalyptic scenarios were created by Thomas Malthus, who in his *Essay on the Principle of Population* from 1798 predicted that due to rising population numbers as well as insufficient crop yields, there would soon be a severe food shortage and an increase in child mortality and epidemics (14).

Added to these anxieties surrounding nature and its resources were other social and economic fears: the excesses of terror in the wake of the French Revolution revealed the dark side of the idealistic dreams of freedom. The aftermath of the Napoleonic Wars left many people impoverished and looking for work; rapidly growing numbers of poor people were flooding into the European cities, hoping for a better life but, more often than not, being confronted with even greater squalor there (Horn 60).

Topical issues were also reflected in the so-called *fin de siècle* Gothic, i.e. the Gothic of the end of the nineteenth century, represented by works such as *Dr Jekyll and Mr Hyde*, *Dracula*, Oscar Wilde's *The Picture of Dorian Gray* and H. G. Wells' *The Time Machine*. These works evoked:

> [S]omatic fears, anxieties over Empire and the purity of identity, phobias occasioned by perceived decadence, feminization, homosexuality, the threat of empire's others, and the widespread sense of social and cultural degeneration, given pseudo-scientific valorization in the works of eugenicists and anthropologists such as Cesare Lombroso and Max Nordau. (Wolfreys 103)

Twentieth-century Gothic continued some of the tendencies of the nineteenth century, but also intensified them and created new approaches. For instance, due to the discoveries of Sigmund Freud regarding the unconscious, there was a significant increase in psychological Gothic, as evidenced by the disturbed mental states of the protagonists in H. P. Lovecraft's "The Outsider" and Kafka's *The Trial*. The Gothic more and more featured a variety of marginalized individuals such as women, homosexuals and subjects of empire. It spread to new media, and, from the 1970s onwards, it became increasingly commercialized.

This commercialization does not merely imply a general over-use of the term 'Gothic', due to which it may have become emptied of its meaning altogether (see e.g. Lévy; Warwick; Jones). It rather signifies that the Gothic may lose its bite – so to speak – as evil monsters like Lovecraft's Cthulhu are turned into cuddly toys and blood-thirsty vampires become controlled, vegan teenaged versions of themselves in films and TV series. Thereby the Gothic's "darkness dragged into the light" (Botting, *Gothic Romanced* 14) is transformed into what Fred Botting has alternately described as "Candygothic" ("Candygothic" 133), "Aftergothic" ("Aftergothic" 277) or "Disneygothic" (*Limits* 3). He expounds that the Gothic, which has always been a populist form, in recent decades may have become "a matter of lifestyle, consumer choice or personal taste, […] one genre among many, normalised, commodified, with a hint of the delicatessen about its taste for blood, the macabre lifted by camp flavourings" (*Limits* 40).

'Candygothic' also signals a certain reassuring conservatism, which harks back to the "conservatism and moral violence of earlier traditional gothic fictions" (Botting, *Candygothic* 136), such as those written by Ann Radcliffe. This seeming assimilation and delimitation of the Gothic to mainstream consumerist culture begs the question of where the transgressive aspects of commercialized Gothic may lie – if they exist at all – and how the Gothic will continue in days to come. Another question may be: if the future Gothic still seeks to be transgressive and scary, how can the growing "demand for more thrilling horrors" (Botting, *Candygothic* 135) be met in a time when it arguably becomes increasingly difficult to shock readers and viewers?

The articles in this volume explore these and other issues concerning the various border crossings of the Gothic which still need to be analysed in further detail. In doing so, they examine what it may be that makes the Gothic 'Gothic'. Depending on the context, this problem of defining the concept can take on very different forms. For instance, the question may be: "Can there be Gothic before the Gothic?" This is the main concern underlying the contributions in the first section of the book, which is entitled "Proto-Gothic". It aims to identify the Gothic mode in texts published before the rise of the Gothic novel in the mid- and late 1700s.

While this approach may seem paradoxical at first glance, it is perhaps
fitting that the transgressive Gothic mode even transgresses its own
inception. Following Borges' *dictum* that "every writer *creates* his own
precursors" (201; emphasis in the original), the articles in this section
trace motifs, themes and settings that are best described *post hoc* as
Gothic or Proto-Gothic.

One literary period that can arguably be viewed through such a Gothic
lens is the English Renaissance, particularly Elizabethan and Jacobean
drama. This is not only because of the use of supernatural elements such
as ghosts in these plays, some of which can already be traced back to
Seneca's tragedies. It is rather most probably due to the fact that such
Renaissance dramas combine dark elements with concepts that paved the
way for modern autonomous individualism as well as modern notions of
liberty vs. tyranny, which – as was discussed above – can be regarded as
crucial features of the Gothic. Two recent volumes of essays are devoted
to connections between Shakespeare and the Gothic: *Gothic Shakespeares*, edited by John Drakakis and Dale Townshend, and *Shakespearean Gothic*, edited by Christy Desmet and Anne Williams. These
volumes examine traces of Shakespeare's oeuvre in Gothic works and
include Gothic analyses of Shakespearean drama.

Jeaneen Kish's "Pre-Gothic Goths: Shakespeare's Usage of the Goths as
Gothic Monsters in *Titus Andronicus*" not only explores this direction
even further, but also takes the word 'Gothic' back to its roots, as she
analyses the portrayal of the Goths in Shakespeare's perhaps most violent
play. As Kish shows, the brutal disruption which *Titus Andronicus*
ascribes to the Goths invading Rome reflects contemporary anxieties
about religious strife and the perceived threat of Catholicism in
Elizabethan England, which is similar to the anti-Catholicism of later
Gothic novels. At the same time, the distinctions between English
Protestantism and 'foreign' Catholicism are blurred. Thus, Kish
maintains, what makes a Gothic reading of the English Renaissance so
rewarding is that its drama fictionalizes existing socio-political anxieties
about broken boundaries and doubtful delimitations. Fred Botting aptly
argues that "[u]ncertainties about the nature of power, law, society,
family and sexuality dominate Gothic fiction" (*Gothic* 5) – and the same
can be said for the majority of Elizabethan and Jacobean plays.

These notions of uncertainty are also central to Susanne Gruss' article
"Jacobean Gothic and the Law: Revengers and Ineffectual Rulers on the

Early Modern Stage", which similarly discusses the violent excesses of Renaissance revenge tragedy as manifestations of the Gothic mode. Gruss focuses on what she terms 'Jacobean Gothic', as the transgressive horror of Jacobean plays has obvious parallels to Gothic texts. However, she identifies a shared preoccupation with the law as an even more relevant connection between early modern drama and the Gothic. Gruss reads the excessive violence and sexuality of John Marston's *Antonio's Revenge* and Philip Massinger's *The Duke of Milan* as a Gothic examination of the absence and breakdown of the law. In these plays, the tyrannical ruler figures as well as the avenging vigilantes taking justice into their own hands personify a both social and individual transgression of the law.

However, while Renaissance drama may have offered specifically brutal excesses that can be interpreted as Gothic, other historical and literary periods also brought forth texts which express their respective anxieties about specific limitations and transgressions. Kerstin Frank's article "'[Y]ou must see the Sun through the Cloud, and relish Light by the help of Darkness': Morality, Rationality, and the Proto-Gothic Atmosphere in Daniel Defoe's *An Essay on the History and Reality of Apparitions*" analyses how even the late seventeenth and early eighteenth centuries, often considered to constitute the Age of Enlightenment, spawned an entire tradition of texts that can be read as being part of the Gothic mode – the apparition narrative. Providing an overview of the genre's history and development, which is centred on supernatural apparitions of various kinds, Frank particularly concentrates on the ways in which Defoe takes up the conventions of earlier apparition narratives, but suffuses them with rational empiricism and satirical subversion. As Frank suggests, the moral and generic ambiguity created through this suffusion anticipates the structural uncertainties and ambivalent morality of later Gothic texts.

Historical delimitations are only one kind of border disrupted by the Gothic; less controversially and more commonly, the mode transgresses the generic and national borders that seem to define the concept. The second section, "Gothic Adventures: Thematic Experiments", details two of these boundary crossings. Firstly, as an encompassing mode, the Gothic is not limited to horror literature of any specific kind, but may take the form of rather different genres – for instance that of a fantasy novel. One of these conjunctions of fantasy and Gothic is illuminated by Oliver Plaschka in "Distressing Damsels: Gothic Chivalry in James Branch Cabell's *Biography*". Plaschka explores the idiosyncratic oeuvre of James Branch Cabell, one of the most important writers of early twentieth-century fantasy, and pays special attention to Cabell's ambivalent portrayal of female characters. Reflecting the author's biographical experiences, these figures oscillate between different romantic stereotypes, particularly the *femme fatale* and the damsel in distress, who abound with Gothic imagery. However, Plaschka illustrates how Cabell constantly uses disillusioning realism and satire to undercut such clear characterizations as well as the conventions of the fantasy romance. The main transgressive element of Cabell's writing may thus be the distinctly ambivalent realization that any male attempt at categorizing femininity is futile.

Secondly, the contemporary Gothic mode may also transgress the national borders of its origins. Often seen as a particularly British concept, which spread to countries such as France, Germany and the US, where Romanticism and Transcendentalism created like-minded interests, the Gothic may nowadays surface in various cultural and national contexts all over the world. In order to describe this development Glennis Byron coined the term 'Globalgothic' and edited a ground-breaking eponymous volume on this topic. An analysis of Gothic manifestations in different cultural and political settings of course also has to consider the specific socio-cultural and political anxieties which these texts address. This is the focus of Franziska Schneider's "From Bullerby to Blackeberg: Gothic Themes and National Settings in the Writings of John Ajvide Lindqvist". In her article, Schneider locates the transgressions of the Gothic in the seemingly rather tranquil and well-ordered national context of Sweden, namely in the fiction of Swedish horror writer John Ajvide Lindqvist. As she illustrates, Lindqvist's narratives adhere to markedly Gothic conventions, but insert them into archetypically Swedish settings and structures. Lindqvist's writing constantly undermines socio-cultural Swedish myths of the late twentieth century and thereby expresses a distinctly Gothic spirit of transgressing the dominant national discourse. Such a usage might be applicable to many more cultural contexts as every nation may be said to have its Gothic sides.

In light of the generic transgression of the boundary between Gothic and fantasy novel mentioned above, the next step is to look at the ways in which the Gothic as a mode may mix with another encompassing mode, encroaching on its 'territory', but also interacting with its conventions and attitudes to express something new. This intermodal interaction is central to the next section, "Intermodal Gothic: Sinister Idylls", whose title already hints at its special focus on depictions of nature. Indeed, when it comes to describing the natural world, the Gothic commonly competes with a mode that expresses an entirely different and seemingly contradictory world-view: the pastoral. Contrasting the two modes, one cannot help but see them as direct opposites, depicting either natural order or uncertainty, tranquillity or excess, nostalgia or horror. This opposition between the two modes makes the title of Andreas Schardt's contribution, "Terror in the Garden: The Gothic as (Anti-)Pastoral in H.P. Lovecraft's 'The Colour out of Space'", appear almost paradoxical – how can the pastoral and the Gothic be equated? However, Schardt demonstrates how the two modes actually share certain assumptions about the position of individuals in the world and about their interactions with nature, and analyses how the pastoral and the Gothic may occur concurrently in certain texts. He illustrates this by reading H.P. Lovecraft's short story "The Colour out of Space" as a text which details the transgressive destruction and subversion of a pastoral place by an external Gothic force. The powerlessness of humanity in the face of this corruption is a dark echo of the human insignificance commonly depicted by classical pastoral texts, a conjunction that even nowadays still manifests itself in various texts.

A similarly ambiguous view on nature and its relation to humanity is explored by Susan J. Tyburski in "Seduced by the Wild: Audrey Schulman's EcoGothic Romance", in which she discusses Schulman's Arctic novel *The Cage*. As Tyburski argues, Schulman's fiction blends the Gothic notion of an uncaring and threatening wilderness with the conventions of the romantic mode, resulting in a very distinct EcoGothic view. EcoGothic, a concept applying ecocritical ideas to Gothic texts, has been increasingly gaining attention in recent years, as the eponymous volume edited by Andrew Smith and William Hughes in 2013 demonstrates. Tyburski uses the term to describe human reactions to the Arctic wilderness, which oscillate between existential fear and erotic fascination as the individuals need to come to terms with their own insignificance. Despite experiencing hardship and death, Schulman's protagonist recognizes her own animalistic nature and strength and thus her liberation from the shackles of civilization. Schulman's EcoGothic not only transgresses the distinction between the Gothic and the romantic mode but also reaches beyond established ideas about the relationship between humankind and nature.

One of the essential features of a transgressive Gothic mode is that it is not bound to a certain medium. In the twentieth and twenty-first centuries, the number of media the Gothic may appear in has grown enormously. What has also increased is the intricacy of the intermediality of the Gothic itself. Nowadays, a large variety of different semiotic and technical channels are employed to create a Gothic effect. This is the focus of this volume's fourth section, "Intermedial Gothic: Woodcuts, Comics and Films". As the title indicates, most of these intermedial representations are distinctly visual in nature, which is again something inherent to the mode. Elizabeth McCarthy writes, "the issue of the visuality in Gothic horror is as old as the genre itself" (341), addressing the unimaginable sublime or the graphically gruesome. It is therefore necessary to examine the ways in which different visual cues may evoke a Gothic effect.

One medium with its very own Gothic possibilities is described in Erik Redling's "Monstrous Woodcuts: Experiments with Scary Word-Image Relations in Lynd Ward's Gothic Work". He analyzes the woodcuts of American artist Lynd Ward, who only used images for his 'wordless novels', a form deeply connected to the Expressionist Modernism of the early twentieth century. As Redling shows with regard to Ward's *God's Man*, a Faustian tale of an artist selling his soul, these woodcut narratives manage to express Gothic themes and plots entirely with visual means, inserting only a few textual cues. Supported by their rich intermedial connections, Ward's expressive images construct a symbolically complex narrative and a highly charged Gothic atmosphere that also surfaces in his illustrations of Mary Shelley's *Frankenstein*. His visualization adds new meaning to this classic Gothic narrative, while showcasing the intricate storytelling potential of visual literature.

Transgressing both types of media in order to create a new form of expression, Ward's blending of images and words finds its continuation in the graphic novels of the late twentieth and early twenty-first centuries. Winning new critical recognition for the often maligned medium of comics, the format of the graphic novel also uses primarily visual narrative means, usually integrating typographic words and drawings in a seamless way. Nevertheless, these narratives may still express a Gothic world of disruption and ambiguity, as Christian Schneider's article "'«It» forever': *Black Hole* as a Gothic Graphic Novel" demonstrates. Schneider reads Charles Burns' *Black Hole*, a graphic novel about a group of teenagers threatened by a mysterious disease, as a Gothic text. On the one hand, the comic addresses typically Gothic themes of body horror and dangerous adolescence, portraying puberty as a time of violent social and biological transgressions. On the other hand, similar to Ward's woodcuts, Burns uses visual symbolism and the effect of his black-and-white drawings to create a surreally nightmarish atmosphere. His graphic depictions of excessively mutated and mutilated bodies also connect the graphic novel to the earlier tradition of the Comix Underground. Yet, Schneider also points out the liberating and hopeful aspects of *Black Hole*'s adolescent transgressions.

Substituting the static page for moving images, film is nowadays the most prevalent intermedial and visual channel in current culture. Its formal expression has also been employed to create Gothic manifestations, even beyond the stereotypical conventions of the horror film genre. As Ellen Redling shows in her article, "Gothic Nightmares Then and Now: The Oneiric Descents in Edgar Allan Poe's Short Stories and Falling Dreams *ad extremum* in Christopher Nolan's Film *Inception*", an extremely successful blockbuster movie such as *Inception* may use strikingly Gothic elements to create its visual presentation of dreams and nightmares. Redling focuses in particular on the intermedial link between Christopher Nolan's film and Edgar Allan Poe's short stories "A Descent into the Maelström" and "The Fall of the House of Usher". Both the film and the stories depict the oneiric situation of falling and descending as well as its psychological effects. As Redling details, the notion of descent – and more specifically that of the 'falling dream' – can be read as particularly Gothic, as one loses any control over one's body and one's position in space. Redling discusses how the ever-growing desire for thrills might have resulted in Nolan's filmic means aiming to transgress more traditional Gothic methods and effects.

Finally, the last section of this volume, "Gothic Ltd: The Current Commercialization of the Gothic", asks the question of whether or not the transgressive Gothic has transgressed itself in the light of 'Candygothic', 'Aftergothic' or 'Disneygothic'. In this context, one especially relevant point of discussion is the current extreme popularity of one of the Gothic's most obvious figures: the vampire. Without wishing to over-use any clichéd metaphors about the vampire's un-dead nature, one might still say that the ceaseless appearances of the vampire in ever new literary fiction, films or TV shows is remarkable. In her article "'No Sex Please, We're Vegetarians': Marketing the Vampire and Sexual Curiosity in *Twilight*, *True Blood* and the *Sookie Stackhouse* Novels", Simone Broders explores the vampire's success in contemporary popular culture. Analyzing Stephenie Meyer's enormously popular *Twilight* series and their film versions as well as Charlaine Harris' similarly well-liked *Sookie Stackhouse* novels and their TV adaptation, *True Blood*, Broders looks at their cultural and commercial success particularly in terms of their respective treatment of transgressive sexuality, a long-established trait of vampire figures in popular fiction. She discusses the complex relationship between and ambiguity of subversiveness and conservatism in these works by, for instance, looking at how sexual politics may be depicted in accordance with traditional and commercialized concepts, while sexuality and romance as such are celebrated and indulged in.

The erotic aspect of the commercialized Gothic mode also plays a major role in Anna Powell's "Enchanted Objects: Steampunk Fetishes and Machinic Desire". Powell explores the Gothic potential of Steampunk, an increasingly popular cultural and subcultural phenomenon evoking an anachronistic alternate vision that blends current technological achievements with Neo-Victorian visuals and sensibilities. Its alienating aesthetics and its obsession with an imagined past render Steampunk a more than just superficially Gothic form of expression. In her article, Powell particularly focuses on the fetishism of objects and machines as magical talismans, erotically charged objects and commercialized consumer goods, which transgresses the established borders between humanity and technology. However, Steampunk's fetishism of material objects as part of a general consumer culture and its ahistorical glorification of Victorian culture can also attract criticism; Steampunk may be the most objectifying aspect of 'Candygothic'.

As can be seen in various forms in all of the contributions in this volume, the transgressive nature of the Gothic brings with it an essential ambivalence. Transgression means a disturbance of borders; thus it both considers these borders and breaches them, creating a grey area of uncertainty, which is at the same time the main source of its vibrant energy and allure. The Gothic mode's constant excess, its transcendence of all established delimitations, opens up ever new fields of examination, new questions and interactions with other critical concepts. However, it also prevents any fixed categorization. This is not necessarily something to be lamented; as the articles make clear, such ambivalence may still provide us with a wide variety of detailed analyses, convincing interpretations and stimulating discussions, thereby both enriching and extending the scholarly importance of the Gothic. In turn, these articles can open up doors for new queries regarding yet again new delimitations to be breached.

Today's Gothic may have to some extent transgressed itself, but it has certainly not cancelled itself out. We could perhaps talk about a Post-Gothic mode, surfacing in a multitude of media and genres, interacting with other modes, crossing national and cultural borders and becoming part of a multi-faceted commercialized world. One may venture to predict that as long as there exist some aesthetic, social, political, ethical or cultural theories and boundaries, the Gothic may in some form or another aim to test and breach them.

Works Cited

Borges, Jorge Luis. "Kafka and his Precursors." Trans. James E. Irby. *Labyrinths: Selected Stories and Other Writings*. Eds. Donald A. Yates and James E. Irby. New York: New Directions, 2007. 199-201.

Botting, Fred. *Gothic*. London: Routledge, 1996.

---. "Candygothic." *The Gothic*. Ed. Fred Botting. Cambridge: Brewer, 2001. 133-151.

---. "Aftergothic: Consumption, Machines, and Black Holes." *The Cambridge Companion to Gothic Fiction*. Ed. Jerrold E. Hogle. Cambridge: Cambridge University Press, 2002. 277-300.

---. *Gothic Romanced: Consumption, Gender and Technology in Contemporary Fictions*. London: Routledge, 2008.

---. *Limits of Horror: Technology, Bodies, Gothic*. Manchester: Manchester University Press, 2008.

Burke, Edmund. *A Philosophical Enquiry into the Origin of our Ideas of the Sublime and Beautiful*. Ed. Adam Phillips. Oxford: Oxford UP, 1990.

Byron, Glennis, ed. *Globalgothic*. Manchester: Manchester University Press, 2013.

Chandler, Anne. "Case Studies in Reading 1: Key Primary Literary Texts." *The Eighteenth-Century Literature Handbook*. Eds. Gary Day and Bridget Keegan. London: Continuum, 2009. 70-95.

Desmet, Christy and Anne Williams, eds. *Shakespearean Gothic*. Cardiff: University of Wales Press, 2009.

Drakakis, John, and Dale Townshend, eds. *Gothic Shakespeares*. London: Routledge, 2008.

Dryden, Linda. *The Modern Gothic and Literary Doubles: Stevenson, Wilde and Wells*. Basingstoke: Palgrave Macmillan, 2003.

Dülmen, Richard van. *Die Entdeckung des Individuums: 1500-1800*. Frankfurt am Main: Fischer, 1997.

Gray, Martin. *A Dictionary of Literary Terms*. Harlow: Longman, 1994.

Horn, Eva. *Zukunft als Katastrophe*. Frankfurt am Main: Fischer, 2014.

Jones, Timothy G. "The Canniness of the Gothic: Genre as Practice." *Gothic Studies* 11.1 (2009): 124-133.

Lévy, Maurice. "'Gothic' and the Critical Idiom." *Gothick Origins and Innovations*. Eds. Allan Lloyd-Smith and Victor Sage. Amsterdam: Rodopi, 1994. 1-15.

Malthus, Thomas Robert. *An Essay on the Principle of Population as it Affects the Future Improvement of Society*. London: Johnson, 1966.

Martin, Philip W. "Romanticism." *The Handbook to Gothic Literature*. Ed. Marie Mulvey-Roberts. Basingstoke: Macmillan, 1998. 195-199.

McCarthy, Elizabeth. "Gothic Visuality in the Nineteenth Century." *The Gothic World*. Eds. Glennis Byron and Dale Townsend. London: Routledge, 2014. 341-353.

Punter, David. *The Literature of Terror: A History of Gothic Fictions from 1765 to the Present Day*. London: Longman, 1980.

Sage, Victor. "Gothic Novel." *The Handbook to Gothic Literature*. Ed. Marie Mulvey-Roberts. Basingstoke: Macmillan, 1998. 81-89.

---. "Gothic Revival." *The Handbook to Gothic Literature*. Ed. Marie Mulvey-Roberts. Basingstoke: Macmillan, 1998. 90-103.

Smith, Andrew, and William Hughes, eds. *EcoGothic*. Manchester: Manchester University Press, 2013.

Waage, Peter Normann. *Ich: Eine Kulturgeschichte des Individuums.* Trans. Lothar Schneider. Stuttgart: Urachhaus, 2014.

Warwick, Alexandra. "Feeling Gothicky?" *Gothic Studies* 9.1 (2007): 5-19.

Wellington, Jan. "Learning to Transgress: Embedded Pedagogies of the Gothic." *Pedagogy: Critical Approaches to Teaching Literature, Language, Composition, and Culture* 8.1 (2008): 170-176.

Wolfreys, Julian. *Transgression: Identity, Space, Time.* Basingstoke: Palgrave Macmillan, 2008.

Jeaneen Kish

Pre-Gothic Goths: Shakespeare's Usage of the Goths as Gothic Monsters in *Titus Andronicus*

When looking at British literature from the Elizabethan era, specifically 1559 to 1594,[1] one can see it as a time of great social and political upheaval, with political and religious issues occurring in Britain and France, as well as between Britain and Spain. Although Shakespeare is not traditionally read as a political author, if we read his play *Titus Andronicus* in light of the political happenings of the day, we can come away with a richer understanding of his time period. And while Gothic literature did not appear until the 1760s, if we read Shakespeare's work as if it were a Gothic work,[2] the reader can see ways in which Gothic tropes were beginning to develop at this time, especially through the representations of the Goths and the purpose of their usage. Even though Shakespeare did not have the use of the Gothic monster to express the deepest fears of the English about what was happing to their country, he did have the image of the historical Goths themselves. By exploring Gothic tropes such as the *doppelgänger* and theatrical tropes such as the *Quem Quaeritis*, we are able to see the Goths as the monsters that are Othered by society and better understand the ways in which the atrocities they commit in the play mirror those actions many Protestants in Shakespeare's age feared the Catholics would commit.

---

[1] Some critics argue that *Titus Andronicus* was an early play of Shakespeare's. However, according to Clare Asquith, "the playhouse records mark it as 'new' in 1594" (91). For the purposes of this essay, I will use this as the publication date of the play.

[2] Two seminal works have been published exploring Shakespeare's work in light of the Gothic: *Gothic Shakespeares,* edited by John Drakakis and Dale Townshend, and *Shakespearean Gothic,* edited by Christy Desmet and Anne Williams. Both works look at the relationship between Shakespeare and Gothic literature, and examine the influence his work has had on the Gothic genre. With my essay I hope to continue their work by scrutinizing Shakespeare's relationship with the Gothic and further explore "the line between Shakespeare and his Gothic heirs [, which] is indeed a tangled one" (Desmet and Williams 10).

I. Historical Background

Before unfolding my interpretation of the play, we must explore the historical events that have significance in regards to this reading. Approximately forty years prior to the writing of the play, Mary I's reign came to an end. She sat on the English throne for five years, and in that time changed the national religion from the Protestant faith back to the Catholic faith. Jane Dunn explains her reign was one known for "reactionary extremism and bloodshed" (3). In fact,

> [t]he fanatical purges of heresy by her decree, and the torture and burnings of hundreds of martyrs, would earn Mary the epithet 'Bloody Mary' from generations to come. The country grew ever more tired and repelled by the bloodshed. The dreadful spectacles had become counterproductive, alienating her subjects' affections for their queen and strengthening the reformers' support. (Dunn 6)

Another issue with her reign "had been her insistence on marrying Philip II of Spain, for the English hated foreigners meddling in their affairs, and they hated the Spanish most of all" (Dunn 6). Even though her reign would have been long past for the contemporary audience of *Titus Andronicus*, the effects of her reign were still in the cultural memory, and, therefore, caused a great deal of fear about another Catholic taking the throne in England, whether as Elizabeth I's consort or as her heir.

In addition, the play was written approximately twenty years after the Saint Bartholomew's Day massacre, which began on 23 August 1572 and lasted for several weeks. After the attempted assassination of Gaspard de Coligny, the French king was said to take steps to stop any repercussions of this effort. However, on the 23rd of August, not only was Coligny killed in a second attempt on his life, other Huguenot nobles, present in France for the marriage of the king's sister, were also murdered. Afterwards, "the mob and the city militia began; methodical, too, but far less discriminating ... they went from house to house through the city's commercial quarter dispatching any Huguenots they found" (Budiansky 12-13). The King of France "went forth to address the Parlement of Paris ... and declared that the massacre of the Huguenots had been necessary to thwart a vile conspiracy hatched by Admiral Coligny and his followers" (Budiansky 14). According to Donald Stump and Susan M. Felch, "as many as 10,000 Protestants were killed" (183) during the massacre.

While this occurred in France, the killing of the Protestants also affected many in England and caused fear that such slaughter would occur there as well. Stump and Felch claim, "[m]ore than any other single event, the massacre strengthened the resolve of leading English Protestants ... to keep Catholic Europe at bay. It also encouraged suspicion of foreigners and convinced loyal English men and women of the favoured status of their own nation" (186).

Another historical occurrence that affected the way Catholics were perceived was the various treasonous plots of Mary Queen of Scots. Queen Mary believed, as did many Catholics, that she had a more legitimate right to the English throne than Elizabeth I. In fact, Elizabeth, "had been declared a bastard by an act of Parliament in 1536 that banned her from making any claim 'as lawful heir' to her father, and, despite the 1544 Act of Succession, the declaration of 'bastard' had never been officially revoked" (Stump and Felch 74). As such, throughout her life, Mary Stuart aspired to gain the throne from Elizabeth. Her claim to the throne was especially dangerous because of Elizabeth's hesitancy to name an heir should something happen to her. She was finally executed on 8 February 1587 after being implicated in the Babington plot (Dunn 398-399; 408).

The final historical event to be addressed is the Spanish Armada. On 19 July 1588, "[a] hundred and thirty [Spanish] sail in all, a staggering force" (Budiansky 208) were spotted off the coast of England. After ten days of fighting and manoeuvres, the English were able to overcome the Spanish fleet with a combination of skill and luck. Because the weather played a large role in their victory, the English felt that God favoured them over the Spanish. While the victory raised the spirits of the British, such a large fleet sent after them showed the strength of the Catholic foreign element and its great ability to send forces against them in an attempt to unseat Queen Elizabeth. With all of these Catholic plots, the country at that time lived in fear of the Catholics taking over again and bringing back a reign like Bloody Mary's. The association of the Goths with Catholicism then can lend a reading showing that Britain was expressing its fears of the Catholics taking over from within.[3]

---

[3] Traditionally, the Goths are associated with anti-Catholicism and anti-Papism because of their struggle against the Roman Empire. However, when reading *Titus Andronicus*, we can equate them with Catholicism because of the

II. The Gothic Monster

One way *Titus Andronicus* uses Gothic conventions is to express the fear of the nation during times of war and political upheaval. According to Judith Halberstam in *Skin Shows: Gothic Horror and the Technology of Monsters*, "[i]f the Gothic novel produces an easy answer to the question of what threatens national security and prosperity (the monster), the Gothic monster represents many answers to the question of who must be removed from the community at large" (3). As we can see from Halberstam's interpretation of the Gothic monster, it represents that which the society fears the most, what it deemed to be a terrorist element. During times of political turmoil and war, then, we often see the Gothic monsters representing the current political enemy feared at the time. They embody the Otherness of the 'terrorist' in order to help the community delineate that element and feel safe that in the end it will be defeated, as are many of the traditional Gothic monsters. If we read the Goths of *Titus Andronicus* through this lens, we could see them as the Catholic sector of society. The Catholics during the Elizabethan era were viewed as the terroristic element due to the events discussed above. Their actions, then, may have caused them to be seen as monsters residing within English society.

Another important feature of Gothic literature is that many Gothic authors wish to show what one should fear the most is what is inside of one: "[…] we ought to be very afraid – and of nothing so much as ourselves" (Edmundson 11). The history of England illustrates why this would be a concern for authors throughout the Elizabethan era. The enemy was not always a clearly demarcated foreign element, but instead a fellow British citizen. Not only was the average citizen a potential suspect, but also at the time when Shakespeare wrote *Titus Andronicus*, Elizabeth had not yet married and produced an heir, which was more than doubtful since she was approximately in her late 50s and early 60s. The choice of her successor was a very controversial issue because several potential candidates were either Catholic or had strong Catholic ties. British citizens would have worried about the potential religious upheaval they would have to go through did Elizabeth choose a Catholic to succeed her; in fact, "[w]orries over the civil strife that might ensue should she die without a successor led to renewed pressure [on Elizabeth I] to name an

---

correlation of the British Empire with the Roman one.

heir" (Stump and Felch 436). While Shakespeare did not have the use of the Gothic monster to express his society's deepest fears about what was happening to his country, he did have the image of the Goths themselves.[4]

III. The Silencing of Lavinia

When considering the history of the English Protestants and Catholics and the fears held by many Elizabethans, the ways in which the play's Goths embody monstrous behaviour become visible when adopting this perspective. One of the scenes that most strongly highlights their monstrosity is the rape and mutilation of Lavinia, Titus' daughter. Lavinia is raped by the Goths Demetrius and Chiron and then has her tongue and hands cut away. This removal of body parts could be seen as connected to the *Quem Quaeritis* trope in theatre, which, according to Anthony Kubiak in *Stages of Terror: Terrorism, Ideology and Coercion as Theatre History*, is "a responsorial chanted during the Mass in Eastertide that reenacted the visit of the three Marys to the tomb of the crucified Christ" (51). As Kubiak further explains, "the image of the effaced body becomes a metaphor for the operational principle of terror essential to drama, the terror of disappearance and disaster represented by the body 'under erasure'" (48). Therefore, the terror caused by this trope is in reaction to the missing body of Christ, specifically, the tortured, crucified body. The Goths perpetrate a similar action of terror, making parts of Lavinia's body disappear. Relating this notion back to the

---

[4] One of the biggest contemporary controversies in Shakespeare studies is the nature of Shakespeare's religion. Up until recently, most people assumed that Shakespeare was a Protestant. However, new scholarship has emerged challenging this notion. As Clare Asquith explains, up until recently Shakespeare's works were read with the assumption that he did not reference the politics of his time (xiv-xv). Scholars such as Asquith are revealing through their readings the ways in which the plays surreptitiously speak on the politics of the time and do so through the lens of a Catholic. In my reading, I will be looking at the ways in which the play reveals the fears of the society at large, rather than focusing on the politics of Shakespeare in particular. In this way, the play is addressing the politics of his time. For further reading on the subject of Shakespeare's Catholic ties, see the works of Joseph Pearce, Carol Curt Enos and David N. Beauregard.

political state of the time, Catholics were frequently considered violent terrorists who would do anything to re-establish themselves in the Church and the government. When we read the Goths in the play as the Catholics, by cutting Lavinia's body into pieces, they are reflecting the fear of people that the Catholics would, piece by piece, destroy the country until there was nothing left.

Not only do they make parts of her body disappear, they also attempt to silence Lavinia by cutting off her tongue and hands. Such an action could illustrate the fear held by a large number of Protestants that did the Catholics come to power again, they would silence the Protestants, not allowing them to practice their religion or have a say in their government. It is significant that they cut off her hands as well so that she could seemingly not write what happened to her. At this time, a great many writings by Protestants existed, expressing their views on how the country should be run as well as how their religion should be practiced (Budiansky 56-57). It was a time of "the growing power of print, which brought rapid and effective communication direct to the people, supplementing the official message of the state or church" (Dunn 367). This disappearance of the hands and the tongue and thereby the ability to write and speak may also express a fear of not only losing their voice but also their ability to affect their society through their writings.

Lavinia's – and Titus' – loss of hands is significant in another way as well. Elizabeth I was known to cut off the right hand of political dissenters who published tracts against her and her government. In fact, she did not limit this punishment to Catholics. In 1579, she was in the middle of marriage negotiations with the Duc d'Alençon. He was twenty-two years her junior and a proclaimed Catholic. According to Dunn,

> [...] Elizabeth was capable of acts of savage retribution when threatened, for instance, by the power of print to disseminate dissension and revolt. The writer and distributor of a tract published in September 1579 entitled, 'The Discovery of a Gaping Gulph whereinto England is like to be swallowed by another French marriage ...,' were sentenced immediately to have [*their right hands hacked off.*]" (367; emphasis added).

Dunn further points out that

> [t]he offending work expressed in intemperate language what most of her populace believed to be the case – that the Valois

princes were sly papists and worthless reprobates, that Elizabeth was too old for Alençon and he could not love her, that she anyway was past childbearing. In short, he was a rat who should not have been allowed even to look on their Queen. (367)

As this example illustrates, anyone, Protestant or Catholic, was in danger of losing hands if what he or she printed was in opposition to the Queen's beliefs. Thus, the loss of hands by both Lavinia and Titus then would have called to mind the dangers one faced when publishing a political tract, even if it seemingly supported Elizabeth and her reign.

However, one must note at this point that the attempt to silence Lavinia through both speech and writing does not work. Not only is she still able to indicate that she was raped, she does so through writing. First, she implies what happened to her by pointing out the story of Philomel in her nephew's books (Shakespeare 4.1.49-52). Then she manages to write the name of her rapists in the sand: *"She takes the staff in her mouth, and guides it with her stumps, and writes"* (Shakespeare 4.1.77; emphasis in the original). Here we are shown that even though Demetrius and Chiron attempted to silence her, she can still give voice to her thoughts. In this way, the passage can be read as a warning of sorts to Catholics. No matter how the Catholics both from outside and inside the country may try to silence the Protestants, the Protestants will still communicate their political opinions. Even if those were silenced, Lavina's ability to communicate despite her loss of tongue and hands shows that there are other ways of conveying one's message to those who need to hear it.

Another example of the *Quem Quaeritis* trope in the play is the literal disappearance of the bodies of children through death. The play begins with us finding out that "of five-and-twenty valiant sons" of Titus, only four remain (Shakespeare 1.1.79). The rest have been lost in the wars with the Goths. Danielle A. St. Hilaire in "Allusion and Sacrifice in *Titus Andronicus*" shows that these children are important because "[t]hroughout the play, offspring, particularly sons, fulfill a vital role, as parents continually pass their agency down into their children's hands", thereby making them "necessary to the survival of Rome, for only through succession, through the passing down of agency from parent to child can the future of the society beyond the parent's generation be ensured" (312). By making these bodies "disappear", the Goths are destroying the Roman culture's ability to maintain itself and insure its prosperity in the future. It makes sense that the play would encompass these fears. *Titus Andronicus'* publication date is approximately 1594, and as mentioned above, the country feared a war if Elizabeth did not name an heir. One must also recognize that these bodies, the ones interred in the Andronicus family tomb, will never return, unlike the body of Christ. These bodies are ones that have been obliterated forever, so the audience is left with the terror of a permanent erasure. Much like the Protestant martyrs, Titus' children died for the cause and will only live on in the memory of their deeds. Their bodies will never return. In this way, the children of these families are being literally eradicated by the struggle between the two religious groups. By the end of the play, only one Andronicus son and one grandson remain. If not for their survival, the entire line would have disappeared.

IV. The Significance of Borderlines

In addition to the mutilation of Lavinia, Titus is encouraged to enact his own self-mutilation by cutting off one of his own hands. This loss of body parts by several characters is significant because in literature of this time period, according to Mikhail Bakhtin in *Rabelais and His World*, "[t]he accent was placed on the completed, self-sufficient individuality of the given body. Corporal acts were shown only when the borderlines dividing the body from the outside world were sharply defined" (29). By both characters losing body parts, we can see that firstly they are not the traditionally completed bodies represented in Elizabethan literature. Secondly, their borderlines are continually changing and in some ways are not 'sharply defined'. Lavinia is raped, an act that can be read as a breach of borders. In essence, their bodies are open to the outside world, allowing them to interact rather than maintaining a sharp border. This changing border of the body could reflect the borders of the Roman city. According to Alexander Leggatt in *"Titus Andronicus*: A Modern Perspective", "in the course of the play, that border [between Rome and the Goths] becomes remarkably porous" (248). This blending of the Self and the Other, the inside and the outside, could have caused a great deal of fear in the audience. Even today, people are very uncomfortable with the notion that our enemies could blend in with us. We like there to be clear distinctions so that we can easily identify who and what is the cause of terror and thereby remove or defeat that "terrorist". Shakespeare's audience could have felt a comparable discomfort at not being able to distinguish between a Protestant and a Catholic.

While the brothers commit the aforementioned act of erasure concerning Lavinia, ironically at the end of the play, they become the victims of it as well in another crossing of borders. Titus bakes the brothers into a pie as part of his revenge against Tamora and her sons for the atrocities committed against his family. To finish this act of revenge, he then serves the pie to Tamora, not telling her of its contents until she has already consumed them: "Why, there they are, both baked in this pie, / Whereof their mother daintily hath fed, / Eating the flesh that she herself hath bred" (Shakespeare 5.3.61-64). Alexander Leggatt describes the scene as designed for "Chiron and Demetrius to enter Tamora's body, making her the final image of the hole in the earth that swallows men" (246). Significantly, she swallows not just any men, but specifically her sons. If she represents the Catholics during Shakespeare's time, then her consumption of her sons can represent the ways in which warring with the state will consume or destroy the young men who would be expected to fight. Those Catholics who would be put to death by the English government for treasonous acts would in essence disappear and be swallowed up by the cause, thereby relating to the notion of the "body 'under erasure'". Markman Ellis defines the "cannibal, [as] an ideologically motivated rhetorical device deployed to demonstrate and establish the moral superiority of civilized colonial authority over the barbarous slaves" (208). While we are not looking at the situation of a colonizer over a slave, the definition still holds true for the Protestants and Catholics. The Protestants were considered civilized and the Catholics mostly as barbarous. By including the cannibalism committed by Tamora, the notion commonly held at the time that the Catholics are savage enough to consume their own kind is reinforced.

However, Tamora is not the only one to 'consume' her progeny. Before Titus serves Tamora her sons in the pie, he kills his own daughter (Shakespeare 5.3.47). Titus claims that he is doing so to eliminate Lavinia's shame, but it is probable that his action has more to do with her delimitation. Immediately before killing her, he says, "And with thy shame thy father's sorrow die!" (Shakespeare 5.3.47). The violation committed to her 'borders' must be eliminated. As long as Lavinia has her wounds, she shows not only that she has been breached, but the Goths also might have impregnated her. If she bears the child of her rapists, there would be no way to tell the difference between that child and one who is a 'pure' Roman. Therefore, she must die before such a breach can happen. Again, we can see here the fear of not being able to identify one's enemy by sight as well as the need to maintain the Roman state in its purity.

The confusion regarding borders and who or what is evil is further reinforced when the border between Roman and Goth becomes blurred during Act 5. In Scene 1, Lucius, whilst on stage at the head of a Gothic army, says, "I have received letters from great Rome, / Which signifies what hate they bear our emperor/ And how desirous of our sight they are" (Shakespeare 5.1.2-4). Here we have a situation where the Romans want Lucius to come into Rome to save them from the problems occurring. While a Roman, he is entering the city at the head of an army of its enemies, those very people whose presence causes the troubles in the first place. Were it not for the loss of Titus' sons to this army, the events of the play may never have happened. One of the Goth soldiers further strengthens this notion of blending when he says "Brave slip sprung from the great Andronicus, / Whose name was once our terror, now our comfort / [...] Be bold in us. We'll follow where thou lead'st / [...] And be avenged on cursed Tamora" (Shakespeare 5.1.9-16). At this point it is hard to tell whether the soldiers were Gothic or Roman in their allegiance. Here we have a literal blending of the Goth and the Roman in addition to the Goths penetrating the Roman city's borders.

What might be the ultimate example of internal evil and the ability to infiltrate borders is the position Tamora holds after entering the city as a prisoner of war. Once Titus brings Tamora to Rome, he introduces her to Saturninus, who takes her as wife once he is named emperor. Tamora goes from Gothic prisoner of war to Roman empress showing her ability to permeate the Roman state. As such, "[...] the distinction between the city and its enemies, between Us and Them, collapses" (Leggatt 248). Once again we have the notion of the entity to be most feared found internally.

V. The Use of the *Doppelgänger* and the Fear of the Other

Another Gothic trope found in the story is the use of the double, particularly the *doppelgänger*, being the evil entity and the doubled character, the good. Mark Edmundson explains the Gothic double as "[t]he idea of a second self – of a horrible other living unrecognized within us, or loosed somehow into the world beyond ..." (8). In *Titus Andronicus*, however, it becomes difficult to decide which character is good and which is evil in the end. The two characters who double each other the most are Titus and Tamora. Both characters have lost children to each other and both are looking for revenge against the other. In the beginning of the play, Titus sacrifices Tamora's oldest son, and later in the play, Tamora tells her remaining sons to rape Titus' only daughter. In this way, they begin a spiralling cycle of revenge that blurs the lines between which one is good and which is evil. One of the uses of the Gothic double is to illustrate that what one needs to fear is internal rather than external.[5] In the case of the doubling between these two characters and the confusion it causes, we can see this same warning being transmitted. Tamora is the insidious Goth trying to infiltrate and destroy the culture, but Titus acts in a similar manner. While one would think that Shakespeare would make Titus the clearly good character, if we read it through this trope, we can interpret Titus' role as a warning. Because he embarks on a path of revenge that quickly gets out of control, thereby marking him as evil as Tamora, he can be read as a warning that acting the same way as the opposition will cause one to become evil as well. This was happening during Shakespeare's time period; we can see it with Elizabeth I. According to Dunn, "[i]n a much longer reign [Elizabeth] executed more Catholics than her sister Mary I burned heretics" (286).

Another instance of the notion of internal evil can be viewed in Tamora's and Aaron's baby. In the scene where Aaron is showing Tamora's sons her newly birthed child and they reject it because of its skin colour, Alexander Leggatt reads Aaron's reaction of enforcing the notion that the baby is their brother as "[...] not so much a plea for common humanity as

---

[5] One of the most famous examples of this use of the *doppelgänger* is found in Robert Louis Stevenson's *The Strange Case of Dr. Jekyll and Mr. Hyde*. Jerrold E. Hogle explains "When the lawyer Utterson sees Stevenson's Hyde as 'troglodytic' in *The Strange Case of Dr. Jekyll and Mr. Hyde*, then, he is speaking to the deep fear of regression to a violent animality in us ..." (222).

a challenge to recognize in the self the evil that is too easily projected onto the Other" (249-250). Once again we see the internal evil. Within the world of the play, a baby born of a Goth and a Moor would have been a true monstrosity, one that even the Goths would not accept. What would have probably been particularly frightening to Shakespeare's audience was the fact that the baby might have passed for a legitimate offspring of the emperor if not for the colour of its skin. Only its appearance marks it as Other, the offspring of the Moor. Throughout the play there is the emphasis on the importance of the eldest son, because of primogenitor laws. The eldest son was expected to inherit any land or titles held by the father. The child Tamora gives birth to might have become emperor someday if not for its skin colour; otherwise, there would have been no other way for the child to be marked as Aaron's progeny: "Did not thy hue bewray whose brat thou art, / Had nature lent thee but thy mother's look, / Villian, thou mightst have been an emperor" (Shakespeare 5.1.28-30). Elizabethans would have felt a sense of comfort that this perceived monstrosity could not pass for a Roman baby in this case. Elizabeth herself played on this fear held by her subjects by emphasizing "[h]er claim that her blood was unsullied by foreign taint [, which] reinforced the chauvinism, superiority and suspicion shown towards foreigners that was beginning to characterize her people" (Dunn 354). In this way, the fear caused by an inability to identify British Catholics based on their appearance is also reflected in the child. While Aaron is often read as the villain of the piece, the child is more frightening because of its potential to pass for that which it is not.

VI. Conclusion

What may arguably separate Shakespeare's play from a work of Gothic fiction is its lack of the traditional tropes. It does not have the castles, the supernatural, the medieval setting, but so many contemporary Gothic works lack those elements as well, and it is the Goths, the 'monster' in the play, that perpetrate the actions that cause our reaction. Noël Carroll in *The Philosophy of Horror* claims in Gothic fiction "[t]he monsters are regarded to be violations of nature, and abnormal [...]. [The other characters] not only fear such monsters; they find them repellent, loathsome, disgusting, repulsive and impure" (54). While Tamora might be a truly reprehensible and vile person, she does not inspire the aforementioned emotions in most of the other characters; she is not a 'violation of nature'. In fact, Saturninus finds her desirable enough that he is willing to break his betrothal to Lavinia, which could have created problems between him and Titus.

What may be more important, however, is the response of the audience. If acted in a certain way, the play could prompt the audience to react to the scenes as though they were comedic. In fact, Harold Bloom claims, "[b]oth performances of *Titus Andronicus* that I have attended – one in New York, one in London – had similar effects upon their audiences, who never knew when to be horrified and when to laugh" (77). With the rape, murder, fragmentation of bodies, and cannibalism, one would expect the audience to have some kind of visceral reaction, even though it may not be directed toward the characters as Carroll required; in fact, "if not laughed off the stage, it [*Titus Andronicus*] requires extra paramedics to cope with the number of fainting spectators" (Holden 103). While reading the play may not incite a reaction of fear per se, watching the violence enacted live may cause such a response in audience members, and when interpreting most plays, one must always remember that the original purpose of plays is performance. According to an article from the *BBC News*, a contemporary production of the play was so gruesome that the Globe warned audiences of its nature and expected a higher than normal number of patrons to faint during the performance ("Globe Warns"). So should this then be taken into consideration in our interpretation of *Titus*? At least to some degree it has to be. If watching a woman walk on stage who has had her tongue cut out, her hands cut off, and her body sexually ravished does not produce a negative reaction of some sort, I am not sure what might.

The fluidity of the Gothic genre and its ability to question and break down borders allows us to look at its definition to see if other works can be read as if they were Gothic texts in order to open up a new way of looking at the work. In Shakespeare's play, *Titus Andronicus*, he uses what would later be defined as Gothic tropes in order to express the political upheaval prevalent in England at the time and the consequences of that upheaval. Through the use of Gothic conventions such as the *Quem Quaeritis* trope and doubling, we are able to see the Goths as the monsters who are Othered by society and better understand the ways in which the atrocities they commit mirror those actions many Protestants feared the Catholics would commit.

Works Cited

Asquith, Clare. *Shadowplay: The Hidden Beliefs and Coded Politics of William Shakespeare*. New York: PublicAffairs, 2005.

Bakhtin, Mikhail. *Rabelais and His World*. Trans. Hélène Iswolsky. Bloomington: Indiana University Press, 1984.

Beauregard, David N. *Catholic Theology in Shakespeare's Plays*. Cranbury, NJ: Rosemont Publishing, 2008.

Bloom, Harold. *Shakespeare: The Invention of the Human*. New York: Riverhead, 1998.

Budiansky, Stephen. *Her Majesty's Spymaster: Elizabeth I, Sir Francis Walsingham, and the Birth of Modern Espionage*. New York: Plume, 2006.

Carroll, Noël. *The Philosophy of Horror or Paradoxes of the Heart*. New York: Routledge, 1990.

Desmet, Christy and Anne Williams. "Introduction." *Shakespearean Gothic*. Eds. Christy Desmet and Anne Williams. Cardiff: University of Wales Press, 2009. 1-10.

Dunn, Jane. *Elizabeth and Mary: Cousins, Rivals, Queens*. New York: Knopf, 2003.

Edmundson, Mark. *Nightmare on Main Street: Angels, Sadomasochism, and the Culture of the Gothic*. Cambridge: Harvard University Press, 1997.

Ellis, Markman. *The History of Gothic Fiction*. Edinburgh: Edinburgh University Press, 2003.

Enos, Carol Curt. *Shakespeare and the Catholic Religion*. Pittsburgh: Durrance, 2000.

Everitt, Anthony. The *Rise of Rome: The Making of the World's Greatest Empire*. New York: Random House, 2012.

"Globe Warns Over 'Gruesome' Play." *BBC News*. 2 June 2006. Web. 2 June 2014.

Halberstam, Judith. *Skin Shows: Gothic Horror and the Technology of Monsters*. Durham: Duke University Press, 1995.

Hilaire, Danielle A. St. "Allusion and Sacrifice in *Titus Andronicus*." *Studies in English Literature 1500-1900*. 49.2 (2009): 311-331. Web. 7 Aug. 2010.

Hogle, Jerrold E. "Stevenson, Robert Louis (1850-94)." *The Handbook to Gothic Literature*. Ed. Marie Mulvey-Roberts. Washington Square: New York University Press, 1998. 220-223.

Holden, Anthony. *William Shakespeare: The Man Behind the Genius: A Biography*. Boston: Little, Brown, 1999.

Kubiak, Anthony. *Stages of Terror: Terrorism, Ideology, and Coercion as Theatre History*. Bloomington: Indiana University Press, 1991.

Leggatt, Alexander. "*Titus Andronicus*: A Modern Perspective." *Titus Andronicus*. By William Shakespeare. Eds. Barbara A. Mowat, and Paul Werstine. New York: Washington Square, 2005. 241-250.

Pearce, Joseph. *The Quest for Shakespeare: The Bard of Avon and the Church of Rome*. San Francisco: Ignatius, 2008.

---. *Through Shakespeare's Eyes: Seeing the Catholic Presence in the Plays*. San Francisco: Ignatius, 2010.

---. *Shakespeare on Love: Seeing the Catholic Presence in Romeo and Juliet*. San Francisco: Ignatius, 2013.

Punter, David. "Introduction: The Ghost of a History." *A New Companion to the Gothic*. Ed. David Punter. Malden, MA: Wiley-Blackwell, 2012.

Shakespeare, William. *Titus Andronicus*. Eds. Barbara A. Mowat, and Paul Werstine. New York: Washington Square, 2005.

Stump, Donald, and Susan M. Felch, eds. *Elizabeth I and Her Age*. New York: Norton, 2009.

Susanne Gruss

Jacobean Gothic and the Law: Revengers and Ineffectual Rulers on the Early Modern Stage

Gothic tropes have long since moved from primary texts to the articles and monographs analyzing them. In an exemplary passage, one critic describes the text she discusses as "replete with unsettling, slippery images of the interstitial, the in-between: images of dung, poison and blood; of wolf-men, wax figures, witches and lunatics; of mandrakes, hyenas and basilisks; of echoes, shadows and evanescent stains in snow" (Zimmerman, *Early Modern Corpse* 143). In Marie Mulvey-Roberts' *Handbook to Gothic Literature*, another critic links the same text's waxworks to Ann Radcliffe's *The Mysteries of Udolpho* from 1794, and highlights broader topics such as perverted sexuality, morbidity, madness, and male transgression (Butler 275-276). Despite the superabundance of generic markers, neither of these critics is discussing an obscure Gothic novel – both refer to John Webster's Jacobean tragedy *The Duchess of Malfi*, written 1612-13. The works of Shakespeare and his contemporaries – or what I will call 'Jacobean Gothic' – have repeatedly surfaced as an intertextual haunting of Gothic criticism in recent years and could, I will argue in this chapter, be read as generic precursors to Gothic fiction. This Jacobean 'haunting' of the Gothic has recently been complemented by a fairly novel development in early modern studies, the analysis of Renaissance literature through the critical lens of the Gothic, which allows critics to expand the 'limits' of the Gothic into the late sixteenth and early seventeenth centuries.[1]

Focusing on early modern tragedy and its predilection for what one might call a (proto-) Gothic mode, my article will follow a triple trajectory: in a first step, I want to demonstrate the Gothic potential of Jacobean tragedy; by using Webster's *Duchess* as a case study, I will move from the already established 'Shakespearean Gothic' to the 'Jacobean Gothic'. In order to point out the close proximity of Gothic and legal discourses in early modern drama I will then briefly delineate the intersections between the stage and legal practices in Renaissance England, and employ Pierre Legendre's psychoanalytic approach to legal studies to illuminate these

---

[1] See Drakakis and Townshend, as well as Desmet and Williams.

issues.[2] In a last step I will use John Marston's *Antonio's Revenge* from 1602 and Philip Massinger's *The Duke of Milan* from 1623 as exemplary texts to illustrate legal practice in crisis, depicted, in these plays, in the eventual conflation of the figure of the revenger and the ruler as tyrant. In short, I will argue that early modern tragedy shares with the early Gothic novel an intense literary investment in a legal framework that is experienced as endangered or instable, which allows for a Gothic re-reading of Jacobean tragedy as 'Jacobean Gothic'.

I. From Shakespearean Gothic to Jacobean Gothic

"Scratch the surface of any gothic fiction and the debt to Shakespeare will be there" (Clery 30): the notion of 'Shakespearean Gothic' can be understood in a double sense; on the one hand, it can be used to analyze the Gothic atmosphere or proto-Gothic potential of Shakespeare's plays – most notably in tragedies like *Titus Andronicus*, *Hamlet* and *Macbeth*, but also in comedies and romances such as *A Midsummer Night's Dream* or *The Tempest*. On the other hand, 'Shakespearean Gothic' invokes the many ways eighteenth-century writers of the Gothic have used the cultural capital associated with Shakespeare's works in order to legitimize their own writing.[3] This strategy is clearly visible in Walpole's use of Shakespeare in the second preface to *The Castle of Otranto* from 1765, for example, in which he "cites the authority of Shakespeare for the mixture of comedy and tragedy that his narrative contains" (Drakakis 4). Radcliffe quotes Shakespeare in several epigraphs in *The Mysteries of Udolpho* and mentions the bard in her programmatic "The Supernatural

---

[2] In Gothic studies, Sue Chaplin has introduced Legendre's work to the analysis of literary texts, and Peter Goodrich's well-established psychoanalytic approach to legal studies and legal culture in the early modern age also takes account of his theories. However, Legendre has as yet been comparatively marginal to the study of Renaissance literature. Goodrich's *Languages of Law: From Logics of Memory to Nomadic Masks*, especially Chapter 8 – "Law's Emotional Body: Image and Aesthetic in the Work of Pierre Legendre" (262-297) – provides a good introduction to Legendre's *oeuvre*.

[3] See, for example, John Drakakis, who points out that "[o]ne means for a 'popular' literature to assert its own credentials is to align itself with other forms of writing whose cultural capital has already been established" (12).

in Poetry", which was published posthumously in 1826.[4] Christy Desmet and Anne Williams even read Shakespeare as the Gothic's spectral point of reference:

> As 'Shakespeare' materialized as the father of English literature in the eighteenth-century imagination, his figure cast a growing shadow, which from Horace Walpole onwards came to be called Gothic. Beginning with Walpole, enthusiasts of the 'barbarous' and the medieval argued that Shakespeare's plays justified their sensational material, 'monstrosities' of all kinds. Thus, a complete portrait of Shakespeare must include his Gothic 'shadow'. (2)

Variations of this argument can be found in E. J. Clery's "The Genesis of 'Gothic' Fiction" – Clery notes that "[i]t would be impossible to overestimate the importance of Shakespeare as touchstone and inspiration for the terror mode" (30) – or Anne Williams' *Art of Darkness: A Poetics of Gothic*, where she demonstrates how the life of Henry VIII can be read as a Gothic family story and connects the Gothic novel to early modern tragedy in pointing out both genres' foundation in popular culture. Williams argues that what she calls "'Gothic' impulses are inherent in the spectacular politics and political spectacles" (30) of plays by Shakespeare and his contemporaries. What is, I think, surprising in many of these recent studies that take into account the Gothic's debt to the early modern age is the construction of an astonishingly homogeneous connection between the Gothic and Shakespeare, a connection that seems to ignore Shakespeare's equally popular contemporaries almost entirely. At the same time, plays by authors such as John Fletcher, Thomas Middleton, Cyril Tourneur, Webster or Massinger have long lurked close to the surface of Gothic criticism: David Punter notes that "it is the cathartic pretensions and ambiguities of the drama of Webster and Tourneur which reappear in Gothic works" (*Literature of Terror* 85); Punter and Byron argue that Radcliffe's villain Montoni "looks back to precursors in

---

[4] Christy Desmet and Anne Williams stress that "Shakespeare and the Gothic were born together in the eighteenth century. By 'Shakespeare' we mean the canonical figure in place by the 1790s, England's national poet and candidate for the greatest writer of the Western tradition [...]" (1); with reference to Ann Radcliffe, Sue Chaplin highlights the author's persistent evocations of "Shakespeare in order to contextualise and legitimise her Gothic" (11).

Jacobean drama" (186); Williams mentions "the sensational scenes of Jacobean dramatists such as Webster and Tourneur" (30) as an early modern 'Gothic impulse'; Butler introduces Webster's *Duchess of Malfi* as a proto-Gothic text (276); and Punter strengthens his conceptualization of Jacobean texts as 'spectres' haunting eighteenth-century Gothic when he notes that Gothic is "a ghost haunted by another ghost, almost as eighteenth-century Gothic was haunted by Jacobean tragedy, and Jacobean tragedy by the horrors of Greek drama" (*Gothic Pathologies* 14). However, none of these critics has taken the obvious step to include Jacobean tragedy into the consideration of a 'Gothic Renaissance',[5] and none of the references to non-Shakespearean drama that I have quoted results in a more substantial discussion of these plays and their relevance for the Gothic legacy of the early modern age. Taking my cue from these critics, I will make a decisive turn towards a 'Jacobean Gothic'.[6]

Having argued for the introduction of the 'Jacobean Gothic' into the study of Gothic, it is necessary to consider the critical gains of such a step. On a superficial level, it seems almost too easy to categorize Jacobean tragedy as Gothic *avant la lettre*: the plays are set in foreign countries, with Italy and Spain as favourites, ghosts and other supernatural visitations are stereotypical ingredients of the revenge play, as are the plays' notorious depictions of excessive violence and the descent of the revenger figure into madness; anti-Catholicism, latent social criticism and the anxiety about fluctuating and changing gender roles drive the plots of many Jacobean tragedies. Webster's *Duchess of Malfi* is a case in point: the play is famously set at the corrupt court of Malfi, where the eponymous Duchess's twin brother Ferdinand tries to control his sister and becomes increasingly obsessed with her sexuality. As a young widow, the Duchess is presented as a political imponderable due to her potentially uncontrollable ability to procreate. Her rampant sensuality,

---

[5] An international conference in Cologne in 2009, bearing the same title, is the only academic forum to date in which the interconnections between Shakespeare and the Gothic were extended to Renaissance literature as a whole. The collection of essays based on the conference was published in 2014 (Bronfen and Neumeier, *Gothic Renaissance: A Reassessment*).

[6] My use of 'Gothic' denotes a mode of writing rather than a genre, a mode that, as Fred Botting defines it, "exceeds genre and categories" (14), "a writing of excess" that signals "the disturbing return of pasts upon presents and evoke[s] emotions of terror and laughter" (1).

which is largely Ferdinand's fabrication, a projection of his incestuous obsession with his sister and her body, becomes a question of state politics when she marries Antonio, who is lower in rank, and has children with him. In the fourth act, the duke conspires against his sister and tries to drive her insane with the help of a group of madmen and the aforementioned waxwork model, which depicts the dead Antonio and the couple's children. When the Duchess prevails and, surprisingly, manages to preserve her sanity, Ferdinand has her killed by Bosola, the play's malcontent figure. However, his sister's death eventually drives Ferdinand mad himself – he succumbs to lycanthropy, deeming himself a werewolf. Patients like Ferdinand, his physicist, observes,

> [...] imagine
> Themselves to be transformed into wolves,
> Steal forth to churchyards in the dead of night,
> And dig dead bodies up: as two nights since
> One met the duke 'bout midnight in a lane
> Behind Saint Mark's church, with the leg of a man
> Upon his shoulder; and he howl'd fearfully;
> Said he was a wolf, only the difference
> Was, a wolf's skin was hairy on the outside,
> His on the inside; (Webster 5.2.9-18)

The proto-Gothic quality of the duke's lycanthropy is palpable in the physicist's description of Ferdinand's condition and nocturnal behaviour and anticipates the Gothic's obsession with the monstrous aspects of the human psyche as well as the dark, twisted humour of the mode, which were to become so characteristic of its male vein.[7] It is therefore less than surprising that the play has repeatedly been connected to the Gothic. In an introduction to the works of Webster, for example, David Coleman explicitly reads the text as developing "from a political tragedy of state [...] to a proto-gothic tragedy of supernatural horror" (90). Coleman focuses on Act 4 and also notes the ghostly, supernatural echo of the dead Duchess's voice, which reaches her husband Antonio as a warning in 5.3.

---

[7] While the female Gothic is almost always associated with Ann Radcliffe's novels (or romances) of sensibility, her poetic realism and the frequently parodied element of the explained supernatural, the male Gothic has become almost identical with Matthew Lewis' sensationalism, violence and the transgressive existence of the supernatural (see Miles 41).

The play also found critical reappraisal in the wake of the nineteenth-century fascination with the Gothic. Coleman highlights Charles Lamb's appreciation of Webster as an author of horror, and points to R. H. Horne's adaptation of the play for a Victorian audience. Horne compared the Jacobean text to "a grand old abbey – haunted, and falling into decay – […], and I had undertaken to reconstruct it anew with as much of its own materials as I could use […] but preserving almost entire its majestic halls and archways, its loftiest turrets, its most secret and solemn chambers" (qtd. in Coleman 110). He thus turned the play into a quasi-Gothic artefact waiting to be unearthed in order to unleash its ghosts on a modern audience. Intriguingly, the *Duchess*'s Gothic potential was also crucial in the critically acclaimed 2012 staging of the play at the Old Vic in London: the scenery was characterized by the slanting angles of steep arches and various intersecting stairways, creating a vaguely labyrinthine, Gothic stage architecture and atmosphere that was heightened by the use of incense and candles and the appearance of monk-like figures clad in cowls, who – in a spectral and uncanny fashion – were employed as observers – or voyeurs – during the course of the play.[8] The proto-Gothic elements of Webster's play are, it seems, hard to overlook, even if critics have only recently begun to explore them more fully.

II. Jacobean Gothic and the Law

In addition to and, quite possibly, more important than these plot-based arguments, I would maintain that the crucial connection that allows for an interpretation of Jacobean tragedy as 'Gothic' – and of the Gothic as 'Jacobean' – lies in these forms' shared obsession with the law. As I have shown elsewhere (Gruss), the analysis of the discursive connections between law and literature has become a veritable critical paradigm in literary and cultural studies during the last fifteen years.[9] Critics have

---

[8] See, for example, Ben Brantley reviewing the play for the *New York Times* – he describes the stage as "a tiered Gothic-cathedral-like space that echoes with intimations of both eternity and decay" (online). For the *Oxford Times*, Christopher Gray notes that the performance was "steeped in Gothic atmosphere" (online).

[9] See, for example, Constance Jordan and Karen Cunningham, Dennis Kezar, Subha Mukherji, Paul Raffield or Erica Sheen and Lorna Hutson.

demonstrated how the heterogeneity of early modern English law as well as the increasing institutionalization and centralization of the English legal system have found their expression in early modern plays. Trials can not only be linked to the stage in their theatricality[10] – early modern legal training at London's Inns of Court is crucially based on the quasi-dramatic experimentation with cases, the so-called moots, a performative teaching method that bears close resemblance to the theatre.[11] The early modern age can be seen as a period of transition – or crisis – in the development of a national jurisdiction in England, as "a moment in which, necessarily, the question of jurisdictional heterogeneity was messier than in either the earlier period, when legal orders alternative to the common law were more efficacious, or the later period, when the dominance of common law received more final expression" (Cormack 27). This transition entails uncertainties that are mirrored in the often radical scrutiny of law and justice in the drama of the age, which is why "a close engagement with literary texts can help us track for a particular historical moment the cultural usefulness of the discovery that law is constituted, at limits at once necessary and contestable, as the processing of an unruliness it cannot quite put in order" (Cormack 21). Literary and legal narratives serve as complementary textual and cultural frameworks that can be used to shed light on each other.[12] Critics tend to argue in passing that the revengers' determination to seek private – or 'wilde' – justice conflicts with established law,[13] but at the same time serves to

---

[10] Richard Schechner, among others, looks at "Trials and Executions as Performance" (211-214). Maria Aristodemou notes that, "[a]s in the court-room, the clustering of signs in the theatre challenges the centrality of the word with signs other than the text contributing to the making of meaning. Although academically we read law as a text, in the court-room law is also a collection of images, performances, signs that influence if not determine the outcome" (77).

[11] See, for example, Karen Cunningham. Kieran Dolin highlights that "the rhetorical culture of the Inns [...] fostered links between law and literature which spread through personal contact and textual transmission well beyond that privileged cultural space. It also led jurists to think of legal writing as a cultural rather than a technical exercise" (81).

[12] See, for example, Stevie Simkin, who has pointed out that the depiction of revenge in Jacobean drama is closely linked to the development of the judicial system and its gradual shift "towards a centrally-organised justice system" (30).

[13] The term 'wilde justice' originates in Francis Bacon's essay "Of Revenge", from his *Essays or Counsels, Civill and Morall*, and refers specifically to

highlight the perceived inability of the government to maintain these laws in meting out justice: "Revenge redresses injustice caused by abuses of power, and the distribution of power in this period was not only hierarchical, but increasingly unstable" (Pollard 59).[14] Reading both Jacobean drama and Gothic literature in terms of the wider context and implications of the Law and Literature-debate would thus allow for re-evaluations of both genres.

The interest of early modern drama in the law can also be found in classic Gothic: both David Punter and Sue Chaplin explore paradigmatic Gothic novels such as *The Castle of Otranto* in legal terms and thus provide an interconnection of Jacobean tragedy and the Gothic novel that opens up a field of interest worth investigating. As Punter has noted, eighteenth-century Gothic is obsessed with the law, with justifications and limits at a time when the limitations of the British legal system become obvious. Gothic, Punter points out, has always "known the problem of the thin line between justice and persecution, has known the moments when the state order is stretched to breaking point and the law appears either as naked force or as weakened beyond recall" (*Gothic Pathologies* 16). In a somewhat similar argument, Sue Chaplin suggests that the emergence of the Gothic in the eighteenth century is linked to the still precarious status of the evolving legal system:

> The Gothic emerges in the eighteenth century as a fissured, disruptive literary form that throws into question a juridical economy that can no longer necessarily guarantee the authority and authenticity of its fictions. Gothicism began to develop in this period as one of the most potent aesthetic modes of critical engagement with the modern rule of law.[15] (12)

---

revenge.

[14] See also Stevie Simkin, who points out that "the state's failure to deliver justice [... as] a result of its own insidious corruption" is a central concern of revenge tragedy (38). Linda Woodbridge argues that "[i]n revenge plays, a resort to private retaliation is a vote of no confidence in the official bodies charged with providing fair treatment" (6).

[15] Chaplin also explores narratives of the English constitution as 'Gothic', *i.e.* as based on ancient customs and linked to both folklore and romance – see, for example, her reading of William Blackstone's *Commentaries on the Laws of English* (1765-69), in which "the labyrinthine narratives of English common law [are depicted as] reaching back to a fictive 'Gothick' past" (102).

It is therefore possible to read both Jacobean tragedies and the Gothic as forms of literature that develop from a shared concern of the early modern age and the late eighteenth century to deal with anxieties that stem from an evolvement of the hierarchical structure of patriarchy as well as from an evolvement of the legal system as 'Law'.

In adopting the critical framework of Pierre Legendre, I will opt for a relatively expansive understanding of law as 'Law' or 'law of the father' in the remainder of this essay, a framework that, at least in parts, mirrors early modern political thinking at the Jacobean court: James I, famously a proponent of royal absolutism, articulates what critics have termed the "patriarchal model of royal authority" (Clegg 10) in texts such as *The Trew Law of Free Monarchies*, first published in 1598, where he makes use of the familiar trope of the ruler as *pater patriae*, whose word becomes quite literally the law of the father.[16] Legendre, a trained Lacanian psychoanalyst and historian of law, prioritizes law over language in the development of subjectivity and thus identifies a juridical component in the formation of the subject: "For each subject," Legendre argues,

> Law is a function played by the father, or what we call the father, according to a triangular Oedipal logic. The entire structure of legality is built upon these foundations, because these are the principles of authority and legitimacy. Institutions, therefore, have a primary relation to the mechanism of human desire and to its genealogical recognition.[17] (117)

Legendre's approach to legal thinking is, as this quote demonstrates, enmeshed in psychoanalytical thinking, especially in concepts on the formation of the individual, and posits an inherently intimate and familial connection of the individual to the Law. Law in Legendre becomes the foundational social principle of authority, a paternal principle – similar to Freud's construction of the social in terms of the family or Lacan's theorization of society in terms of the Symbolic order, the *non/nom du père*. As a social and familial principle, Law also affects the role of each

---

[16] Cyndia Susan Clegg stresses that, "[a]ccording to James's use of the trope, the father is the source and originator of law" (13).

[17] See also Chaplin, who points out that Legendre "theorises human subjectivity as *juridical* subjectivity: self-identity is constituted through a system of lineage institutionalised as law" (57).

subject within the family, within a given institution or within a society, and highlights the instability and constructedness of these structures. As Legendre emphasizes, a "legal system is first and foremost a social technique of communication; it is the only technique which can assure the entry of human subjects into the order of Law" (103). Peter Goodrich points out that Law, "for Legendre, is intrinsic to the formation of the individual subject, and law is both historically and theoretically at the centre of the symbolic order in relation to which individual identity is formed" ("Introduction" 6). Within the context of the Jacobean Gothic, a breakdown of the law, or of authority, must consequently lead to a breakdown of the symbolic as the 'law of the father', and therefore of individual identity. Clearly influenced by deconstruction, Legendre's symbolic order of Law is based on a source of authority that is forever absent, an "unsayable or immutable yet invisible source of law, which can only be represented or symbolised in the various figures of the power of law" (Goodrich, "Introduction" 13).[18] Regarding the legal framework which informs so many early modern plays, the excessive or transgressive violence that is so typical of these plays and the revengers' defiant insistence on a revenge that always goes wrong seem to lend themselves to a reading that borrows elements from Legendre's and Goodrich's legal theories, which argue for an unconscious or 'dark side' of legal thought that resonates with Gothic theorizing.[19] In early modern tragedy, it is quite often the figure of the tyrant as *pater patriae*, symbolic father figure and stand-in of the Law, who becomes the point of culmination of these questions.[20]

---

[18] See also Goodrich's interview with Legendre for a more detailed discussion of the impact of psychoanalysis on Legendre's thinking.

[19] In *Law in the Courts of Love: Literature and Other Minor Jurisprudences*, Goodrich explores "minor jurisprudences or forms of legal knowledge that escape the phantom of a sovereign and unitary law" (2) or were suppressed and marginalized by official jurisdiction. These minor jurisprudences, he argues, form the suppressed part of law's unconscious, "a history of the dark side of law, of its other scene, of that which it does not know and so cannot control" (3).

[20] See, for example, the tyrant figures in Thomas Middleton's *The Bloody Banquet* and *The Lady's Tragedy*, Ben Jonson's *Sejanus His Fall*, William Shakespeare's *Richard III* and *Macbeth*, John Fletcher's *Valentinian*, Beaumont and Fletcher's *The Maid's Tragedy*, or Massinger's *The Roman Actor*.

III. John Marston's and Philip Massinger's Proto-Gothic Writings

Even in a very cursory reading, John Marston's *Antonio's Revenge* and Philip Massinger's *The Duke of Milan* reveal their Gothic potential and a generic proximity to what will become the 'male Gothic' tradition in the eighteenth century. They are replete with excessive violence and a sexuality more than bordering on the obscene; and in *Antonio's Revenge*, the ghost of Antonio's father is an integral part of the plot. At the same time, both authors are deeply enmeshed in the legal framework of early modern drama: Marston enrolled at the Middle Temple as a young man and was thus directly involved in questions of legal training.[21] Massinger – even though he never received a formal legal training – quite obviously catered to an audience which was able to "appreciate the characteristically elaborate judgment scenes, complete with accusations, defenses, and argumentative summations that appear in more than half of [his] extant works and distinguish him from collaborators" (Clark 21). For my brief delineation of the Gothic potential of these plays, I will focus on the depiction of the breakdown of symbolic Law as it is demonstrated by the increasing conflation of revenger and tyrant figure in both plays as well as the transgressive sexuality of the tyrant figure in *The Duke of Milan*.

"*Enter* Piero *unbraced, his arms bare, smeared in blood, a poniard in one hand, bloody, and a torch in the other* [...]." (Marston 1.1.1) – this is the introduction of Piero, the tyrant figure of Marston's *Antonio's Revenge*, who has killed Antonio's father Andrugio and Feliche, both known to Marston's audience from his earlier comedy *Antonio and Mellida* from 1602, the romantic 'prequel' to this bloody play.[22] Throughout the first scene, Piero is boasting about his violent deeds – "I am great in blood, / Unequalled in revenge" (Marston 1.1.17-18) – but he is soon surpassed by Antonio, introduced as a sensitive young lover in *Antonio and Mellida*, who turns into a bloodthirsty psychopath when his father's ghost spurs him on to take revenge. Antonio kills Piero's innocent son Julio in a brutal act of onstage violence, revels in the gore of his deed, and then sprinkles his father's hearse with the child's blood in what might be

---

[21] The definitive study of Marston's cultural context is still Philip J. Finkelpearl's *John Marston of the Middle Temple: An Elizabethan Dramatist in His Social Setting.*

[22] See Finkelpearl, who notes that *Antonio and Mellida* and *Antonio's Revenge* form "a unique comic-tragic diptych" (140).

called a displaced act of cannibalism, as Andrugio's corpse soaks up or
'drinks' the blood of Antonio's victim; only a little while later, Antonio is
depicted as entering the stage "*his arms bloody, [bearing] a torch and a
poniard*" (Marston 3.5.13). By the middle of the play, then, the revenger
Antonio has come to visually replicate the subject of his revenge, Piero –
and their identities have already become precariously similar to one
another. This play, as Rick Bowers has pointed out, "deconstructs notions
of sanity and society and the cause-and-effect relationships that purport to
hold a society together" (73).[23] *Antonio's Revenge* has, consequently,
often aroused reactions of either bewilderment or outright disgust in
critics and can therefore be easily described as a play that privileges
transgression in its exploration and deconstruction of the social and moral
order of its fictional world. This Jacobean Gothic play seems to invite a
reading that is concerned with the Law in the text; notions of order and
the symbolic are debunked as fabrications at the same time as they are
evoked. Antonio's urge to revenge his father not only prompts him to
commit deeds that transform him into the visual equivalent of the
monstrous Piero – a bloody *doppelganger*, one might say; his final plot to
kill the tyrant also seems to surpass his opponent's cruelty in its bloodlust
and psychological as well as physical violence. Together with his
conspirators, he lures the ruler to a banquet which contains a dish created
especially for the Duke: "Here lies a dish to feast thy father's gorge. /
Here's flesh and blood which I am sure thou lovest" (Marston 5.5.48-49).
Even though it remains unclear whether Piero is in effect forced to
consume the dish with his son Julio's remains – the revengers have just
cut out his tongue and leeringly displayed it to the audience, and the stage
directions do not indicate an explicit cannibalistic act – the play uses the
challenge of cannibalism as its climactic transgression.[24] With reference
to cannibalism in general, Raymond J. Rice notes that the "consumption
of human flesh represents the symbolic order's limit point, a threshold
that must not be crossed" (298). Even though the act of incorporation is
not explicitly executed in Marston's play, the symbolic/legal order of the

---

[23] Famously, Marston's play is transgressive in plot as well as in its language;
see Ben Jonson's *Poetaster* for his popular parody of Marston's often
exaggerated and hyperbolic speeches.
[24] Other early modern tragedies include more explicit scenes of cannibalism. See,
for example, Shakespeare's *Titus Andronicus* or Middleton's *The Bloody
Banquet*.

play is unhinged as cannibalism becomes less 'the symbolic order's limit point' than just one among many transgressions. Rice goes on to argue that the transgression of Antonio and his fellow revengers in the eventual murder of Piero is integral to the maintenance of the symbolic Law of the play: "Revenge is thus shown to be a *precondition* of Law, a ritualistic subversion that underscores the Law's necessity and, in fact, legitimates the Law itself" (313; emphasis in the original). In contrast to this affirmative reading, I would argue that, in a play in which distinctions are collapsed so decisively, the Law necessarily breaks down with these distinctions. While on the surface of the play it is true that the victims of Piero's tyranny impose justice, justice is annihilated in the cruel bloodiness of their act of revenge. It is crucial for Marston's play that Antonio, the solitary revenger, eventually becomes the leader of a communal plot of revenge. As Philip J. Finkelpearl has convincingly argued, "Piero's accumulated outrages have transformed the activity from private revenge into a political assassination with all elements of society allied against him" (158). With the multiple stabbings of Piero, moral distinctions and order in the play are irrevocably obliterated, as the ending demonstrates. While plays such as Thomas Middleton's *The Revenger's Tragedy* seem to maintain at least a semblance of order due to the eventual imprisonment of Vindice, Marston's revengers are not punished: when one of the Senators asks, "Whose hand presents this gory spectacle?" (Marston 5.6.1), the revengers embark on a darkly comic competition in which they want to prove their participation in the deed: "I pierced the monster's heart / With an undaunted hand" (Marston 5.6.5-6), Antonio boasts, only to be cut off by Pandulpho who affirms that "'twas I; / 'Twas I sluiced out his life-blood" (Marston 5.6.7-8). Instead of punishment, the second Senator offers blessings to the murderers: "Blest be you all, and may your honours live / Religious held sacred, even for ever and ever" (Marston 5.6.10-11). The world that Piero has created is monstrous, and in the worldview that his murderers have adopted, there is no Law that could punish the revengers' 'wilde' justice. If subjectivity is, as Legendre has it, always also juridical, then in this play, both legal frameworks and those of individual identity have collapsed.

Massinger's *The Duke of Milan* is based on Shakespeare's *Othello* in the depiction of the Duke's jealousy and clearly modelled after Middleton's *Lady's Tragedy*, which, in turn, is inspired by Josephus' account of the

myth of Herod and Mariam.[25] Dramatic tyranny is often linked to a
confusion of the sexes in general and to the effeminacy of the tyrant
figure more specifically, and this is certainly true for Massinger's *The
Duke of Milan*. The Duke's erotic bond with his wife Marcelia is
completely incompatible with the integrity of his political position;
Sforza can only act as a responsible politician whenever he is separated
from his wife and her influence.[26] *The Duke of Milan* also uses
necrophilia and the taboo of the dead body as an erotic object to
showcase the breakdown of legal boundaries. In this play, the interconnection between the Gothic, Law and identity becomes quite explicit.
Sforza, the eponymous Duke of Milan, kills his wife Marcelia in a fit of
jealous rage. The Duke makes clear that he is the representative of the
Law when he threatens to order the execution of his sister – "She hath
blaphem'd, and by our Law must dye." (Massinger 4.3.124-125) – and
when he stabs Marcelia he comments: "I being now (*Stabs her.*) / In this
my Iustice" (Massinger 4.3.286-287). Law and 'justice' in this play are
based on a weak man's blind passions, and the killing of Marcelia, who,
like Desdemona, has not, in fact, betrayed her husband's trust, leads to a
collapse of not only the Law, but also to a literal breakdown of the
Duke's identity. In denial of his wife's murder, Sforza goes mad and
comforts himself with the delusion that his wife's bloody corpse is still
alive – an illusion that can only be sustained temporarily, as one of his
doctors points out: "The body to, will putrifie, and then / We can no
longer couer the imposture" (Massinger 5.2.135-136). The play's
revenger figure, Francisco, wants to avenge his sister Eugenia, who has
been seduced and then abandoned by Sforza before his infatuation with
Marcelia. Disguised as an artist, Francisco can at least visually bring
Marcelia back to life by applying artful – if poisoned – makeup. When
the Duke kisses the corpse, he dies. In contrast to the revengers in
Antonio's Revenge, Francisco *is* punished for his deed and accepts his
fate willingly: "I leaue the world with glory; they are men / […] / That
wrong'd doe right themselues before they die" (Massinger 5.2.254-255).
Order is thus seemingly restored with the destruction of Sforza, the

---

[25] This version of the Herod legend, which explicitly mentions his necrophilia,
can be found in the *Babylonian Talmud* (see Zimmerman, "Animating Matter"
225).
[26] When he negotiates a new political alliance with Charles, King of Spain, he
presents himself as a good diplomat and constant ruler (see Massinger 3.1)

necrophiliac ruler who neglects a state in crisis because of his possessive love for his wife,[27] and the impending execution of the revenger. However, the endangerment of the legal framework remains a source of anxiety. Sforza dies before he can utter his last words, and the courtiers decide to "giue him funeral, / And then determine of the state affaires" (Massinger 5.2.266-267). The problematic state of affairs in Milan is intensified by the women's perceived unfeminine behaviour, which complements the Duke's emasculation; the aggressiveness of female characters in the play lays open male inactivity. Mariana, Sforza's sister and Francisco's wife, for example wishes "[t]hat it were lawfull / To meete her [Marcelia] with a Ponyard, and a Pistoll; / But these weake hands shall shew my spleene" (Massinger 2.1.180-182). It is the allegation of unmanliness which unites Sforza and revenger Francisco – and when Francisco's sister Eugenia presses her brother to "Aske thy feares, / Thy base vnmanly feares, thy poore delayes, / Thy dull forgetfulnesse equal with death" (Massinger 5.1.67-69), the 'unmanly' revenger has become almost interchangeable with the effeminate Duke. In a play in which women are more aggressive than men, the representative of the Law loses his mind over his wife, and tyrants and revengers are effectually interchangeable, the legal framework must remain seriously troubled.

Both of my case studies therefore not merely attest to early modern tragedy's obsession with the instability of legal frameworks. This obsession is also acted out on stage in decidedly – male – Gothic terms in the plays' focus on the supernatural, madness, the loss of identity, violence, the instability of gender and sexual transgression or perversion. As I have demonstrated, an approach to these plays which combines the postmodern psychoanalytical legal framework created by Pierre Legendre and Peter Goodrich with knowledge of the Gothic mode can shed new light on plays the full potential of which is still being rediscovered by critics. Rather than constrict the 'Gothic' perspective on the early modern age to Shakespeare, whose influence on canonical Gothic writing is

---

[27] At the beginning of the play, courtiers note that the Duke, as well as his realm, "Appeares now shaken" (Massinger 1.1.50), his political career "Being now at stake" (Massinger 1.1.53). With reference to this scene, Maurizio Calbi points out that "[t]he inappropriateness of Sforza's passionate attachment is enhanced by the fact that it is enunciated at the most critical of moments, as his dukedom is threatened by military invasion" (86).

undeniable, my broader notion of a 'Jacobean Gothic' helps to understand the topical similarities that can be found in Jacobean plays and Gothic literature; it also allows us to reconceptualize our understanding of the relationship between two forms that are characterized by a shared interest in excess, the possibilities of its representation and the ways to contain it. The function of the Gothic as a mode could then become a central tool in the analysis of the role of excess in early modern drama, an excess that migrates into a different literary discourse in the late eighteenth century, which can be characterized by a similar crisis of legal thinking. Jacobean drama is proto-Gothic – or should we rather call the Gothic works post-Jacobean?

Works Cited

Aristodemou, Maria. *Law and Literature: Journeys from Her to Eternity.* Oxford: Oxford University Press, 2000.

Bacon, Francis. "Of Revenge." *The Major Works: Including* New Atlantis *and the* Essays. Ed. Brian Vickers. Oxford: Oxford University Press, 2002. 347-348.

Botting, Fred. *Gothic.* New York: Routledge, 1996.

Bowers, Rick. *Radical Comedy in Early Modern England: Contexts, Cultures, Performances.* Aldershot: Ashgate, 2008.

Brantley, Ben. "Britain, Amid Austerity, Turns Rather Cutthroat." *The New York Times*, 28 June 2012. Web. 16 June 2014.

Bronfen, Elisabeth and Beate Neumeier. *Gothic Renaissance: A Reassessment.* Manchester: Manchester University Press, 2014.

Butler, Charles. "Jacobean Tragedy." *The Handbook to Gothic Literature.* Ed. Marie Mulvey-Roberts. Basingstoke and London: Macmillan, 1998. 275-276.

Calbi, Maurizio. *Approximate Bodies. Gender and Power in Early Modern Drama and Anatomy.* London: Routledge, 2005.

Chaplin, Sue. *The Gothic and the Rule of Law, 1764-1820.* Basingstoke and London: Palgrave Macmillan, 2007.

Clark, Ira. *The Moral Art of Philip Massinger.* Lewisburg: Bucknell University Press, 1993.

Clegg, Cyndia Susan. *Press Censorship in Jacobean England.* Cambridge: Cambridge University Press, 2001.

Clery, E. J. "The Genesis of 'Gothic' Fiction." *The Cambridge Companion to Gothic Fiction.* Ed. Jerrold E. Hogle. Cambridge: Cambridge University Press, 2002. 21-39.

Coleman, David. *John Webster, Renaissance Dramatist.* Edinburgh: Edinburgh University Press, 2010.

Cormack, Bradin. *A Power to Do Justice: Jurisdiction, English Literature, and the Rise of Common Law, 1509-1625.* Chicago and London: University of Chicago Press, 2007.

Cunningham, Karen J. "'So Many Books, So Many Rolls of Ancient Time': The Inns of Court and *Gorboduc.*" *Solon and Thespis: Law and Theater in the English Renaissance.* Ed. Dennis Kezar. Notre Dame, IN: University of Notre Dame Press, 2007. 197-217.

Desmet, Christy and Anne Williams, eds. *Shakespearean Gothic.* Cardiff: University of Wales Press, 2009.

Dolin, Kieran. *A Critical Introduction to Law and Literature.* Cambridge: Cambridge University Press, 2007.

Drakakis, John, and Dale Townshend, eds. *Gothic Shakespeares.* London: Routledge, 2008.

Drakakis, John. "Introduction." *Gothic Shakespeares.* Eds. John Drakakis and Dale Townshend. London: Routledge, 2008. 1-20.

Finkelpearl, Philip J. *John Marston of the Middle Temple: An Elizabethan Dramatist in His Social Setting.* Cambridge, MA: Harvard University Press, 1969.

Goodrich, Peter. "Introduction: Psychoanalysis and Law." *Law and the Unconscious: A Legendre Reader.* Ed. Peter Goodrich. London: Macmillan, 1997. 1-36.

---. *Languages of Law. From Logics of Memory to Nomadic Masks.* London: Weidenfeld, 1990.

---. *Law in the Courts of Love: Literature and Other Minor Jurisprudences.* London and New York: Routledge, 1996.

Gray, Christopher. "*The Duchess of Malfi*: The Old Vic, London." *The Oxford Times*, 4 April 2012. Web. 16 June 2014.

Gruss, Susanne. "Thomas Middleton's Gothic Nightmares: *The Revenger's Tragedy*, *The Bloody Banquet* and *The Lady's Tragedy*." *Zeitsprünge: Forschungen zur Frühen Neuzeit / Studies in Early Modern History, Culture and Science* 16.3/4 (2012): 225-242.

Jordan, Constance and Karen Cunningham, eds. *The Law in Shakespeare*. Basingstoke: Palgrave Macmillan, 2007.

Kezar, Dennis, ed. *Solon and Thespis. Law and Theater in the English Renaissance*. Notre Dame, IN: University of Notre Dame Press, 2007.

Legendre, Pierre. *Law and the Unconscious: A Legendre Reader*. Ed. Peter Goodrich. London: Macmillan, 1997.

Marston, John. *Antonio's Revenge*. Ed. W. Reavley Gair. Manchester: Manchester University Press, 2006.

Massinger, Philip. *The Plays and Poems of Philip Massinger*. Eds. Philip Edwards and Colin Gibson. Oxford: Clarendon Press, 1976.

Miles, Robert. "Ann Radcliffe and Matthew Lewis." *A Companion to the Gothic*. Ed. David Punter. Oxford and Malden, MA: Blackwell, 2000. 41-57.

Mukherji, Subha. *Law and Representation in Early Modern Drama*. Cambridge: Cambridge University Press, 2006.

Pollard, Tanya. "Tragedy and Revenge." *The Cambridge Companion to English Renaissance Tragedy*. Eds. Emma Smith, Garrett A. Sullivan Jr. Cambridge: Cambridge University Press, 2010. 58-72.

Punter, David, and Glennis Byron. *The Gothic*. Malden, Oxford and Victoria: Blackwell, 2005.

Punter, David. *Gothic Pathologies. The Text, the Body, and the Law*. Basingstoke and London: Macmillan, 1998.

---. *The Literature of Terror. A History of Gothic Fictions from 1765 to the Present Day*. Vol. 1: *The Gothic Tradition*. New York: Longman, 1996.

Raffield, Paul. *Images and Cultures of Law in Early Modern England: Justice and Political Power, 1558-1660*. Cambridge: Cambridge University Press, 2004.

Rice, Raymond J. "Cannibalism and the Act of Revenge in Tudor-Stuart Drama." *Studies in English Literature, 1500-1900 (SEL)* 44.2 (2004): 297-316.

Schechner, Richard. *Performance Studies: An Introduction.* London and New York: Routledge, 2013.

Sheen, Erica, and Lorna Hutson, eds. *Literature, Politics and Law in Renaissance England.* Basingstoke: Palgrave Macmillan, 2005.

Simkin, Stevie. *Early Modern Tragedy and the Cinema of Violence.* Basingstoke: Palgrave Macmillan, 2006.

Webster, John. *The Duchess of Malfi.* Ed. John Russell Brown. Manchester: Manchester University Press, 2009.

---. "Introduction." *Shakespearean Gothic.* Eds. Christy Desmet, and Anne Williams. Cardiff: University of Wales Press, 2009. 1-10.

Williams, Anne. *Art of Darkness. A Poetics of Gothic.* Chicago: University of Chicago Press, 1995.

Woodbridge, Linda. *English Revenge Drama. Money, Resistance, Equality.* Cambridge: Cambridge University Press, 2010.

Zimmerman, Susan. "Animating Matter: The Corpse as Idol in *The Second Maiden's Tragedy.*" *Renaissance Drama* 31 (2002): 215-243.

---. *The Early Modern Corpse and Shakespeare's Theatre.* Edinburgh: Edinburgh University Press, 2005.

Kerstin Frank

"[Y]ou must see the Sun through the Cloud, and relish Light by the help of Darkness": Morality, Rationality, and the Proto-Gothic Atmosphere in Daniel Defoe's *An Essay on the History and Reality of Apparitions*

I. Introduction

In keeping with literary historians' predilection for clearly delineated movements and counter-movements, beginnings and endings, the close of the eighteenth century has long been regarded as the start of something new, alongside the return of something that had been repressed. The scientific revolution, the cultural forces of the Enlightenment and the rise of Realist fiction,[1] so the story goes, had displaced representations of the irrational, the liminal, and the supernatural in the course of the eighteenth century. The vigorous return of these themes in the form of the Gothic novel came to herald the beginning of modern Fantasy.[2] These shifts in world-view, literary modes and taste did not occur overnight, however, nor did 'new' genres neatly supersede those that had previously existed. While attitudes towards knowledge, truth, physics and metaphysics gradually changed during the seventeenth and eighteenth centuries, literary texts that contained supernatural elements continued to be written and read.[3] They did not present fossilized, archaic forms, but genres

---

[1] 'Realist' fiction is capitalized here in order to emphasize its emergence as a distinct literary form of writing in the eighteenth century, in contrast to the more general – and problematic – idea of realism as the depiction of extra-literary 'reality'. For a similar distinction see Brooke-Rose (65). Doody gives an account of the rise and characteristics of this particular kind of Realism in the eighteenth century (287-291).

[2] See e.g. Mendlesohn and James (3), Jackson (95) and Boone (173). Punter calls this traditional opposition between Realism and Gothic fiction, both in a generic and in a historical sense, "a commonplace of literary history" (10).

[3] 'Supernatural' here denotes phenomena which at the time appeared to contradict the laws of nature and were ascribed to metaphysical forces. Of course, these distinctions are notoriously vague and subject to historical change and cultural differences.

which developed along with cultural and scientific transitions and incorporated the discourses of the time.

Stories of apparitions in particular remained popular throughout the seventeenth and eighteenth centuries and proved to be remarkably versatile.[4] A brief overview in the following chapter will show how they were adapted during the second half of the seventeenth century to negotiate the shifting and uncertain boundaries between the physical, the metaphysical, and the – merely – illusionary. In the course of the eighteenth century, however, apparition narratives again changed their functions and techniques, as English society was faced with new challenges in the form of economic, political and social developments, which made this-worldly moral considerations seem more pressing than deliberations on the afterlife.

Daniel Defoe's *An Essay on the History and Reality of Apparitions* from 1727 takes a prominent position within the development of apparition narratives in the eighteenth century.[5] It displays both traditional features and radical changes in relation to epistemology, ontology, and morality, and is unique in its complex use of narrative techniques. The *Essay* presents itself as a treatise on apparitions, but it makes use of many concrete examples and cuts across the boundary between argument and narrative. This study reveals how Defoe's *Essay* changes the functions of the supernatural within apparition narratives by shifting the emphasis from epistemological or theological to moral concerns, and analyzes the intricate narrative set-up of the text. Defoe's carefully constructed narrator-figure on the one hand emphasizes his stance as sober critic and theologian while on the other hand indulging in narrative detail and an uncanny atmosphere. The text thus playfully confounds religious conviction, rational argument, proto-Gothic elements, and circumstantial Realism, and ultimately satirizes its own attempts at rationalizing the irrational.

---

[4] In this study, the term 'apparition' will be used, since it leaves the ontology of the appearing entity open, while 'ghost' more specifically indicates the return of a dead person (see Davies 2).

[5] Hereafter, the title will be abbreviated as *Essay*.

II. The Development of Apparition Narratives, 1660-1727

Stories about apparitions have been a popular source of entertainment at all levels of society ever since people first gathered around a fire to spin a yarn. During the English Restoration and at the beginning of the eighteenth century, however, they reached new heights of popularity and underwent significant changes in style and tone in order to serve other purposes within a changing theological, scientific and cultural climate.[6] As the scientific revolution generated different attitudes towards knowledge and established specific methods for obtaining it, empirical evidence gained in importance, and 'truth' had to be compatible with rational argument. McKeon describes this as "a transformation from metaphysics and theology to epistemology" (83). With the new focus on the empirical, 'natural' world, 'supernatural' entities were increasingly relegated to the realm of superstition and old wives' tales, and the emerging opposition contained strong political hierarchies in terms of social class, gender, and marginalized religious groups.[7] Somewhat paradoxically, however, stories of supernatural occurrences were also incorporated into epistemological debates and refashioned in a way that made them appropriate support for theological arguments.[8] Authors like Joseph Glanvill, Richard Baxter, George Sinclair and Richard Bovet collected and retold apparition narratives as empirical data to buttress belief in the afterlife, the realm of spirits and God's providential participation in worldly affairs.[9] On the one hand, their texts absorbed the rational argumentation and empirical data confirmed by reliable witnesses of the new scientific discourse, but on the other hand the authors employed it in order to strengthen beliefs which transcend the empirical realm for which these discourses were designed. The texts thus contained a fundamental contradiction or "structural instability"

---

[6] For a more detailed account of this development see Handley (23).

[7] The politics of class and gender in this context are explored further by Boone (174-178).

[8] Brian Easlea explores the complex relation between the changing world-view and the belief in occult forces, particularly in witchcraft, in his *Witch-Hunting, Magic and the New Philosophy: An Introduction to Debates of the Scientific Revolution 1450-1750*.

[9] These collections do not exclusively focus on apparition narratives, but also include other supernatural occurrences, particularly those attributed to witchcraft.

(McKeon 87) within themselves, which surfaces in their "rhetorical anxiety" (Boone 173).

In addition to epistemological and theological functions, apparition narratives also answered other purposes: the creation of stability and a sense of coherence within the Church after the shattering experiences of the civil war and the splintering off of various dissenting groups. Concerns about the threat which a materialist world-view posed to religion united people from different denominations (Handley 36). Besides, for the publishers these increasingly popular texts represented an important economic gain. Finally, apparition narratives also served social and moral functions since they gave a voice and power to underprivileged members of society who were exploited by those with money and status. In George Sinclair's *Satan's Invisible World Discovered* (19-22), for example, a yeoman gets his housekeeper pregnant and has her sent away and killed, but her ghost appears to a miller living not far away and causes him to reveal the yeoman's deed. While the argumentative framework of the collections points towards their theological function, the tales themselves, as in this example, invariably focus on the moral evaluation of individual actions – cases of warnings, punishments and atonement are related to sinful deeds driven by greed, personal spite, sexual desire or the need for social recognition and respectability.

Within the range of apparition narratives published, however, argumentative priorities and narrative styles vary widely. While Glanvill, for instance, is most concerned with the epistemological question, Sinclair's collection, although based on Glanvill's work, shows more attempts at stylistic variety and techniques for creating suspense and atmosphere (Parsons, "Introduction" vii; xvi). Nathaniel Crouch, a bookseller and publisher, in turn strengthens the sensational and terror-inspiring elements, whereas Baxter emphasizes the moral function and responsibilities of the individual (Capoferro 113; 120). Bearing in mind these stylistic and argumentative variations, it is difficult to trace a clear, linear development in the genre towards the end of the seventeenth and the beginning of the eighteenth century. Nevertheless, critics have been tempted to suggest such developments. In an early outline of apparition narratives, Parsons proposes a definite "shift from propaganda to pastime, from indoctrination to literary entertainment" ("Ghost-Stories" 293) towards the end of the seventeenth century.[10] Handley links this transformation into a more literary genre to developments in the market and in literary theory, as different formats of publication, the Stamp Act of 1712, and a general debate about the differences between fact-related and fictional genres pushed towards more precise categorization at the beginning of the eighteenth century (95-96). She also attests a shift in emphasis from the epistemological to the moral function of the texts: "The truth or falsity of ghost stories gradually became less significant than the moral lessons that they taught, helping to explain how ghost stories gradually shaded into the genres of poetry, drama and novels" (18).

This description of change within the genre certainly does more justice to its variety and flexibility than the idea of a clear dividing line between the functions of different genres, as McKeon describes it: "In the arguments and [apparition] narratives that I have discussed in this chapter, the assertion of historical truth aims to serve the end of inculcating Christian faith. In the early novels it will seek to aid the cause of teaching moral truth" (89). Assigning just one function to apparition narratives neglects both the variety and developments that occurred within the genre. Their appeal relies on the tension generated by the uneasy relationship between epistemological quandaries, moral judgments, and more and more aesthetically refined and entertaining ways of narrating the stories. This tension and complexity also made them flexible enough to meet the moral and social challenges of the new century.

Daniel Defoe's journalistic and literary works responded to these challenges posed by changes in English society and in the economy. His novels create convincing and complex characters whose life histories and actions dramatize the doubts, hopes and inner conflicts of the individual faced with the beginnings of modernity, when traditional social and moral frameworks were crumbling and the emerging consumer society presented a myriad of new opportunities, but also responsibilities and dangers. Most of these novels reveal a tension between this modern, secular outlook on the one hand and considerations of metaphysical and supernatural forces on the other (Baine 5-9; Mullan 268-269; Bostridge

---

[10] Clery sees this process as inevitably linked to the nature of these narratives, proposing that the "'real' supernatural [...] was always, irresistibly, on the way to becoming a 'spectacular' supernatural, a species of fiction" (*Rise* 24).

113-115). In other texts, Defoe dealt more explicitly with supernatural
occurrences and other-worldly influences on the actions of individuals,
most famously in his apparition narrative, "A True Relation of the
Apparition of One Mrs Veal" from 1706.[11] Among his articles on the
supernatural and his demonological treatises,[12] the *Essay* stands out in the
way it combines the arguments of a treatise with the literary merits of a
collection of apparition narratives in an intriguing amalgam of narrative
modes, as the following analysis will show.

III. Daniel Defoe's *An Essay on the History and Reality of Apparitions*: Epistemological and Ontological Arguments

In contrast to the pivotal collections of apparition narratives from the
seventeenth century, Defoe's *Essay* unfolds a more extensive theoretical
argument. It not only uses recent stories of apparitions, but also includes
examples from the Bible and classical antiquity. Within the narrator's
argument, epistemological considerations, i.e. the question as to how we
can know that spirits exist, get relatively short shrift:

> I shall therefore spend but very little time to prove or to argue for
> the Reality of Apparition. Let Mr. *Glanville* [...] and his Antago-
> nists [...] be your Disputants upon that Subject [...]. If there is an
> invisible World, and if Spirits residing or inhabiting are allowed
> to be there, or placed there by the supreme governing Power of
> the Universe; it will be hard to prove, that 'tis impossible they
> should come hither [...]. Reason does not exclude them, Nature
> yields to the Possibility, and Experience with a Cloud of Witness-

---

[11] "A True Relation of the Apparition of One Mrs Veal" adds important new
features to the genre, as discussed e.g. in Handley (96-97) and Capoferro (130-
132). Its authorship has, however, been questioned by George Starr, in his essay
"Why Defoe Probably Did Not Write The Apparition of Mrs Veal". To comment
on this debate would go beyond the scope of this study.
[12] Defoe's major demonological treatises besides the *Essay* are *The Political
History of the Devil* from 1726 and *A System of Magick* from 1727. For his
treatment of witchcraft in the *Review* see Bostridge (124-128). Novak discusses
several articles about supernatural topics from *Applebee's Original Weekly
Journal* which show strong parallels to Defoe's other works and might have
sprung from his pen (594-595).

es [...] in all Ages confirm the Reality of the affirmative. The Question therefore before me is not so much whether there are any such things as Apparitions of Spirits; but WHO, and WHAT, and from WHENCE they are; what Business they come about, who sends them or directs them, and how and in what manner we ought to think and act, and behave about them, and to them; and this is the Substance of this Undertaking. (Defoe, *Essay* 46; emphasis in the original)

The 'fact' of spirits' existence is thus not detached from the fundamental 'if' that precedes it.[13] The aim of the argument is to consider their ontological position, their place in the system of invisible, metaphysical entities. This system is very clear and follows a strict hierarchical order starting with God, his angels or good spirits, moving down to evil spirits, and finally, to the souls of men. Of these entities, only good spirits and evil ones can appear to human beings (Defoe, *Essay* 128-130). Among the (good) angels, there is a difference between those in heaven, next to God, who will not appear on earth again, and the "lower" angels, who are placed close to us "at or near the outer Circumference of the Earth's Atmosphere", know about our human affairs, and can "converse with this World, either by Apparition, Voices, Noises, good or bad Omens, or other sensible Conveyances to the Mind, by which they can give Notices of Good or Evil, and can intimate to Man many things useful to him in the Conduct of his Life". When they choose to appear, they "can assume Bodies, Shape, Voice, and even can personate this or that Man or Woman" (Defoe, *Essay* 166; see also 79-82).

A central part of this argument is that the narrator strongly opposes the notion of ghosts in the sense of human souls returning to the earth after their death. Any stories in which someone sees a dead person must be interpreted either as a psychological phenomenon which happens only in the mind of the spectator, or as a good angel who chooses to assume the form of a dead person in order to impart a message (Defoe, *Essay* 115; 120). This argument is not unusual among Protestant writers, but some of Defoe's predecessors, such as Glanvill or Sinclair, do not exclude the

---

[13] In other places, the narrator asserts the reality of spirits more forcefully – e.g. "There must certainly be a World of Spirits" (Defoe, *Essay* 79) – but the subject of their existence is not central to his argument.

possibility that ghosts exist (Baine 86).[14] If apparitions cannot be revenants, apparition narratives lose a major theological function, since they no longer lend support to the belief in life after death. It also follows that they do not transgress or play with the boundary between life and death, which is a central theme and atmospheric element in traditional ghost stories and in Gothic writing. Yet even if in theory this subject is foreclosed, it remains present in many stories included in the *Essay*, since spirits seem to have a distinct predilection for appearing in the guise of a revenant.

The narrator combines empirical evidence in the form of narratives and logical reasoning to reach a middle ground between absolute scepticism, i.e. the negation of all supernatural entities, and extreme credulity or superstition, which takes even the most improbable tales of supernatural occurrences at face value (Defoe, *Essay* 39; Starr 3). This stance is gauged to appeal to the world-view and mind-set of Defoe's target group, "respectable" and "well-heeled" readers (Handley 103), who are interested in supernatural phenomena, but steeped in rational discourse, and would neither want to be taken for credulous fools, nor be considered as consumers of vulgar entertainment. The middle position informs both the ontology and the argumentative techniques of the *Essay*: its key concern is with a middle class of spirits that are not in heaven, but not quite in our world either. This argument presupposes that the whole metaphysical world, including providence, follows consistent rational principles and can hence be explained by the rational mind: "the Wisdom of Providence too is not known to act inconsistent with itself; and, which is a sufficient Answer to all the rest, we are allowed to judge of all these things by our reasoning Powers, nor have we any other Rules to judge by" (Defoe, *Essay* 110). The narrator exercises and demonstrates his powers of reasoning by including several stories where the supernatural occurrence turns out to have a natural explanation, being either based on a hoax or on the hallucinations of a disturbed mind. The narrator then gleefully satirizes the credulity and simple-mindedness of people who believe these stories to be true. However, it will be argued later on in this essay that these seemingly clear-cut distinctions do not always hold, and

---

[14] The question remains whether Defoe's disbelief in ghosts dated from early on in his career, an argument which Starr (421) uses to questions his authorship of "A True Relation …," or whether he changed his attitude, "swinging […] with the pendulum of contemporary belief" (Parsons, "Ghost-Stories" 297).

that 'real' and 'hoax' supernatural occurrences tend to be entangled in the stories, thus destabilizing the opposition.

The litmus test for the truth of a story in the *Essay* is its rational compatibility with the proposed system of the invisible world. In contrast to this, the claims of authenticity found in former collections of apparition narratives were based primarily on the authority of their sources. In Defoe's *Essay*, the narrator carefully distinguishes between reliable and more dubious sources, but a questionable witness does not lead him to exclude a powerful story from his collection:

> 'Tis very unhappy in the Case before me, that it is impossible to attest the Truth of all the Stories which are handed about upon such a Subject as this is; and therefore tho' I might make Flour-ishes of the Truth of the Particulars in all Cases, as others do; I chuse rather to insist upon the Moral of every Story, whatever the Fact may be, and to inforce the Influence, supposing the History to be real, or whether it be really so or not, which is not much material. (Defoe, *Essay* 271)

Here, the narrator makes his priorities clear: the moral impact of the story is more important than its truth value. In this significant "shift of emphasis from the historicity or truth of ghosts stories to their moral utility", Sasha Handley sees the *Essay*'s importance "for easing the transition of ghost stories into new fictional genres over the course of the eighteenth century" (104).

IV. Morality, Class, and Individual Responsibility

In fact, the very ontology of the hierarchy of spirits in the *Essay* connotes a move towards human morality. Those supernatural entities who still interfere with human affairs, i.e. the lower spirits, both good and evil, are restricted in their power to help or hurt human beings and can, in effect, only give advice, however threatening or powerful they may choose to appear (Defoe, *Essay* 85). The responsibility for moral decisions and actions therefore rests with the individual. This emphasis is created not only by the restrictions on metaphysical intervention, but also by a far more radical break with tradition: while traditional ghost stories and apparition narratives often hark back to past events, the stories in the

Essay are on the whole more concerned with the present moment of moral decision-making. Owen Davies summarizes the most typical reasons why revenants return in medieval and early modern ghost stories: "to haunt the sinful and plague the consciences of moral transgressors" (4-6). These motives predominantly refer to deeds committed in the past. The apparitions in the *Essay*, in contrast to that, mostly come to issue warnings or to help the good party in a conflict by frightening their opponents. Individual, non-supernatural feelings of guilt now take over the function of haunting the offenders: "Conscience, indeed, is a frightful Apparition itself" (Defoe, *Essay* 112). Alternatively, the Devil in some cases comes to haunt them, but not for moral reasons – he just likes to inflict pain for its own sake (Defoe, *Essay* 172). The good spirits follow a kinder and more pragmatic approach: they only intervene when they can make a real difference, not merely to punish. In most of the stories they appear in the role of helpers, who are not to be feared, but to be welcomed. Sometimes – even more humbly – they recruit disinterested third parties as human helpers by appealing to their benevolence and sense of justice (e.g. Defoe, *Essay* 243-245). Even bad spirits can, in the narrator's point of view, only be a cause for fear if they point to an already existing guilt (Defoe, *Essay* 174-175). This shift of the source of fear and terror from the supernatural to the human mind is an important step towards the Gothic and will be discussed further in the next chapter.

While good spirits as helpers represent the virtue of disinterested engagement for others, the central plots of the stories mostly revolve around the danger of loss and the duty of guarding and keeping a valuable possession – one's life, one's sexual virtue, or, in most cases, one's material property. Hence, the function of the supernatural is mainly conservative in the literal sense of the word. In terms of social class, it appears that the value which is to be protected by supernatural intervention often concerns established property rights of middle- or upper class protagonists, whose claims seem to be more worthy of the spirits' attention: the narrator pours scorn on the traditional idea that apparitions "come to help you to find out Money [...]; nor do I recommend it to you to believe those Trifles; they are most certainly the Apparitions of Fancy" (Defoe, *Essay* 268). For the recuperation or protection of large estates, it seems, apparitions do go to some trouble in the stories (Defoe, *Essay* 243-246; 148-157). Social class does not, however, justify the intrusion or appropriation of other people's property.

This becomes clear in the story where an apparition assumes the shape of a living clergyman to prevent a woman from losing her virtue to a gentleman who is her social superior and on whom her livelihood indirectly depends (Defoe, *Essay* 133-147).[15] Here, the supernatural occurrence protects the rights and chances of the weaker party, both in relation to her gender and social standing. This function is also traditional in the history of apparition narratives, which often strengthen the authority of the socially powerless, in particular women (Handley 105). On the whole, the moral alignment of the stories contains traditional elements from the history of apparition narratives. At the same time, the stories also emphasize material possession, female sexual virtue, and benevolence, and therefore endorse the value system of the middling classes as it develops in the course of the eighteenth century.[16]

The emphasis on individual responsibility fits into this moral and social framework. Many of the stories' protagonists struggle with moral decisions and different forms of pressure. Indeed, the supernatural helpers seem to favour these troubled souls, i.e. those who are weak enough to be tempted to transgress moral boundaries. In the story about the prevention of the loss of virtue, the female protagonist is on the brink of meeting the man when the apparition intercepts her and sends her away, and only later does she realize how close she came to social and moral ruin (Defoe, *Essay* 140). As it turns out, the young man loves her "the better for her so seasonably recovering her Virtue and good Principles" (Defoe, *Essay* 145). The woman is at a disadvantage both in terms of class and gender, but the incident with the apparition supports her sense of justice and her recognition of her own rights, and she grows steadily in confidence and self-assurance, consequently impressing her lover and even reforming him: "it made him be quite another Man in his Way of living than ever he was before; and particularly he was very thankful that he had been prevented being so wicked with her as in all Probability he had been, if this had not happen'd" (Defoe, *Essay* 147). Another narrative (Defoe, *Essay* 148-157)[17] depicts a man whose second wife pressures him to disinherit his son from a first marriage, who is abroad. He defends the

---

[15] For later readers, this situation is highly reminiscent of Samuel Richardson's *Pamela*, only with a supernatural addition.

[16] For the importance of benevolence in the moral code of the emerging middle classes, see Nünning (23).

[17] A similar story is mentioned in Davies (5).

rights of his son, but her constant cajoling and threatening weaken his resolve; twice he is on the verge of giving in when an apparition of his son intervenes and frightens his wife while bringing him to his senses and discouraging their legal executors. It is precisely the husband's weakness of character that necessitates the supernatural intervention.

The most elaborate of the stories thus eschew an idealized dualistic morality of good versus evil, and the effects of suspense and fear are not created by the opposition between a villain and his innocent victim but by moral conflict within the characters themselves. While the stories lack some of the stock characters found in later Gothic fiction, the depictions of the figures' inner turmoil anticipate the treatment of moral topics in the Gothic novel. The temptation of desire or material greed and the guilt and self-inflicted terror produced by a bad conscience are basic expressions of moral conflicts both in Defoe's *Essay* and in the Gothic. They represent the unstable and conflicting concepts of individual identity and duty in the rapidly changing social fabric of the eighteenth century.[18] The following chapter reveals how, in the *Essay*'s complex narrative set-up, moral quandaries in the stories are supported by proto-Gothic atmospheric elements which stand in contrast to the narrator's overall stance of sober rationalism.

V. Conflicting Narrative Modes: Rational Control and Proto-Gothic Terror

From the outset, the narrator of the *Essay* proceeds in a rational manner and tackles difficult theological and epistemological questions from a position of common sense. It was shown in section III that he advocates a middle position between absolute materialist positivism and extreme superstition. His weapons against these extremes are abstract rational argument and textual criticism of his narrative examples, but also satire and entertainment. His rational argument is displayed when he describes the ontology of the system of higher and lower metaphysical levels mentioned above. When he introduces texts to support the logic of these assumptions, he acts as critic, interprets the stories and relates them to his system. His own apparition narratives ostensibly support his arguments,

---

[18] Kilgour summarizes interpretations of the Gothic which focus on its problematization of identity (5-6).

but he also quotes from well-known collections of ghost stories and confronts the aspects that clash with his ideas, for example by pointing out "some little Incongruity [...], which renders it inconsistent" (Defoe, *Essay* 171), or by suggesting "that the several Hands thro' which the Relation has pass'd, have made up the Speech for the Ghost, and committed some Blunders in it" (Defoe, *Essay* 172). On occasion, he also compares and contrasts different versions of a story (Defoe, *Essay* 233-239; 243). The narrator in this way both undermines and strengthens the authority of his narratives: on the one hand, his suspicion that various narrators have changed and edited the story reveals the unreliability of such stories in general. On the other hand, he presents himself as a shrewd critic who separates the core story from narrative embellishments and purges older material, rendering it suitable for retelling and interpretation. He creates a link to traditional storytelling and asserts its value, but also emphasizes his modern treatment of it.

The narrator's tone switches back and forth between theological and moral seriousness, satire and mockery of other points of view,[19] and jocular remarks about his own narrative and argumentative process. In the act of praising a character's innocence and "the Comfort of a good Conscience", he checks himself and goes on "which, as the World goes now, I must be cautious how I lay too much stress upon, or moralize too much upon, lest I should be call'd Religious and Grave, which is as much as to say Mad" (Defoe, *Essay* 14). Earlier in the text, he elaborates on this view of modern taste:

> But hold! whither am I going? This looks like Religion, and we must not talk a Word of that, if we expect to be agreeable. Unhappy Times! where to be serious, is to be dull and grave, and consequently to write without Spirit. [...] Well, we must comply however; the Humour of the Day must prevail; and as there is no instructing you without pleasing you, and no pleasing you but in your own Way, we must go on in that Way; the Understanding must be refin'd by Allegory and Enigma; you must see the Sun through the Cloud, and relish Light by the help of Darkness; the Taste must be rectify'd by Salts, the Appetite whetted by Bitters;

---

[19] Objects of his mockery are, for example, the shallowness of fashionable society (Defoe, *Essay* 267) and ancient and modern believers in ghosts as revenants (Defoe, *Essay* 165; 72; 232).

in a word, the Manners must be reform'd in Masquerade, Devotion quicken'd by the Stage not the Pulpit, and Wit be brighten'd by Satyrs upon Sense. (Defoe, *Essay* 72)

The metaphors of light and darkness, in particular, represent the *Essay*'s conflict between its rational, 'enlightened' argument and the stories which are meant to support the argument. These stories inevitably introduce an element of mystery, doubt and fear, which renders the topic more palatable, but also confuses its clarity and focus. The narrator constantly plays with this tension, so that his grudging concession to modern taste does not appear convincing in the face of his apparent delight in his own "Masquerade". The playful oscillation between rational control on the one hand and vivid, concrete fictional scenes, dense with atmosphere and provocative of emotional response, is the hallmark of the *Essay*.

Within the stories, there is a further dualism between a rather condensed summary of events and elaborate, detailed scenes in a style which Baine calls "dramatic and realistic" (79). The two aspects which set these stories apart from previous apparition narratives are their wealth of circumstantial detail and their expert use of dialogue in direct or reported speech. The fictional scenes in the *Essay* move further into the realm of entertainment and emotional appeal. There are some very comic scenes, particularly in the story about the woman whose virtue is saved by the apparition of a clergyman. In most tales, the use of detail and dialogue contribute more to a dark, sinister atmosphere. This is enhanced by the use of uncanny spaces like deserted moors and lonely country lanes in the middle of the night; characters like banditti, highwaymen, and murderers; proto-Gothic plots, focusing on revenge, guilt and the threat to innocent people's lives, possessions or virtue; and, of course, eerie supernatural apparitions in the shape of people known to be dead. This is not to say that the stories are all thoroughly steeped in a proto-Gothic atmosphere. The typical settings are normal private homes, not haunted by the past, and the supernatural appearances, far from introducing chaos and disorder,[20] carry messages of civilized behaviour, as has been shown. The spirits can, however, assume very threatening shapes if it is necessary to achieve their ends. One particularly striking example is an old man whom

---

[20] Punter emphasizes these aspects of the Gothic and pits them against the order of the 'classical' (5).

a gang of banditti breaking into a house encounter in three different rooms at the same time and who suddenly "chang'd into the most horrible Monster that ever was seen [...]": "[I]nstead of his Hands [...], there were two large fiery Daggers, not flaming, but red hot, and pointed with a livid bluish Flame". The narrator adds his suspicions, however, that "the Rogues were so frighted, that their Imagination afterwards form'd a thing in their Thoughts more terrible than the Devil himself could appear in" (Defoe, *Essay* 102).

This scepticism is part of the narrator's stance as a shrewd and sober critic who carefully edits and comments on the stories he has chosen. It also reveals that in the *Essay*, the effects of fear and terror are more important than their actual sources. These sources can be supernatural or natural or a combination of both: for example, in the case of the banditti, their fear of the monstrous apparition increases shortly afterwards as a result of some hand grenades that the steward of the house and his helpers throw down the chimneys, and which seem to the banditti to be part of the supernatural protection of the house. The stories accordingly introduce a certain amount of relativity to the source of terror. Even if it is supernatural, the terrifying aspect of the spirits is not part of their essence or being, but a performance intended for a certain effect. Defoe's narrator explains that "the Spirits I speak of, know how to make themselves be better regarded, know how to make themselves considerable, can come clothed in Terror if they please, and have done so where occasion has call'd for it" (Defoe, *Essay* 269). The fact that they seem so often to appear in the shape of a dead person is ascribed in one example to their intention "to add as it were a Solemnity to the Message" (Defoe, *Essay* 238). The moral end here seems to justify the means, and neat ontological distinctions behind the means lose their importance. Part of this logic is the narrator's basic assumption mentioned above that fear can only be produced on the basis of guilt. Essentially, any feeling of terror has to be grounded in individual moral aberrations and the consciousness of them. The supernatural cannot be the real cause for fear. This shifting of the source of fear away from the supernatural and into the human psyche represents a remarkable departure from earlier apparition narratives and foreshadows Gothic varieties of terror.

From this shift, it is only a small step to a scenario where the same effect can be reached without any supernatural intervention whatsoever. There are several stories of this kind in the *Essay*. In the narrator's classification, they are set apart from the stories where 'real' apparitions occur, but in fact there seems to be very little difference between them and the supernatural stories. The most elaborate of these stories of the 'supernatural explained'[21] concerns a murderer who has been on the run for many years, but who becomes so tormented with guilt that he has repeated visions of the murdered person, and in the end is driven to return to England in order to receive his punishment. The narrator argues that the apparition is clearly only a product of the murderer's guilty conscience, but the scene of his return to England unfolds in great detail, full of atmosphere and with many decidedly uncanny coincidences: his boat from Billingsgate to Westminster is damaged in an accident, leaving him, at dusk, close to the place where he had committed the murder. When he hears people shouting and running after a thief, he assumes they are after him and runs away. He finally falls over, confuses his followers with his stammered confession of murder and is taken to the authorities, where he receives his punishment. Incidentally, the narrator adds, the place where he falls over "was just against the very Door of the House where the Person liv'd that he had murther'd" (Defoe, *Essay* 119). The night scene of solitary walking, persecution, delusion and arrest is presented in great detail and atmospheric density, and even if the man's sense of guilt explains his fear and his visions, it does not in itself provide a reason for the uncanny coincidences of his involuntary return to the place of his deed, the pursuit of another person just at that moment, and his fall in front of the house belonging to his victim. Here, the narrator seems to get carried away by the dramatic potential of the story and defeats his own purpose of separating the natural from the supernatural by presenting an atmosphere that seems charged with supernatural possibilities. In addition, the narrator suddenly lets the supernatural in through the back door: "he was harrass'd by the Reflection of his own Guilt, and the Sluices of the Soul were set open by the Angels or Spirits attending, and who by Divine Appointment are always at hand to execute the vindictive part of Justice, as well as the more merciful Dispensations of Heaven" (Defoe, *Essay* 120). The man's fear is in his mind, his actions betray him and then he suffers the this-worldly justice, while the supernatural is relegated to the role of a dubious psychological influence. The effects of

---

[21] See Clery for this variety of Gothic fiction as represented most famously in Ann Radcliffe's novels (*Rise* 105). Starr also compares this story's techniques to Radcliffe's methods (26).

strangeness and uncanny terror are meanwhile produced by strange coincidences within the plot, on which the narrator does not comment. This story exemplifies best of all how the *Essay* shifts the functions of the supernatural from the epistemological to the moral. It also shifts its place, as the supernatural no longer appears as an intrusive external entity, but resides in the characters' minds and emotions – and in the dynamics of sensational storytelling. All of this links the *Essay* to some of the core themes and features of Gothic fiction.

It becomes clear that the *Essay* shows a complex amalgam of narrative modes which is hard to categorize. Firstly, the narrator's theoretical, argumentative passages stand in contrast to the stories. Secondly, within the stories, the way atmosphere, plot and character unfold is constantly kept in check by the narrator's intrusive moral or theological comments and textual criticism. Conversely, the narrator's control is undermined and challenged by those passages in the stories where, as Starr phrases it, they "develop a narrative momentum that carries them beyond Defoe's explanations" (27). This way of putting it identifies the narrator's rational voice with Defoe himself and suggests that the text transgresses the boundaries of his sober intentions against his will. Keeping in mind, however, Defoe's masterful grasp of the subtleties of narrative techniques in his other, more prominent works, the question arises whether the narrator of the *Essay* might not be seen as a construct, a figure whose insistence on the possibility of rational access to the metaphysical realm is threatened or at least counterbalanced by occasional glimpses into the power both of the irrational part of people's minds and of the emotional, atmospheric effects of vivid storytelling. This is not to say that most of the narrator's theological convictions are not Defoe's own; this is a different matter.[22] However, Defoe is an author who, in his best work, shows an intense awareness of the tensions and predicaments of his time and creates intricate narrative ways of representing the way the modern individual is torn between the different force fields of moral values, social hierarchies, metaphysical considerations, and personal goals and desires. It is only to be supposed that the construction of a narrator who exudes confidence in rational control, but repeatedly seems on the brink

---

[22] For summaries of the debate among critics concerning Defoe's attitude towards the supernatural and metaphysical, see Bostridge (111) and Capoferro (129-130).

of losing it, is another way of creating (and occasionally satirizing) just such an individual struggling for control in a complex and rapidly changing world.

VI. Conclusion

Defoe's *Essay* marks an important step in the development of narratives dealing with the supernatural. It links back to the tradition of apparition narratives serving theological and epistemological arguments as established in the seventeenth century and refines many of this tradition's themes and techniques. It also distances itself from some of its tenets and shifts the emphasis towards the moral and aesthetic functions of apparition narratives. In particular, the more detailed unfolding of atmosphere, scenes and characters in the stories and the psychologizing of terror pre-empt core features and themes of the Gothic novel. However, beyond this idea of an appealing linear development and refinement of literary genres, the *Essay*'s prime significance lies in the ways in which it destabilizes and undermines just such easy categorization. When Starr sees a "Proto-Gothic variety of realism" (25) in it, the uneasy combination of 'Gothic' and 'Realism', two terms which traditionally stand in opposition to each other, demonstrates that the *Essay* works against such oppositions even before they emerge and plays with them in its complex amalgam of narrative modes. The text oscillates between argument and fiction, between rational and pragmatic spirits and the irrational reaction of characters, between sober logic and an emotionally charged atmosphere. It thus not only transgresses, but zigzags back and forth across the artificial, retrospectively imposed conceptual boundaries between Enlightenment thinking and Realist fiction on the one hand and superstition and Gothic fiction on the other.[23]

The Gothic itself, even within the first 50 years after Horace Walpole's founding work, *The Castle of Otranto* from 1764, comprises radically

---

[23] Of course, not all critics base their work on these simplified categories. For studies which challenge the clear-cut opposition between Realist fiction/Enlightenment thinking and the Gothic, see for example Schlaeger and Carson.

different varieties and incorporates myriad previous genres,[24] rendering it unfit to serve as a consistent foil against which to define other literary forms. Defoe's *Essay* is certainly not simply a link in a chain which connects apparition narratives with the rise of Gothic fiction. It reveals several parallels to themes and motives which are later developed more fully in Gothic novels, but these are placed within a very specific and un-Gothic narrative and argumentative framework which playfully defies simple expectations of moral and theological tenets, generic traditions, und established narrative techniques.

Works Cited

Baine, Rodney. *Daniel Defoe and the Supernatural*. Athens, GA: University of Georgia Press, 1968.

Baxter, Richard. *The Certainty of the Worlds of Spirits*. London, 1691.

Boone, Troy. "Narrating the Apparition: Glanvill, Defoe, and the Rise of Gothic Fiction." *The Eighteenth Century* 35.2 (1994): 173-189.

Bostridge, Ian. *Witchcraft and Its Transformations, 1650-1750*. Oxford: Clarendon Press, 1997.

Bovet, Richard. *Pandaemonium, or, the Devil's Cloyster*. London, 1684.

Brooke-Rose, Christine. *Invisible Author: Last Essays*. Columbus: The Ohio State University Press, 2002.

Capoferro, Riccardo. *Empirical Wonder: Historicizing the Fantastic, 1660-1760*. Bern: Peter Lang, 2010.

Carson, James P. "Enlightenment, Popular Culture, and Gothic Fiction." *The Cambridge Companion to the Eighteenth-Century Novel*. Ed. John Richetti. Cambridge: Cambridge University Press, 1996. 255-276.

Clery, E. J. *The Rise of Supernatural Fiction, 1762-1800*. Cambridge: Cambridge University Press, 1995.

---

[24] Kilgour (4) and Capoferro (104) name some of these genres. Kilgour stresses the variety of Gothic fiction and calls it a "confused and self-contradictory form" (5).

---. "The Genesis of 'Gothic' Fiction." *The Cambridge Companion to Gothic Fiction*. Ed. Jerrold E. Hogle. Cambridge: Cambridge University Press, 2002. 21-39.

Davies, Owen. *The Haunted: A Social History of Ghosts*. London: Palgrave Macmillan, 2007.

Defoe, Daniel. "A True Relation of the Apparition of One Mrs Veal, the Next Day after her Death to one Mrs. Bargrave at Canterbury, the 8th of September, 1705." 1706. *Daniel Defoe and Others: Accounts of the Apparition of Mrs Veal*. Ed. Manuel Schonhorn. Los Angeles: University of California Press, 1965.

---. *The Political History of the Devil*. 1726. *Satire, Fantasy and Writings on the Supernatural by Daniel Defoe*. Vol. 6. Ed. John Mullan. London: Pickering and Chatto, 2005.

---. *A System of Magick*. 1727. *Satire, Fantasy and Writings on the Supernatural by Daniel Defoe*. Vol. 7. Ed. Peter Elmer. London: Pickering and Chatto, 2005.

---. *An Essay on the History and Reality of Apparitions*. 1727. *Satire, Fantasy and Writings on the Supernatural by Daniel Defoe*. Vol. 8. Ed. G. A. Starr. London: Pickering and Chatto, 2005.

Doody, Margaret Anne. *The True Story of the Novel*. New Brunswick: Rutgers University Press, 1996.

Easlea, Brain. *Witch Hunting, Magic and the New Philosophy: An Introduction to Debates of the Scientific Revolution, 1450-1750*. Brighton: The Harvester Press, 1980.

Ellis, Markman. *The History of Gothic Fiction*. Edinburgh: Edinburgh University Press, 2000.

Glanvill, Joseph. *Saducismus Triumphatus*. 1681. Ed. Bernhard Fabian. Hildesheim: Olms, 1978.

Handley, Sasha. *Visions of an Unseen World: Ghost Beliefs and Ghost Stories in Eighteenth-Century England*. London: Pickering and Chatto, 2007.

Hogle, Jerrold E. *The Cambridge Companion to Gothic Fiction*. Cambridge: Cambridge University Press, 2002.

Jackson, Rosemary. *Fantasy: The Literature of Subversion*. London; New York: Routledge, 1981.

Kilgour, Maggie. *The Rise of the Gothic Novel*. London: Routledge, 1995.

Mendlesohn, Farah, and Edward James. *A Short History of Fantasy*. London: Middlesex University Press, 2009.

McKeon, Michael. *The Origins of the English Novel, 1600-1740*. Baltimore: The Johns Hopkins University Press, 1987.

Mullan, John. "Swift, Defoe, and Narrative Forms." *The Cambridge Companion to English Literature 1650-1740*. Ed. Steven N. Zwicker. Cambridge: Cambridge University Press, 1998. 250-275.

Novak, Maximillian. "Daniel Defoe and Applebee's Original Weekly Journal: An Attempt at Re-Attribution." *Eighteenth-Century Studies* 45.4 (2012): 585-608.

Nünning, Vera. "From 'Honour' to 'Honest': The Invention of the (Superiority of the) Middling Ranks in Eighteenth-Century England." *Journal for the Studies of British Cultures* 2.1 (1995): 19-41.

Parsons, Coleman E. "Ghost-Stories Before Defoe." *Notes and Queries* (July 1956): 293-298.

---. "Introduction: George Sinclair's War against Satan." Sinclair, George. *Satan's Invisible World Discovered*. Ed. Coleman E. Parsons. Gainesville: Scholars' Facsimiles and Reprints, 1969. v-xxviii.

Price, Fiona. "'Myself Creating What I Saw': The Morality of the Spectator in Eighteenth-Century Gothic." *Gothic Studies* 8.2 (2006): 1-18.

Punter, David. *The Literature of Terror. A History of Gothic Fictions from 1765 to the Present Day*. Vol. 1: The Gothic Tradition. London: Longman, 1996.

Schlaeger, Jürgen. "Die Unwirtlichkeit des Wirklichen: Zur Wandlungs-dynamik des englischen Romans im 18. Jahrhundert." *Poetica* 25.3 (1993): 319-337.

Sinclair, George. *Satan's Invisible World Discovered*. 1685. Ed. Coleman E. Parsons. Gainesville: Scholars' Facsimiles and Reprints, 1969.

Smith, Andrew. *Gothic Literature*. Edinburgh: Edinburgh University Press, 2007.

Starr, George. "Why Defoe Probably Did Not Write The Apparition of Mrs Veal." *Eighteenth-Century Fiction* 15.3-4 (2003): 421-450.

Thomas, Keith. *Religion and the Decline of Magic: Studies in Popular Belief in Sixteenth and Seventeenth-Century England.* London: Weidenfeld and Nicolson, 1971.

Walpole, Horace. *The Castle of Otranto: A Gothic Story and The Mysterious Mother: A Tragedy.* 1764. Ed. Frederick S. Frank. Peterborough, ON: Broadview, 2003.

Oliver Plaschka

Distressing Damsels: Gothic Chivalry in James Branch Cabell's *Biography*

While James Branch Cabell liked to call himself a writer of romance, he is seldom considered to be a representative of the Gothic mode. Today, what little of his popularity remains is owed to the efforts of authors like Lin Carter or Neil Gaiman, who stress his importance as an early writer of fantasy. Indeed, his imaginary province Poictesme with its capital Storisende, situated in southern medieval France, abounds with castles, knights, magicians and creatures of myth. All the same, scholars such as Edmund Wilson and Louis D. Rubin, H. L. Mencken, Leslie Fiedler, or James D. Riemer have studied him in his capacities as Southern writer, late Decadent, satirist, enemy of modernism or even precursor of postmodernism.

Cabell might well be all of these, as an even cursory glance at the 18-volume Storisende Edition of his *Biography of the Life of Manuel* in all its delightful intricacy and inconsistency will prove. So his inclusion in a 'Gothic' collection should come as no surprise, either. As Nick Freeman notes, Cabell has "treated the Gothic as a rich reservoir of characters, situations, and tropes to be subverted, undermined, and satirized", so as to "refine and reconfigure Gothic characteristics, delighting in torturous genealogies and improbable encounters" (103). Above all, this article will focus on the equally improbable *characters* encountered, which Cabell, as a self-proclaimed romantic, could not "ever, quite, regard [...] as human beings" (*Eve* xiii):[1] women.

---

[1] All of the page numbers that are provided regarding Cabell's major monographs refer to the illustrated editions. The chapter numbers are indicated in addition where appropriate to help locate the sources in different editions. Works not relevant to the discussion of the illustrations are listed as part of the Storisende Edition (SE) in the list of works cited.

I. Lovers How They Come

Cabell was very much raised within the traditions of previous centuries. Born into an old, wealthy and scandal-ridden family in Richmond, Virginia, in 1879, he attended the William and Mary College in Williamsburg from 1894-98. A gifted student, he soon fell under the tutelage of college librarian Charles Washington Coleman and the spell of childhood friend Gabriella Brooke Moncure. They would become the "parents of the literary figure who emerged in the first two decades of the twentieth century. Coleman put the pen in his hand and Moncure gave him inspiration" (MacDonald 76).[2]

Cabell played the part of the youthful courtier and Gabriella the one of the noble lady, "alternately defensive and receptive" (80). Still, his efforts exclusively led to the production of a remarkable amount of poetry and ultimately to the separation from Gabriella when they moved to different cities. But even in 1913, fifteen years after college, Cabell's friends were surprised, and Gabriella apparently hurt, by his marriage to Rebecca Priscilla Bradley Shepherd, a widowed mother of five children (92). In 1915, another son, Ballard Hartwell, was born.

Cabell continuously reiterated his biography in his fiction, which also explains the somewhat tautological title *Biography of the Life of Manuel:* "It was really a Biography with a capital *B*" (93). Gabriella kept playing the part of the unattainable beloved and Priscilla the one of the domestic wife. Both archetypes surface in almost all of Cabell's major works, and many allusions only make sense in the light of the letters he and Gabriella used to write to each other; some of his prose passages are really disguised love poetry, the line breaks having been removed (92-93).

Cabell's fame peaked in 1920 when the New York Society for the Suppression of Vice had *Jurgen* banned for its sexual innuendos. For two years, Cabell arguably enjoyed the public attention until *Jurgen* was finally cleared. *Figures of Earth, The High Place, The Silver Stallion* and *Something about Eve* expanded his intricately-linked universe. They were followed by new editions illustrated by Frank C. Papé which presented "a

---

[2]   Biographical information, unless indicated otherwise, is taken from MacDonald's *James Branch Cabell and Richmond-in-Virginia*. A vague account of the rumours of homosexuality overshadowing Cabell's last months at college is also provided by Glasgow.

matching of minds and of styles" even from a more critical point of view, "getting [Cabell] the illustrator that [he] most deserved" (Cobb 111). The final step was to rework all of his publications into the uniform Storisende Edition, comprising monographs, short stories, essays, poetry and one play. By the time he was fifty, Cabell had completed his life's work.

His fame diminished from the 1930s onwards. Cabell's imposing oeuvre was deemed to be too Mannerist, and the sometimes far-fetched intertextual references of the Storisende Edition made it seem the more inaccessible the less a given reader was willing to delve into it. While in the 1920s critics like H. L. Mencken or Carl Van Doren reliably sang his praises, Cabell's golden rule – "to write perfectly of beautiful happenings" (*Jest* 24:133) – made later critics dismiss Poictesme as "a cloud-cuckoo land, having no purpose other than to divert and to amuse" (Rubin, *Richmond,* 129). Still, he did not let go of the unattained. The tell-tale collection *The Witch-Woman: A Trilogy About Her* was published as a late afterthought to the *Biography* in 1948.[3]

After Priscilla's death, he married editor and decorator Margaret Waller Freeman, who saw to it that after his death and burial in 1958, both he and Priscilla were moved to another cemetery so Margaret could lie next to him.

II. Manuel's Daughters

Following the inner logic of the Storisende Edition, the *Biography* is not so much about Dom Manuel, the roguish culture hero of early thirteenth-century Poictesme, but about the principles he – allegedly – embodies. These principles live on in his children and grandchildren, over many generations from medieval France to modern Virginia, guiding them on their quests for meaning in a seemingly meaningless world.

---

[3] *The Witch-Woman* contained "The Music from Behind the Moon", first published in 1926 and reprinted in SE IV along with *Domnei* in 1928; "The Way of Ecben", first published in 1929 and reprinted in SE XVIII along with *Townsend of Lichfield* in 1930; and "The White Robe", first published in 1928 and also reprinted in SE XVIII.

Despite being denied an active part in most of these quests, it is the daughters of Manuel, not his sons, that play pivotal roles in them: Melicent, Dorothy, Ettarre and their many guises. They are the princesses and witches that inspire and sometimes doom the interchangeable heroes. Oscillating between conflicting stock characters of the romantic and Gothic tradition, e.g. the damsel in distress and the *femme fatale*, they beg closer examination.

Bram Dijkstra, in his comprehensive study *Idols of Perversity*, identifies several archetypal male fantasies that pervade the fiction and visual arts of the late nineteenth century, from the devoted 'household nun' to the dream-like 'women of moonlight and wax', who, along with the many incarnations of Lilith, Circe and Salome, struggle "over the eternal essence of man" (217), thereby constituting the old dichotomy of "the virgin and the whore, the saint and the vampire" (334).

In Cabell's case, this type of struggle is most likely based on his own *psychomachia*: with Gabriella as the model for the saintly moonlight ladies courted by his heroes, as well as for most of the less-saintly enchantresses crossing their way; and Priscilla as the mother of the plain, down-to-earth types the same heroes end up marrying. For all its fanciful meandering, *The Biography* is more about the Gothic trials and tribulations of male-female relations than anything else.

III. Women That Cannot Be Reached

In *Domnei: A Comedy of Woman Worship*,[4] Perion has to rescue Manuel's eldest daughter Melicent from various kidnappers. But dripping in blood after the final "magnanimous butchery" (30:231), he suffers an unexpected defeat: for when Melicent offers up her body in exchange for Perion's life, her captor Ahasuerus declares that he is not in love with a "handsome piece of flesh" (30:230) but with her "shrewd and dauntless soul" (30:228) instead. Winning for her "all which righteousness and honour could not win", he releases her, exclaiming: "do you now conquer Perion" (30:231).

The meaning of this last remark becomes clear when the lovers meet again and realize they can hardly reconnect: "Their love had flouted Time

---

[4] The word 'domnei' is Old Provençal, meaning just that: "woman worship".

and Fate. These had revenged this insolence, it seemed to Perion, by an ironical conversion of each rebel into another person" (30:233). Melicent is not the same girl he set out to rescue anymore; nor does Perion resemble the man she longed for all those years. Neither of them can find fulfilment. All there is left to do for Perion, bereft of his illusions, is to kneel, granting her, as the intruding narrator comments, "her high hour of triumph" (30:235).

As a spectre of the past, Melicent *cannot be reached*. Revised and published just two months before making his vow to Priscilla and acquiescing in marital life at the age of 34, this singular ending for an otherwise "modern medieval romance" (MacDonald 149) can also be read as echoing Cabell's ongoing attempts to exorcize Gabriella. When comparing the text with its earlier versions, the first of which was published in 1911 as "The Soul of Mervisaunt", it is interesting to note that the eponymous soul changed from being described as "wise and naked" (675) to the harsher sounding "shrewd and dauntless". Cabell also added a remark to Perion's final deliberations about "the divine and stupendous unreason of a woman's choice, among so many other men, of him", along with a comment about "women and their love [...]: 'They are more wise than we; and always they make us better by indomitably believing we are better than in reality a man can ever be'" (30:234). These new paragraphs also foreshadow the Faustian morale about the merits of Eternal Womanhood that is expressed in *Jurgen*.

The Cream of the Jest: A Comedy of Evasions moves from Poictesme to early twentieth-century Virginia, establishing the duality at work in most of Cabell's romances: on the one hand, the banality and homeliness of domestic life and old age – on the other, the idealized Arcadian dream-world (see Fig. 1).

Married writer Felix Kennaston is plagued by dreams of Ettarre, Manuel's youngest daughter, whom he courts in the guise of Horvendile.[5] The dreams are cloak-and-dagger episodes, the "topsiturviness" of which

---

[5] Horvendile is the *alter ego* which from now on allows Cabell to enter "his own books in masquerade [...] while Ahasuerus peformed a similar function for *Domnei*" – enabling Cabell to capture and release Melicent in person (Cranwell 24). Judging from his name, which can be traced back to the *Gesta Danorum*, Horvendile is a distant relative of both Shakespeare's Hamlet and Tolkien's Eärendil, and to some extent also of Lucifer (Plaschka 125).

Frank C. Papé depicted in his plates as two medievally-clad lovers wandering weightlessly through the air, and a Dalí-legged archer striding through a surreal landscape, sporting an enormous phallic quiver under his tunic (see Fig. 2 and 3).

But Kennaston's love must stay unfulfilled: every time he tries to touch Ettarre, the dream ends and he awakes. Ettarre, just like her sister Melicent, cannot be reached, this time in a very literal sense. She is the proverbial dream-woman – an arresting, but also a mutually dependent existence, as two minor Papé illustrations show: one depicting Ettarre trying to step out of a book, the other as the evasive lover, drawn in almost a single line with her suitor (see Fig. 4 and 5).

To complicate matters, Kennaston uses what he believes to be one half of a magical sigil to enter his dreamworld. When he discovers the second half in his wife's bathroom cabinet, he becomes ashamed – for what if Kathleen has been using *her* half of the sigil all along – what if she is Ettarre, just like he is Horvendile? Later on, the sigil is revealed to be just the fancifully designed lid of his wife's cold cream jar, *Crème Cleopatre*. The cream of the jest turns out to be just that – *the cream* of the jest. Unbeknownst to Kennaston, his key to immortal love is only his wife's humble claim to youth.[6]

IV. Women That Should Not Be Reached

Jurgen: A Comedy of Justice tells of the adventures of middle-aged pawnbroker Jurgen, "part Faust, part Don Juan" (Weir 160), on his quest to rescue his wife Lisa from the claws of the devil, while being secretly in love with Manuel's second daughter Dorothy la Désirée. Of course, neither of these romantic obligations presents an obstacle for the countless amorous adventures that ensue.

---

[6] The inscription of the sigil in Papé's illustration has always been a favourite among Cabell scholars and fans. It reads, upside down: "|iames branch cabell made this book so that he who wills may read the story of mans eternally unsatisfied hunger in search of beauty | ettarre stays inaccessible always and her lovliness is his to look on only in his dreams | all men she must evade at the last and many ar the ways of her elusion" [sic].

The narrative structure takes the form of what Patricia Merivale termed a "Gothicized godgame", devised by "a Magus, devil-god and stage-director [...] to reinforce his didactic manipulations of the hero"; a "Gothic pedagogy" providing the hero with an "astonishing, terrifying, yet phantasmagorical sequence of lessons" (146). Appropriately, the journey begins and ends on Walpurgis Night – as is the case with many of Cabell's works – and crosses several times between the realms of magic, the past and the imagination.

Jurgen enlists the services of Mother Sereda, the patron saint of Wednesdays and therefore of mediocrity, talking her into loaning him one of her 'used' Wednesdays she does not need anymore (see Fig. 6). Still, Sereda does not approve of Jurgen's antics. As the price for his regained youth, she puts him under the surveillance of her shadow, "a shadow that renders all things not quite satisfactory" (43:279-280). When trying to win the young Dorothy, Jurgen learns a lesson similar to Perion's: despite his self-assessment as a "monstrous clever fellow" (43:284), "confident he could always say whatever was required of him" (23:138), he cannot reclaim the lost love of his past, no matter how hard he tries.

What follows is an impious parody on chivalric conduct and Arthurian motives which takes Jurgen through the lands of history and myth. The episode in which he rescues Guenevere the "orthodox" way satirizes the convention of the Sleeping Beauty in her fetishized, death-like state (see Dijkstra chapter II): helpless, submissive and clinging to the man, providing him with a welcome carte blanche for his infidelity (see Fig. 7).

> Her eyes were closed. She was, even so, the most beautiful creature Jurgen had ever imagined. 'She does not breathe. And yet, unless memory fails me, this is certainly a living woman in my arms. Evidently this is a sleep induced by necromancy. Well, it is not for nothing I have read so many fairy tales. There are orthodoxies to be observed in the awakening of every enchanted princess. And Lisa, wherever she may be, poor dear! is nowhere in this neighborhood, because I hear nobody talking. So I may consider myself at liberty to do the traditional thing by this princess. Indeed, it is the only fair thing for me to do, and justice demands it'.
>
> In consequence, Jurgen kissed the girl. Her lips parted and softened, and they assumed a not unpleasant sort of submissive

ardor. Her eyes, enormous when seen thus closely, had languorously opened, had viewed him without wonder, and then the lids had fallen, about half-way, just as, Jurgen remembered, the eyelids of a woman ought to do when she is being kissed properly. She clung a little, and now she shivered a little, but not with cold: Jurgen perfectly remembered that ecstatic shudder convulsing a woman's body: everything, in fine, was quite as it should be. So Jurgen put an end to the kiss, which, as you may surmise, was a tolerably lengthy affair. (9:57)

Still, Jurgen's love for Guenevere does not prevent him from cheating on her, living up to Schopenhauer's doubtful insight that "man's love diminishes perceptibly from the moment it has obtained satisfaction; almost every other woman charms him more than the one he already possesses" (542). This holds true even when that other woman is an "amateur ghost" asking him to re-enact her violent demise so that "at three o'clock the White Turret is haunted to everyone's satisfaction" (16:103). On discussing the circumstances of her murder, the ghost of Queen Sylvia remarks:

'It was not that I minded. Smoit killed me in a fit of jealousy [...]. No, a worse thing than that befell me, Jurgen, and embittered all my life in the flesh.' And Sylvia began to weep.

'And what was that thing, Sylvia?'

Queen Sylvia whispered the terrible truth. 'My husband did not understand me.'

'Now, by Heaven,' says Jurgen, 'when a woman tells me that, even though the woman be dead, I know what it is she expects of me.' (17:107)

Cabell's play with these alleged 'expectations' is a play both with literary and societal conventions. It is the same kind of insubordination that informed the twist ending of *Domnei* or "the great law of living" as expressed in *The High Place:* "Thou shalt not offend against the notions of thy neighbor" (30:308). Its most famous form is the venerable motto of Poictesme, *mundus vult decipi.*[7]

---

[7] This is probably a shortened version of Petronius' *mundus vult decipi, ergo decipiatur,* "the world wishes to be deceived, therefore let it be deceived" (Cranwell 32).

So it was that the tragedy swelled to its appalling climax, and subsided handsomely. With the aid of Caliburn, Jurgen had murdered his temporary wife. He had dragged her insensate body across the floor, by the hair of her head, and had carefully re-membered first to put her comb in his pocket, as Queen Sylvia had requested, so that it would not be lost. He had given vent to several fiendish 'Ha-ha's' and all the old high imprecations he remembered: and in short, everything had gone splendidly when he left the White Turret with a sense of self-approval and Queen Sylvia Tereu. (17:105-106)

This Gothic interlude arouses the curiosity of Anaïtis, the visiting Lady of the Lake. The sorceress takes Jurgen with her to the land of Cocaigne, where "there is no law [...] save, Do that which seems good to you" (22:135). Feeling religiously compelled to live an infamous life, she introduces him to even stranger practices, involving an altar, black candles, a crucified toad and an elaborate mockery of Crowlian sex magick.

Still, for all the excesses, discontent catches up with Jurgen, for soon he "lived with Anaïtis the Sun's daughter very much as he had lived with Lisa, who was daughter to a pawnbroker" (24:149). The major obstacles he cannot escape are his own vanity and inflated ego. His first encounter with the good-natured dryad Chloris, with Jurgen sitting by a pool and once again in love with himself, calls to mind the doomed affair of Narcissus and Echo. Soon he complains:

'She does not understand me, and she does not always treat my superior wisdom quite respectfully. That is unfair, but it seems to be an unavoidable feature of married life. Besides, if any woman had ever understood me she would, in self-protection, have refused to marry me. In any case, Chloris is a dear brown plump delicious partridge of a darling: and cleverness in women is, after all, a virtue misplaced.' (28:183)

Actually, however, Chloris seems to be the rare female character who recognizes him as an impostor but still loves him: "O foolish man of mine, you are determined to be neither fish nor beast nor poultry: and nowhere will you ever consent to be happy" (28:185).

The source of Jurgen's misfortune is readily identified as Queen Helen, famously the most beautiful woman there ever was. For Jurgen she symbolizes the ideal of his youth which makes him incapable of loving anyone else. His obsession with her leads him all the way into her chambers; but standing right next to her bed, he hesitates:

> 'And I do not know what thing it is that I desire, and the will of Jurgen is a feather in the wind. But I know that I would like to love somebody as Chloris loves me, and as so many women have loved me. And I know that it is you who have prevented this, Queen Helen, at every moment of my life since the disastrous moment when I first seemed to find your loveliness in the face of Madame Dorothy.' (30:197)

To protect himself and his ideals, he does not wake her, but lets go of her robe and leaves.[8] For he is wise enough to realize that attaining one's desires can never be so fulfilling as the desire itself, and that one has to maintain one's illusions for one's own sake.

The Gothic odyssey continues. In hell, Jurgen undertakes to comfort the vampire Florimel, who is seriously at odds with her "sad fate" as "a lovely peril, a flashing desolation, and an evil which smites by night, in spite of my abhorrence of irregular hours" (37:238). Eventually he resumes his original quest – however, his wife Lisa is nowhere to be found in hell, and neither is she in heaven. Jurgen has to call on Koshchei "who made things as they are" (41:263), the highest authority in Cabell's pantheon. But contrary to Jurgen's convictions, Koshchei has neither arranged nor even cared about his pedagogic journey: Cabell's world is solely governed by free will (Merivale 149). This also means that Lisa's fate depends on Jurgen alone.

At the memorable end of the novel, his ladies visit him once more in a final act of temptation. But he feels too mundane for Guinevere's faith; too languid for Anaïtis' depravity; and too untrue to his own ideals for Helen (see Fig. 8). One by one, he renounces these "avatars of the Goddess" and the "allegorical possibilities which they represent" (Merivale 154). Instead he asks to be reunited with Lisa. His wish is granted, and his scolding wife takes him home again. Only for a short

---

[8] This episode can be seen as an inversion of the summoning of Helen ending the first Act of *Faust II*, where she kisses sleeping Paris and Faust's rash intervention destroys the dream.

moment – a "moment which did not count" (50:324) – does he sneak back to Dorothy. Then he returns to his old, familiar life of "congenial" illusions (41:270) and thereby "circles, like a good hero of internalized romantic quest, back to the doubtfully Goethean Ewig Weibliche who was his starting point" (Merivale 148).

Dorothy and Helen represent the kind of ideal women that *should not be reached* in order to retain one's dreams; the quest itself is all that counts. Reality always destroys the ideal, for wherever he goes, Jurgen is followed by his own shortcomings, which are personified by Sereda's shadow. "Life in each of the various lands is characterized by the same annoyances and irritations of Jurgen's old world" (Riemer 14) – most notably the inability of men and women to form a meaningful connection, the chief prize of any traditional romance, even a Gothic one. As Jurgen remarks during his visit to hell:

> 'What is the meaning of this insane country? […] There is no sense in it, and no fairness at all.'
>
> 'Ah,' replied Satan, in his curious hoarse voice, 'you may well say that: and it is what I was telling my wife only last night.'
>
> 'You have a wife, then!' says Jurgen, who was always interested in such matters. […] 'And how do you get on with her?'
>
> 'Pretty well,' says Grandfather Satan: 'but she does not understand me.'
>
> '*Et tu, Brute!*' says Jurgen. (35:225)

A similiar lesson is to be learned from several of Cabell's later stories: in *The Music from Behind the Moon,* the exiled Ettarre sends her eponymous music to the harper Madoc. Her song is of such a beauty that Madoc realizes that he can never hope to create anything like it. But when he follows Ettarre's siren call, the prize for her rescue is her forgetting the melody. That's when Madoc, not unlike Jurgen, discovers that it was the song he desired, not the singer – and that "doubt and discontent are beautiful and true in their own right" (Riemer 49).

Florian de Puysange, the anti-hero of *The High Place: A Comedy of Disenchantment*, frees and wins his Sleeping Beauty on the very first pages by selling his first-born son to the devil. But once again, domesticity counteracts any hope for the ideal. Towards the end of his bargained year, Florian's only wish is to get rid of his once-magical wife;

attaining what he desired only led to disappointment and misfortune. The tale concludes with the ambiguous realization that it is better to "let sleeping ideals lie" (312).

V. Women Fatal and Triumphant

Camus' famous saying that "a man is always a prey to his truths" (31) applies all the same to Cabell's protagonists. And since the latters' "truths" are usually personified by their lovers, the last joke in many of his 'comedies' is on the husband, as the following examples of their amorous pitfalls and *katabases* might illustrate.

In "The White Robe", Ettarre is desired by Odo "le Noir". She rejects him, but the Lord of the Forest provides Odo with an ointment that can turn him into a werewolf, allowing him to feast on the babies of the village and excel at other monstrous deeds. When he is eventually brought to court, he incriminates Ettarre and pursues a career in the church while she is tortured to death. But having become a saint, she returns to send Odo to hell, which constitutes the final excess in a dark and blasphemous Gothic parody.

"Concerning Corinna", one of the episodes included in *The Certain Hour,* tells of two investigators examining the disappearance of the seventeenth-century poet Robert Herrick, who was notorious for his verses dedicated to imaginary women and his fondness of a black pig named after one of them.[9] They discover that Herrick apparently developed a magic ritual intended to lift the curtain that separates our world from the invisible spheres of fairies and succubi. But Herrick, too, got trapped in hell, and his saviours only succeed in equipping him with a knife, with which he repeatedly stabs himself until he dies and the nightmare is over.

The Silver Stallion: A Comedy of Redemption chronicles the fruitless endeavours of Manuel's former fellowship. Gonfal of Naimes, trying to win the favour of Queen Morvyth with minimal effort, disparages his rivals at court by comparing their bridal gifts to the unattainable ideal. It

---

[9] According to Robert Graves, the pig was white and poured "libations of Devonshire barley-ale from a silver cup" as an expression of Herrick's "devotion to poetic myth" (417). While the details are not documented, accounts of some kind of pet pig have survived (Gross 12).

works reasonably well, until the fair-bearded tattler commits the mistake of reminding Morvyth of her own transience. Morvyth, however, the dark Queen of Inis Dahut and of the four other Isles of Wonder, and convinced that "blondes do not last" (6:32), proves him wrong – by having him beheaded (see Fig. 9).

Meanwhile, Kerin of Nointel is still in search of a higher truth: his wife Saraïde possesses a talisman which allegedly emanates a "golden shining which would proclaim her capture of the truth" (42:211). Since this talisman only works at night, Saraïde routinely receives visits at late hours by numerous male friends she hopes to learn some truth from, at least about herself. Bored with her lecturing husband, she pushes Kerin down a well. Dutifully, he continues his studies in a magic library in the underworld, reading every book ever written while a singing gander in a cage, "the voice of romantic illusion" (Riemer 65), keeps him company. Decades later, he returns home; but Saraïde is not interested in the only truth he discovered, which is that time destroys all beauty. Nevertheless, the golden shining finally brightens their home – when Saraïde uses the piece of paper on which Kerin has written his little piece of wisdom to light a lamp.

VI. Woman Vital and Inevitable

Figures of Earth: A Comedy of Appearances tells the story of Manuel the Redeemer, the founding father of Poictesme. A trickster and a scoundrel, he commonly does the right thing by attempting to accomplish the opposite. He also finds himself torn between several women, which strongly resembles Jurgen's career from Guenevere to Anaïtis back to Lisa.

At the beginning of his adventures, he teams up with Niafer, who is not exceptionally beautiful but much more competent than him; this is the rare exception to the rule that female characters in such tales have no story of their own (Gilbert and Gubar 22). Strikingly, Manuel mistakes her for a man when they first meet; because of this, he treats her as his equal. She is the one who overcomes all obstacles on their journey to the mountain top where "Miramon Lluagor, lord of the nine kinds of sleep and prince of the seven madnesses [...] lives in mythic splendor" and "designs the dreams of men" (1:6). Only on their arrival does Manuel learn that Lady Gisèle, whom he planned to rescue, is in fact married to Lluagor and dictates which kinds of dreams to send to people, and which not. The wizard himself has spread the rumour of her abduction, hoping that some champion will take her away from him.

Manuel falls in love with Niafer. Nevertheless, when they encounter Grandfather Death, he readily sacrifices her life in order to save his own. His next lovers are princess Alianora and sorceress Freydis (see Fig. 10 and 11). Getting tired of both, he wants to have Niafer back. The necessary act of magic requires 30 years of his own life, the Head of Misery – one of many motifs borrowed from Russian fairy-tales – and the tears of both his former lovers. But just like Jurgen, Manuel chooses the imperfect, down-to-earth Niafer over her ethereal rivals.

All the same, he cannot escape his very first love: mysterious Suskind, "who lurks at the edges of the action from the very first chapter onward" (Godshalk 111). In name, she is a "sweet child", "unkiss'd", and like Dorothy another stand-in for Gabriella: "my heart's delight, and the desire of my desire" (37:251).[10] But Suskind does not consent to being left behind. She possesses a lock of Manuel's hair (a common ingredient for love spells) and rules like a dark fairy queen over a place "where everything stays young" (35:242).

Since Manuel now has a wife and children and is count of Poictesme, Suskind's presence poses a much more immediate threat to him than Dorothy or even Queen Helen did to Jurgen. One day while watching his family from his study, Manuel realizes that one of his windows leads only into darkness; the summer meadow, Niafer, and their daughter Melicent all seem to be mere reflections in the glass. A servant he sends ahead to explore the world beyond that window reports that "all freedom and all delight […] and all horror and all rebellion" are to be found on the other side (35:242). Manuel has to see for himself; the act of secretly climbing out of his window becomes the apt image for his ensuing "excursions from content" (36:245). He spends more time than ever in his study, which has a harmful influence on his family.[11]

---

[10] "My heart" is an allusion to her surname Moncure, from French *mon cœur*; see MacDonald 81.

[11] The triple-windowed "room of Ageus" – usage – is modelled upon Cabell's study in Dumberton Grange, the large county house Priscilla inherited from her first husband. The autobiographical allusions in Manuel's struggles are hard to

When young Melicent encounters Suskind's handsome elf-like brother, who is collecting his sister's "revenues" with an enormous pair of shears (37:251), Manuel decides to save his daughter "from being plagued by the division which has tortured him all his life" (Riemer 35). Unlike Jurgen, he cannot cope with being torn between conflicting truths. "Unhappiness", he declares, "is not the true desire of man [...]. I know, for I have had both happiness and unhappiness, and neither contented me" (38:259). He enters Suskind's magical realm and slays his first love with the same words Jurgen chose as a good-bye: "And so farewell to you, Queen Suskind" (38:258).

But "by eliminating the only one who could preserve his divine dissatisfaction, Manuel in effect removes the impetus of his [...] strivings [...], the discontent which motivated his life" (Riemer 35). "Manuel cannot survive the death of Suskind; they are one heart", MacDonald concurs (93). When Death comes to visit Manuel a second time, he has no choice but to follow him, all the way into the dark waters of Lethe and into oblivion, only to resurface, once more, at the pool of Haranton where his journey began. Manuel has failed to live up to his own legend – he has managed to deceive the world, but not himself. As long as he cannot find a way to reconcile himself to the fragile illusion of a meaningful life, he has to start over again.

Something about Eve presents a more successful, if less heroic quest for illusions. Elderly author Gerald Musgrave is driven out of his body and his reality by demon Glaum. A young man again, he stumbles down the road to Antan, the shimmering, unattainable ideal of 'yesteryear' where he plans to rule as "Fair-haired Hoo, the Helper and Preserver, the Lord of the Third Truth, the Well-beloved of the Heavenly Ones" (37:285). The stations of his journey are anagrams marking his 'progress': Doonham, i.e. manhood, Dersam, i.e. dreams, Lytreia, i.e. reality, Turoine, i.e. routine. In Mispec Moor – compromise – he meets another incarnation of Mother Sereda, whom he comes to know as "Maya of the Fair Breasts" (23:188). Despite her somewhat intimidating conduct (see Fig. 12), he stays with her and procrastinates by chatting with other travellers who are on their way to Antan instead of going there himself, paralleling his writer's block in reality.

---

ignore (MacDonald, "Photographic Essay" 94).

Patterson argues that in an esoteric sense, Maya embodies the female principle Gerald, the male initiand, has to pass through to continue his search for a 'third truth' besides the ones of being born and dying. In the story, she is Circe, turning her male victims into animals. Maya is also the Hindu goddess of illusion, making Gerald wear rose-coloured spectacles. She is Eve, she is Lilith, she is every woman, and in every sense essential for man's existence. She is the one who *must not be escaped.* Sending their illusionary son to Antan, Gerald willingly destroys his dream:

> '[T]he one way for a poet to appreciate the loveliness of a place is not ever to go to it [...]. So a logical poet will always destroy his appointed kingdom, because in this way only he can convert it into a beautiful idea. [...] I can remake the destroyed place several times a day, in my imaginings, and can every time rebuild it more beautifully.' (47:351)

Like most of Cabell's quests, this one ends where it began: Gerald and Glaum switch places again, and Gerald settles in his old familiar body while a young and potent version of himself sets out on his way. "And the eternal quest of Antan continues" (59:369).

VII. Two Truths

Literally a 'man' of letters, Cabell's point of view usually condemns women to remain mere cyphers (Gilbert and Gubar 7; 9). However his writing is never oblivious of the fact that a tale told by a man is only one half of the truth. As Koshchei points out in *The Silver Stallion*:

> 'Did I not make my creatures male and female? and did I not make the tie which is between them, that cord which I wove equally of love and disliking? Eh, sirs, but this is a strong cord, and though all things that are depend upon it, my weaving holds.' (18:89)

The liberal-minded 1920s allow Cabell to both yearn for and ridicule the "attitudes of mythic simplicity" that still pervaded the arts of earlier decades (Dijkstra 188). Likewise, most of his transgressions, refracted by the prism of irony, remain "benevolent" in tone, with "the teeth of Gothic terror [...] filed down, if not extracted" (Merivale 154).

Through his friendship with Ellen Glasgow, Cabell was well aware of the struggles of women for self-determination. Glasgow's heroines (one of them ironically named Gabriella) often have to learn that "lovers come, and pass out of your living […] but no one of them matters deeply" (*Let Me Lie* 234) while still maintaining hope in the future (*Let Me Lie* 237) – themes all too familiar for Cabell. He painfully realized that the very ideals of Southern chivalry he was raised with were to be blamed for the mutual misconceptions and the suffering of both its male and female victims, and saw it as a proof of his conviction that "never while life lasts can the two sexes quite understand each other" (248). A third truth still remained to be found. "I think of Gabriella Carr", he writes in 1938 regarding the protagonist of Glasgow's *Life and Gabriella,* "who […] ran away, in a panic, from the most faithful and the most chivalrous of Virginian gentlemen because she could not endure being married to his delusions" (*Let Me Lie* 246).

In 1935, the New York bookseller Claire Myers Owens published a remarkable feminist response to Cabell's works. *The Unpredictable Adventure: A Comedy of Woman's Independence* is an allegory modelled closely on the style and structure of Cabell's romances, including his fondness for wordplay and anagrams. Following the form of an episodic *bildungsroman*, the young Tellectina travels from the Land of Err into the country of Nithking – Thinking – in search of Mount Certitude. She meets and dismisses various lovers and makes the acquaintance of many fictional and real-life inhabitants of Nithking, including Cabell as the "Prince of Poictesme", who offers to teach her his ironic outlook on life. She realizes that laugher is the highest form of certitude human beings can hope for, but watching the comic enactments of Cabell's narrative works she also learns "how far short of man's dream of her woman could fall"; "and there lurked under her laughter a poignant note of sadness" (388-391). However, as her Jungian twin sister Femina remarks, "no woman can be happy […] because no man of woman's dreaming could ever exist" (411). The disappointment about the fundamental incompatibility of reality and dream holds true for both sexes.

VIII. Lovers How They Part

Between his *Domnei* on the one hand and his meditation on the eternal
'witch-woman' on the other, Cabell's female characters serve a very
different function than their underlying archetypes do in traditional
Gothic texts. Also, Cabell satirizes not so much the distressed damsels as
their conceited knights in shining armour. His aspiring poets might still
maintain the fin de siècle belief that women, having no insight into the
deeper meaning of existence, only understand men sexually and want to
separate them from their "godlike capacity for spiritual transcendence",
dooming their "magnificent dreams of intellectual achievement" (Dijkstra
121; 239-240; vii). But sooner or later they are exposed as the braggarts
they are: as Jurgen learns during his stay with the Lady of the Lake, his
name is derived from "*jargon,* indicating a confused chattering such as
birds give forth at sunrise" (25:157).

So while a strong "male ambivalence […] underlies the traditional
images of such terrible sorceress-goddesses as the Sphinx, Medusa,
Circe, Kali, Delilah, and Salome", who use their charms "both to seduce
and to steal male generative energy" (Gilbert and Gubar 34), in Cabell's
case these seductresses are the very *source* of that energy. Suskind,
Anaïtis, even Maya are projections of his protagonists' need to
desiderate. This favourite word of his literally means to "miss one's star",
and thus to be compelled to search for it; for the stars can be both origin
and destination and grant their followers the fulfilment of their *desires*
when they wish on them, as well as smite them with that special kind of
misery also brought upon by the stars – *disaster* (Plaschka 28).

Cabell employs the element of magic in his fiction so that the sons of
Manuel can create, travel and destroy the worlds of his and their poetic
imagination. These travels range from the allegorical-didactic to the
romantical-fantastic, with the occasional Gothic "peaks" marking the
personal or communal hells the struggling heroes bring to pass. The result
however is most often not so much a Gothic text as a satire on male-
female misunderstanding. In Cabell's fiction, every romantic relationship
carries the seed of Gothic excess within it, since all men are magicians or
megalomaniacs at heart, and all women are princesses that need to be
rescued or sorceresses from whom there is no rescue.

The lure of Eternal Womanhood, in all its guises, is the unifying element
in Cabell's *Biography*, fuelling his "powerful myth of endlessly

unsatisfied desire" (Riemer 93). The circular quest for the ideal informs Cabell's existentialist view on man's (but not only man's) *raison d'être*. Paraphrasing Camus' closing words, the struggle itself is enough to fill a man's heart; one must imagine Jurgen happy (123).

Works Cited

Cabell, James Branch. *The Certain Hour: Dizain des Poètes*. 1916. New York: Robert M. McBride & Co, 1929.

---. *The Cream of the Jest: A Comedy of Evasions*. 1917. New York: Robert M. McBride & Co, 1927.

---. *Domnei: A Comedy of Woman-Worship*. 1920 [1913 as *The Soul of Melicent*]. New York: Robert M. McBride & Co, 1930.

---. *Domnei; The Music from Behind the Moon*. 1920; 1926. New York: Robert M. McBride & Co, 1928.

---. *Figures of Earth: A Comedy of Appearances*. 1921. New York: Robert M. McBride & Co, 1925.

---. *The High Place: A Comedy of Disenchantment*. New York: Robert M. McBride & Co, 1923.

---. *Jurgen: A Comedy of Justice*. 1919. London: John Lane / The Bodley Head, 1921.

---. *Let Me Lie: Being in the Main an Ethnological Account of the Remarkable Commonwealth of Virginia and the Making of its History*. New York: Farrar, Straus and Company, 1947.

---. *The Silver Stallion: A Comedy of Redemption*. 1926. New York: Robert M. McBride & Co, 1928.

---. *Something About Eve: A Comedy of Fig-Leaves*. 1927. New York: Robert M. McBride & Co, 1929.

---. "The Soul of Mervisaunt." *Harper's Monthly Magazine*. April 1911: 663-676.

---. *Townsend of Lichfield: Dizain des Adieux*. New York: Robert M. McBride & Co, 1930.

---. *The Witch-Woman: A Trilogy About Her*. New York: Farrar, Straus and Company, 1948.

Camus, Albert. *The Myth of Sisyphus: And Other Essays.* 1942. Trans. Justin O'Brien. New York: Vintage, 1991.

Cobb, Richard. *Something to Hold Onto: Autobiographical Sketches.* London: John Murray, 1988.

Cranwell, John Philips, and James P. Cover. *Notes on Figures of Earth.* New York: Robert M. McBride & Co, 1929.

Dijkstra, Bram. *Idols of Perversity: Fantasies of Feminine Evil in Fin-de-Siècle Culture.* Oxford: Oxford University Press, 1986.

Fiedler, Leslie A. "The Return of James Branch Cabell; or, The Cream of the Cream of the Jest." *James Branch Cabell: Centennial Essays.* Eds. M. Thomas Inge and Edgar E. MacDonald. Baton Rouge: Louisiana State University Press, 1983. 131-141.

Freeman, Nick. "Cabell, James Branch." *The Encyclopedia of the Gothic.* Eds. William Hughes, David Punter, and Andrew Smith. Oxford: Wiley-Blackwell, 2013.

Gilbert, Sandra M., and Susan Gubar. *The Madwoman in the Attic: The Woman Writer and the Nineteenth-Century Literary Imagination.* New Haven: Yale University Press, 1980.

Glasgow, Ellen. *The Woman Within.* New York: Harcourt, Brace & Co, 1954.

Godshalk, W. L. "James Branch Cabell: The Life of His Design." *James Branch Cabell: Centennial Essays.* Eds. M. Thomas Inge and Edgar E. MacDonald. Baton Rouge: Louisiana State University Press, 1983. 108-121.

Goethe, Johann Wolfgang von. *Faust: Erster und zweiter Teil.* 1808 and 1832. München: dtv, 1997.

Graves, Robert. *The White Goddess: A Historical Grammar of Poetic Myth.* 1948. New York: Farrar, Straus and Giroux, 2013.

Gross, John, ed. *The New Oxford Book of Literary Anecdotes.* Oxford: Oxford University Press, 2008.

MacDonald, Edgar E. *James Branch Cabell and Richmond-in-Virginia.* Jackson: University Press of Mississippi, 1993.

---. "James Branch Cabell: A Photographic Essay." *James Branch Cabell: Centennial Essays.* Eds. M. Thomas Inge and Edgar E.

MacDonald. Baton Rouge: Louisiana State University Press, 1983. 82-107.

Mencken, H. L. "James Branch Cabell." *H. L. Mencken on American Literature.* Ed. S. T. Joshi. Athens: Ohio University Press, 2002. 95-109.

Merivale, Patricia. "Learning the Hard Way: Gothic Pedagogy in the Modern Romantic Quest." *Comparative Literature* 36.2 (1984): 146-161.

Plaschka, Oliver. "Verlorene Arkadien: Das pastorale Motiv in der englischen und amerikanischen fantastischen Literatur – H.P. Lovecraft, James Branch Cabell, Mervyn Peake, William Gibson." *Heidelberger Dokumentenserver.* 2 Dec. 2009. Web. 3 Apr. 2014.

Patterson, Bill. "The Heir of James Branch Cabell: The Biography of the Life of the Biography of the Life of Manuel (A Comedy of Inheritances)." Web. 3 Apr. 2014.

Riemer, James D. *From Satire to Subversion: The Fantasies of James Branch Cabell.* Westport: Greenwood Press, 1989.

Rubin, Louis D. Jr. "A Virginian in Poictesme." *James Branch Cabell: Centennial Essays.* Eds. M. Thomas Inge and Edgar E. MacDonald. Baton Rouge: Louisiana State University Press, 1983. 1-16.

---. "Two in Richmond: Ellen Glasgow and James Branch Cabell." *South: Modern Southern Literature in its Cultural Setting.* Eds. Robert D. Jacobs and Louis D. Rubin. Westport: Greenwood Press, 1974. 115-141.

Schopenhauer, Arthur. "The Metaphysics of Sexual Love." *The World as Will and Representation, Volume II.* 1818. Trans. E. F. J. Payne. New York: Dover Publications, 1966.

Weir, David. *Decadent Culture in the United States.* Albany: State University of New York Press, 2008.

Wilson, Edmund, "The James Branch Cabell Case Reopened" and "James Branch Cabell: 1879-1958." *The Bit Between My Teeth: A Literary Chronicle of 1950-1965.* Ed. Edmund Wilson. New York: Farrar, Straus & Giroux, 1965. 291-321; 322-325.

Figure 1: In the endpapers of "The Cream of the Jest", Papé juxtaposes several pastoral dichotomies: old age vs. vitality, marital estrangement vs. romantic love, city vs. countryside. Even the symbols of freedom and spirituality (the ship, the moon, the temple) correspond only to images of captivity, artificiality and emptiness (the cut flowers, the lamp, the dark area to the left).

Figures 2 and 3: "A dream would usually begin with some light-headed topsiturviness"; "Nightly he went adventuring with Ettarre" (Cream 104; frontispiece). Mocking Kennaston's dreams of omnipotence and courtly romance, Papé exaggerates the sexual undertones in Fig. 2 and plays them down in Fig. 3. As Dijkstra observes, "it is decidedly difficult to imagine engaging in any sort of sustained bodily contact with a woman who is lighter than air" (90).

Figures 4 and 5 (Cream 12; 213): Ettarre, safely "sentenced" and "penned in" by the poetic demiurge (Gilbert and Gubar 5, 13). She is unattainable yet inseparably linked with her demanding creator, attracting and eluding him at the same time.

Figure 6: "Then Jurgen knew with whom he talked" (Jurgen 32). Mother Sereda, the bleacher who deprives life of its colour and joy, depicted as an old and unattractive woman. She seems reluctant to make use of her magic (the goat in her courtyard).

Figure 7: "Upon the middle chest sat a woman" (Jurgen 56). Guenevere as weak and unresisting Sleeping Beauty: barefooted, scantily dressed, a mere commodity at the mercy of the male, malevolent powers that clutch her hair and threaten her private parts with a huge sword.

Figure 8: "And so farewell to you, Queen Helen!" (Jurgen 304). Helen as the centre of all male striving. A similar scene is to be found in Domnei (24); but domnei turns to despair as the man buries his face in the hem of her skirt and begs for her blessing. Helen seems not without compassion; however, the white lilies serve as symbols both of spiritual purity and of death, an interpretation enforced by her spectre-like appearance and Koshchei watching from the darkness, an hourglass on his desk.

Figure 9: "And at her feet one placed the severed head of Gonfal" (Stallion 56) [caption removed]. Papé's Morvyth is a fair-skinned, half-naked Salome with almond-shaped eyes, enthroned between two bejewelled elephant heads. Kneeling before her is the caricature of a chubby, black-skinned executioner with thick lips and big round eyes; the epitome of a Haggardian cliché, were it not for the phallic tusks, the dainty, heart-shaped mirror and the smiling faces on his trousers which turn the scene into ridicule. In the story, the people of Inis Dahut are only identified as "pagan" and – with regard to their tribal religion and their customary sacrifice of children – "Fundamentalists", singing the "Hymn of the Star-Spangled Buttock" (7:40). Morvyth is described as "a lovely girl [...] meditatively [...] prodding with her toe at what remained of Gonfal" (11:57); as Dijkstra characterizes Salome, "not so much evil as wasteful" (384).

Figure 10: "What happened forthwith at the pool of Haranton" (Figures of Earth, frontispiece): Manuel's capture of Alianora the Unattainable Princess is an inversion of the clinging nymphs that often drown heroes like Hylas (see Dijkstra chapter VII). In Cabell's case, it is the swineherd Manuel who literally drags the princess to his level. It is also a violent variation of Fig. 8, with the male ruthlessly following his desires and defiling female purity, as symbolized by the loss of her feather. The quote from the text – hinting at the fact that something happened without really naming it – stresses the scandal-like nature of the scene, with the fish below spreading the gossip and the frog imitating Manuel.

Figure 11: "Then Freydis went away, and the accursed beasts and her castle too went with her, as smoke passes" (Figures of Earth 206). Queen Freydis, along with a panther, a rat and "another creature, such as no madman has ever seen or imagined" (30:204). The beasts frame her like a calyx; the castle gate and the halo-like lines around her head make her look like a dark saint or Madonna. However, despite the demonic mise-en-scène, she is no morbid "idol of perversity" but seems very much sensuous and alive; a "woman of flesh and blood, not a mythologized flower of evil", which by itself would have been a feminist statement only three decades earlier (Dijkstra 392).

Figure 12: "I will give you your dinner, and on top of that your hat" (Eve 188). Maya of the Fair Breasts as a dark-tanned, bare-breasted matron even the devils in her hearth are afraid of, serving Gerald his own genitalia. Her crown is adorned with clubs, spades, hearts and diamonds as called for in the story (187), making her the garish and grotesque counterpart to sexless, cold Sereda.

Illustrations courtesy of the Papé family and the Department of Special Collections and University Archives, Stanford University Libraries. Special thanks to Bill Lloyd of The Silver Stallion website for his helpful advice and Susan Papé for her kind and generous support.

Franziska Schneider

From Bullerby to Blackeberg: Gothic Themes and National Settings in the Writings of John Ajvide Lindqvist

I. Introduction: Sweden and the Gothic

When asking a Swede how he or she would explain a Swedish spirit, a Swedish way of life and behaviour, it is most likely to get an answer that is rather short but not necessarily very precise. The answer might be: *lagom*.[1] *Lagom* is an adjective used relatively often in the Swedish language, despite the fact that it is almost impossible to translate. Itdescribes the state of something lying exactly in the middle. A cup of coffee can be *lagom*, when it is not too cold and not too hot, not too strong and not too light. A book can be described as *lagom* when it is thrilling, but not scary, long enough to be entertaining over a good period of time, but not too long to become boring again. Something *lagom* is right in the middle, nothing too kinky and nothing too exciting, something of substance which is still modest and moderate. In Swedish culture, it is not only a fitting word to describe coffee, but also to describe anything that is important for the society as a whole. The old Swedish dream about building a welfare state is actually the dream about making a country *lagom* for its citizens, 'lagomizing' it in a certain way. As history taught us, this dream did not come true: Sweden has the same problems as the rest of the world and struggles when it comes to, for example, equality, economy, unemployment, racism and crime. But still, Sweden longs to be as *lagom* as possible.[2]

---

[1] The word *lagom* is closely connected to another term that is often used to describe the Scandinavian mentality: *Jantelagen*, which might be translated as 'the law of Jante' and which was established by the author Aksel Sandemose in 1933 in his novel *En flyktning krosser sitt spor* (Eng. *A fugitive crosses his track*). The ten rules of Jante's law can be summarized in one sentence that everybody in Scandinavia is able to recite: "*You are not to think you're anyone special or that you're better than us*" (trans. FS).

[2] The author Mikael Parkvall describes it as follows: "The word *lagom* is often described as the most Swedish word one could imagine. We Swedes not only have the word lagom, we *are* lagom" (9; trans. FS).

When comparing this Swedish spirit with the core of Gothic literature – if it can be said to exist – one might come up with a fairly simple answer: Gothic literature is not *lagom*. In fact, it is as far away from being *lagom* as one could imagine. Gothic literature does not seek to be modest and moderate, careful and sensible: it wants to be scary, uncanny, unhealthy, strong, fascinating and extreme. To use Michel Foucault's words, "[t]he language of terror is dedicated to an endless expense, even though it only seeks to achieve a single effect. It drives itself out of any possible resting place" (65). This image very accurately encapsulates the paradox that lies at the heart of the connection between the Swedish spirit and the Gothic. The Swedish longing for *lagom* represents a desire to really find such a resting place, a little spot in the world where life is neither dangerous nor fast nor loud. Gothic, on the other hand, does not want to rest; it wants excess. A Gothic hero, a Gothic plot, a Gothic text has no interest in resting, nor does it wish to grant its readers the possibility of rest.

It seems almost impossible to combine the Swedish longing for *lagom* with the Gothic desire for excess. Of course some Swedish works do display close ties to the Gothic; one of Sweden's best-known authors, August Strindberg, wrote various novels and plays that show Gothic tendencies and rather uniquely incorporate ideas of excess and unhealthiness.[3] But then, Strindberg is usually not regarded as being very Swedish in Sweden; his works are admired, but not copied. He clearly had the nimbus of a crazy genius, but on the other hand, that is probably not a very Swedish feature.[4]

As far as entertainment and literature for the masses are concerned, Sweden went into a different direction – one that made the country, its landscape and its police officers known worldwide: today, Sweden is

---

[3] Strindberg's Gothic tendencies are most obvious not in his many plays, but in his novels, most of all *Tschandala* from 1889, "a crime novel in the Gothic manner of Edgar Allan Poe" (Johannesson 123). This novel about a 'Gypsy' family "has more than a generous sprinkling of features we associate with the Gothic tale. There is the mysterious setting with its exotic inhabitants and strange events. There are elements of moral depravity: adultery and incest. There are strange transformations: nothing is what it appears to be" (Johannesson 125).

[4] Henrik Berggren and Lars Trägårdh write about Sweden and Strindberg: "As a political ideologist Strindberg is specifically unswedish. Not because of his individualism, but because of his antipathy to both the state and the detaining thought about the law of Jante" (148; trans. FS).

extremely popular all over the world for its crime novels. Henning Mankell started, or, to be correct, restarted this literary tradition in the early nineteen nineties – and still Scandinavian crime fiction is most popular in the rest of the world.[5] These novels are very often brutal, shocking, thrilling and bitter. The evil forces in those stories come from all over the world, enter the little idyllic country that is Sweden and exercise their destructive influence from south to north.[6] Still, these wicked forces are human – a fact which could make the thought of them at least bearable. Swedish crime novels typically tell about people and actions that are absolutely not *lagom*. On the contrary, murder itself, and the most gruesome ways of murder that are included in some of these novels, is horrible, crazy and evil. But, on the other hand, we may still find heroes in these novels such as Henning Mankell's pensive inspector Kurt Wallander; of course, they are not superheroes, just normal police officers or journalists who drink too much coffee, wish that they had more time for their kids, reflect on the way their beloved home country has changed and try to make this evil world a better place. Kurt Wallander is extremely *lagom* – and he is therefore necessary in order to make these novels Swedish and thereby place them firmly within Swedish society and culture. Furthermore, what is probably most important for the genre and its readers – characters like Kurt Wallander guarantee one thing: in the end, there will be justice, of whatever kind.

This promise to the reader of crime fiction is something that Gothic literature, generally speaking, cannot and does not want to provide. In the latter, we normally find a rather different kind of setup: once the evil comes into our world, it will not leave anymore. Nobody will be able to fight it. Gothic writing transgresses borders, and it crosses many

---

[5] In fact, Maj Sjöwall and Per Wahlhöö initiated the success of Swedish crime stories. Their ten-volume series about police detective Beck and the political situation in Sweden was and is one of the most important works in Swedish crime literature, and a far cry from the typical 'Whodunnit' murder mystery. For further details regarding the history and future of Swedish and Scandinavian crime fiction, I strongly recommend Barry Forshaw's *Death in a Cold Climate*.

[6] In the special case of the Wallander mysteries, it truly *is* 'from south to north': Skåne, where Mankell's novels take place, is the southernmost part of Sweden, which belonged to Denmark for a long time and thus represents a part of the country which might be considered more 'continental' than the rest.

boundaries that crime novels are not able to overstep. Fred Botting, for example, stresses the meaning of transgression in Gothic literature:

> The terrors and horrors of transgression in Gothic writing become a powerful means to reassert the values of society, virtue and propriety: transgression, by crossing the social and aesthetic limits, serves to reinforce or underline their value and necessity, restoring or defining limits. (7)

II. Lindqvist and the Gothic

Regarding the above-mentioned contrast between the Swedish spirit and the Gothic, it is surprising to note that not so long ago a Swedish writer stepped onto the international stage of Gothic literature with his vampire novel *Låt den Rätte Komma In* (Engl. *Let the Right One In*), published in 2004, which might be considered to be one of the most important Gothic novels of our time. With the story of twelve-year-old Oskar who falls in love with the vampire Eli, the author John Ajvide Lindqvist became one of the best-known and most important Swedish writers worldwide. A Swede and Gothic, that means *lagom* and excess – does this fit together?

It does indeed. Lindqvist tackles topics that display numerous typical features of Gothic literature: a vampire child, zombies, spooky islands where little children get lost, houses that come to life and start killing people. Yet, Lindqvist's language, his settings, spaces and heroes appear almost perfectly normal – especially at the beginning, but even at various points throughout the story; a little strange perhaps, but still quite usual. All of Lindqvist's novels and short stories certainly begin rather *lagom*.

Let us start with *Let the Right One In*. This novel is set in Blackeberg, a Stockholm suburb which once was built as a planned city during the huge project which was the Swedish welfare state. Lindqvist describes this setting in further detail at the beginning of his novel:

> Blackeberg. It makes you think of coconut-frosted cookies, maybe drugs. 'A respectable life'. […] People must live there, just like they do in other places. That was why it was built, after all, so that people would have a place to live. […] Everything was carefully built for them. Earth-colored concrete buildings scattered in the green fields. (*Let the Right One In* 1)

It is a suburban setting which is not extreme or eerie, spooky or scary in any sense. Any kind of story could begin like this: normal people, familiar types of houses. At this point it is impossible to tell that this is the beginning of a gloomy story about a vampire child who kills innocent people, including children, in order to drink their blood. Indeed, this is exactly how Lindqvist's horror works. It is a horror that is distinctively Swedish. In this context, Blackeberg is not only a suburb, it represents a Swedish dream and a Swedish trauma at the same time; this applies especially to Blackeberg in the 1980s, when the story takes place. Lindqvist describes how people moved to this area to lead good and respectable lives there. They all shared the same dream about equality and wealth. They were pioneers. The whole country was on the move, hoping to be able to create something new thanks to the so-called *Folkhem* – and now, they found all their dreams destroyed. The *Folkhem* – the Swedish model of a welfare state that should guarantee freedom and prosperity for all its citizens – did not work out, as the economy went down, people became unemployed and, with the death of Olof Palme, the whole country lost a hero. People felt betrayed by the politicians since the latter had promised work and wealth for everyone. In a way, Sweden had lost its innocence with the breakdown of the *Folkhem*. So, Blackeberg in the eighties is not just a suburban setting: it represents both a Swedish dream and a Swedish nightmare. The aspect of a collective trauma that is part of everybody's past is an important clue to understanding how Scandinavian and especially Swedish horror might work, as Yvonne Leffler points out: "[I]t should be noted that even if most modern horror deals with the protagonist's individual trauma, Scandinavian horror is more frequently concerned with evoking a collective trauma bound to a common past" (49).

Bearing this traumatic experience in mind, it is interesting to remark that Lindqvist's description of Blackeberg is quite the opposite of what Fred Botting writes about Gothic literature and its settings: "Gothic atmospheres – gloomy and mysterious – have repeatedly signaled the disturbing return of pasts upon presents" (Botting 1). However, Lindqvist describes Blackeberg as a place where

> [o]nly one thing was missing. A past. At school, the children didn't get to do any special projects about Blackeberg's history because there wasn't one. [...] Where the three-storied apartment buildings now stood there had been only forest before. You were

beyond the grasp of the mysteries of the past." (*Let the Right One In* 2)

It appears as if Lindqvist created a setting that was as different from a traditional Gothic setting as could possibly be. The missing link to the past shows not only his independence as a horror writer; it is also part of the Swedish dream to build a new society, a new country. The Swedish *Folkhem* is supposed to be healthy, just, new, and stable – it is therefore the total opposite of anything Gothic. It is quite interesting that the story about a vampire, a creature that is as old as history itself, is set in a place where history itself is lacking. In a certain way, Sweden might be described as obsessed with modernity and progress; Blackeberg stands for these values. It is most effective to destroy this idyll with a horror that represents the total opposite of modernity, health and progress. Thus, it is a logical consequence for Lindqvist to bring a vampire to Blackeberg to destruct this idyllic setting. This is what modern Gothic fiction does: it destroys idylls, dreams, plans; Blackeberg was built as a modern and progressive paradise, and Eli the Vampire embodies the Gothic mode that comes upon this paradise, causing its downfall from within.

The *Folkhem* represents one of the most important Swedish idylls, and although the breakdown of the economy and the death of Olof Palme were regarded as the end of the *Folkhem*, this dream still is very much present in Swedish society. This is why the horror of Blackeberg is something that works better than a horror that might appear in a gloomy castle or a shadowy forest. On the other hand, it is remarkable that Blackeberg and the Swedish *Folkhem* are not destroyed by a vampire: they ruin themselves. There is not even a supernatural force needed to bring down this Swedish paradise. In an interview, Lindqvist answered the question why he had chosen this setting and this plot for *Let the Right One In* with a short sentence: "My idea was quite simple. Horror came to Blackeberg, and I wanted to see what happens" (Redvall; trans. FS). What he does not mention is that horror comes twice: the first horror is the breakdown of the *Folkhem*, the second horror is the vampire that comes to haunt the victims of this breakdown.

III. The Deconstruction of National Idylls

There are three important idylls in Swedish society and literature, and they are loved and adored with great passion: the first one, as I already mentioned, is the *Folkhem*. The second one is childhood. Probably this is the result of Astrid Lindgren's immense success. In her novels, she describes childhood – in the past and present – as some sort of sanctuary. Even if bad things happen, the children in her stories remain pure, innocent and free. The children of Bullerbyhelp each other,[7] the Brothers Lionheart fight for freedom and justice, and Pippi Longstocking uses her money and her superpowers only to buy candy and to do good.

Lindqvist manages to deconstruct this Swedish idyll in almost all of his stories and novels. The children he creates are never allowed to be typical children. Eli, the genderless vampire child, probably never was a normal child. Sometimes s/he appears to be as innocent and helpless as children usually are; in the next moment s/he kills people to drink their blood. Håkan, Eli's 'helper', represents a rather perverted version of the often admired innocent childhood. He is a former teacher, who is sexually attracted to children and stays with Eli because he has fallen in love with the child-like shape of the vampire. Eli's innocence and beauty touch him, but instead of protecting 'his' child, Håkan later tries to rape Eli. He has turned into a monstrous zombie vampire. Eli has to kill him in the end – and, in the Swedish film adaptation at least, it is suggested that s/he does it out of mercy. Children have mercy with their 'parents', not the other way around.

Then there is Oskar, a twelve-year-old who falls in love with Eli. He is obsessed with weapons and violence. His most precious belongings are his knife and his collection of newspaper articles about brutal crimes and murders. When he first meets Eli, he is standing in the yard of his apartment building, trying to kill a tree imagining it was another child.

> The tree didn't answer and Oskar carefully drove the knife into it. Didn't want to damage the fine smooth edge. 'That's what happens if you so much as look at me.' He turned the knife so a

---

[7] In fact, Lindgren's *Bullerby* novels about the peaceful childhood of six kids growing up in a pastoral Swedish village had an immense impact on Swedish culture.

small wedge of wood popped out of the trunk. A piece of flesh.
(Lindqvist, *Let the Right One In* 36)

The children in his school are not any better; they constantly bully Oskar.
When the reader is introduced to Oskar, he is being beaten up by his
classmates in the restroom until his nose starts bleeding: "He [Oskar] got
up and left the bathroom. Didn't wipe up the drop of blood. Let someone
see it, let them wonder. Let them think someone had been killed here,
because someone *had* been killed here. And for the hundredth time" (*Let
the Right One In* 11). In the end, Eli appears as some sort of dark angel of
revenge and kills most of these bullies because they tried to hurt Oskar.
Children kill children, while the adults who should protect them, are
helpless, drunk or simply not interested.

How far apart the spaces of the children and of the adults really are is
very well presented in the two films that were adapted from *Let the Right
One In*; the Swedish one has the same title, while the American remake is
called *Let Me In*. Both films show almost no connection between the
world of adults and the world of children. One scene in the Swedish film,
when Oskar visits his father who lives in the country, away from the
family, shows how the boy longs to establish a connection with the
emotional and actual landscape of his father's world in every possible
way he can. In the beginning it seems to work out, as we see father and
son riding a sledge and laughing together. But as soon as a friend of his
father's comes to visit, the possibility of entering the adult world is closed
again for Oskar. The men start drinking, talking 'adult business' and
Oskar is put in the corner. He then decides to leave on his own, returning
to Blackeberg, i.e. the place of the one person that appears to be a fighter
for his own cause: Eli. In the novel, the situation with his father becomes
difficult as soon as alcohol is involved, and though the reader only gets to
see it all through Oskar's eyes, it is still very obvious that the protagonist's father has a drinking problem and therefore is only in sober periods
really capable of taking care of his son:

> He never got violent or anything. But what Oskar saw in his eyes
> at those times was the absolutely scariest thing he had ever seen.
> Then there was no trace of Dad left. Just a monster who had
> somehow crawled into his dad's body and taken control of it. The
> person his dad became when he drank had no connection to the
> person he was when he was sober. (Lindqvist, *Let the Right One
> In* 256)

So the transformation of his father into another person, a monster, when he drinks, appears to Oskar as the most uncanny change he has ever seen – and we have to keep in mind that he met a vampire only a few days earlier. And yet, the monster his father turns into when he drinks seems more dangerous to Oskar than the monstrous creature that lives next door in Blackeberg.

Let Me In, the American remake of the Swedish film, chose another visual method to show the impossibility of children and adults getting together or finding a connection between their spheres: Oskar lives with his mother, but we never really get to see her. Her face is always blurred, we only hear her voice, see her silhouette, but not the complete person, and there is never a moment that the child Oskar shares with his mother. For the children, and especially for Eli and Oskar, it is 'them against us'.

This is also the motto of the two teenage girls in one of Lindqvist's latest novels, *Little Star* from 2010, a book which is rather different than his other novels so far. No supernatural powers are featured here, no vampires or zombies, just the angst and the wrath of two girls who believe themselves misunderstood by the whole world. Theres and Teresa grow up in different worlds, but as soon as they befriend each other via the internet, they start to form a gang of girls they call the 'Wolves', and their aim is to kill anybody who has ever done them wrong. The grand finale is a massacre during one of Sweden's best-known TV events, the *Allsång på Skansen*, where people gather to enjoy the summer and sing together. On the novel's first pages Lindqvist describes the Skansen setting:

> Sweden's biggest music show will be on air in five minutes, and no one must be allowed to come to harm. There must be these oases of pleasure, where everyday cares are set aside for a while. Nothing bad can happen here, and every possible security measure has been taken to keep this place of enjoyment safe. Screams of pain, of terror, are unthinkable; there must be no blood on the ground or covering the seats when the broadcast is over. There must not be a corpse lying on the stage, with many more on the ground below. [...] The atmosphere must be calm and pleasant. (*Little Star* 1)

With these words Lindqvist makes sure, right at the beginning of his novel, that he is about to cross a line, that his protagonists are going to destroy this Swedish sanctuary that is *Allsång*, that the impossible is going to happen: people are going to be killed during this feast of friendship and joy. They are killed by teenage girls who seem to harbour such reckless hatred and brutal revenge that it becomes unbearable for everyone. Where Eli and Oskar kill to escape or to survive, Theres and Teresa kill because they believe it is their right and their task as wolf girls. In a suicide note Teresa points out that there is not going to be an answer to the question 'Why?': "You will ask why. Why, why, why. [...] In the papers. Big thick letters. [...] And this is our answer (wait for it now): BECAUSE!!!!!" (Lindqvist, *Little Star* 612). This is exactly where the horror of the murdering girls of Skansen lies: in the fact that there is no reasonable explanation for it. The children become murderers because they choose to. The ideas of childhood, of coming of age, and of a family and society that protects its kids – these idylls are utterly perverted during the bloody finale of this novel, as well as one of the country's most protected and beloved events, connecting childhood, nature and the dream of a *lagom* society, the *Allsång*.

Another child in another story, the zombie novel *Handling the Undead,* is Elias. He dies at the age of six, before the plot of the novel even starts. Not much is said about him, only that his mother and grandfather grieve in an almost unhealthy way. When the news spread that for some reason the dead in Stockholm are waking, Elias' grandfather drives to the cemetery and digs out his grandson, since it is impossible for the old man to let him rest. He opens the coffin and takes Elias with him; the latter is now some sort of undead puppet, a perverted creature whose only reason to still exist is to ease his grandfather's grief:

> But this body was not soft, nor warm. It was cold and unyielding, stiff like a reptile. Half-way to the exit he [the grandfather] dared to peek at the face again. The skin was orange-brown, drawn taut so the cheekbones were sharply outlined. The eyes were just a couple of slits and the whole face looked vaguely [...] Egyptian. The nose and lips were black, shrunken. There wasn't much left that resembled Elias except for the brown curly hair tumbling down over the wide forehead. And yet, it was a stroke of luck. (Lindqvist, *Handling the Undead* 83)

Then there is Maja, a child in the novel *Harbour*. Maja does not die, she simply disappears one day. Her parents take her along on a trip to the Lighthouse of Gåvasten, located on one of the islands of the archipelago surrounding Stockholm. Maja vanishes, and while her father Anders is still grieving and looking for his daughter, he does not only find out that the sea around the island of Domarö has a will of its own and demands human sacrifices to be appeased – including child sacrifices. Anders also comes to understand something about his daughter Maja:

> Maja had been dreadful. He had often wished they had never had her. [...] She wept and screamed and kicked as soon as she didn't get her own way. She immediately smashed things that didn't behave in the way she wanted. She had no boundaries. [...] That was the way it had been. Like having a monster in the house, you had to be wary of every step, constantly on the alert to avoid provoking its fury. (John Ajvide Lindqvist, *Harbor* 386)

The child he has been looking for, the sweet and gentle little girl he introduces to us at the beginning of the novel, never existed. Instead his child is compared to a monster.[8]

Lindqvist has created a literary genre that deals with distinctly Swedish topics, but deconstructs them in a very Gothic way. Despite the fact that, as Botting points out, Gothic literature often uses the motif of past events reaching into the present and haunting the protagonists, Lindqvist's work is centred on the future rather than the past; it presents children turning against adults and destroying their carefully built perfect little world.

So we can find two typical Swedish idylls being deconstructed in Lindqvist's novels, the *Folkhem* and childhood. The third idyll is very closely connected to childhood: it is nature. Featuring endless forests, lonely lakes, elks, blooming meadows, dozens of little islands in the famous *skärgården*, the archipelago in the sea, Sweden is frequently regarded as a paradise for those who love nature and seek it in its most original way. Nature has always been important for Sweden, and this is

---

[8] Children are always of some importance in Gothic literature, as Margarita Georgieva points out in *The Gothic Child*. Children usually represent the yearning and nostalgia for "their [the adults'] past childhood" which is "analogous to the human longing for a Paradise that was lost" (Georgieva 111). On the other hand, children are also portrayed as wicked, cunning and even dangerous creatures: "The idea of the child changing from a kind, gentle angel into a wicked demon is frequently mirrored by the image of the doll suddenly springing to life" (Georgieva 188) – a picture that is very close to the Freudian uncanny.

also reflected in famous Swedish works of literature: all the way from Selma Lagerlöf to Astrid Lindgren, nature and its forces play a crucial role in almost every important Swedish novel, including horror novels, as Yvonne Leffler makes clear. This applies not only to novels but also to pop songs, poems or even the little texts found on the back of every bottle of milk. Thus, almost every type of description of Sweden deals with nature. Even the lyrics of the national anthem are mostly constituted by a portrayal of the quiet and joyful landscape. Thus, it is not much of a surprise to find this third Swedish idyll, which is usually defended with a quasi-religious eagerness, deconstructed by John Ajvide Lindqvist.

Deconstruction can be done in many ways. The most obvious is to build an idyll and destroy it again by showing that it is not real, even dangerous; it can be destroyed with powers from outside or from within. This is how Lindqvist deconstructs the idyllic little island world of Domarö in *Harbor*. In this novel, the sea is described as some sort of ancient power that demands yearly sacrifices by the people who live with and from it:

> The sea is a god, an unseeing, unhearing deity that surrounds us and has all imaginable power over us, yet does not even know we exist. We mean less than a grain of sand on an elephant's back, and if the sea wants us, it will take us. [...] To other gods we send our prayer: protect us from the sea. (Lindqvist, *Harbor* 176)

The sea has stolen a child from its parents, and when Anders finally gets to the place where Maja has been taken, he finds a very accurate version of the island Domarö, a picture which is even more perfect than reality itself – and therefore is gloomy and threatening:

> It was late spring. The air was pleasantly mild, and flowers were growing in every crevice. Mayweed and chives danced in a gentle breeze coming off the sea. The lighthouse glowed chalk-white beneath an afternoon sun that was just warm enough. A wonderful day. (Lindqvist, *Harbor* 181)

This is deconstruction via perfection: Lindqvist not only deconstructs the idyllic nature by destroying it or showing its dangers, he simply colours it a little too brightly, a little too perfectly – and achieves almost the same effect: fear.

Deconstruction also can be achieved in another, quite simple way: deconstruction via absence. As I mentioned before, nature is evidently important and present in Swedish literature. The absence of any kind of description of nature or of pastoral elements therefore has a similar effect as the description of nature turning against man: it scares the readers, at least the Swedish ones. *Let the Right One In* is set in a landscape where nature is absent. While the first murder happens in a little forest, the second body is found in a frozen lake, these spaces do not appear as rural, idyllic nature spaces. They appear as perverted parts of the dying town of Blackeberg. The suburb seems to be isolated, to have neither a connection to Stockholm nor to the rest of Sweden, and certainly not to Swedish nature. Nature and its spaces do not play a role in this novel, neither a positive nor a negative one. Nature is part of the past here, before the city was built, nothing more. The horror takes place in shabby apartments or pubs, under bridges and in subway stations and the dangers of this environment are not powers of the nature; the evil does not lurk in the forest, it simply lives next door.

IV. Conclusion

Lindqvist's deconstruction and destruction of Swedish sanctuaries, the welfare state, childhood and nature, shows again how his writing is very closely connected to Sweden. He is able to deconstruct the Swedish ideals and idylls, because he knows them as well as any other Swede. Every nation has its traumatic issues, and national literature deals with these points. From this perspective, Lindqvist's novels are closely connected to national literature. He writes horror fiction, he creates Gothic literature – but his Gothic is enrooted in a highly national context. Gothic is the mode he has chosen for his literature, the aim is deconstruction. His literature is Gothic because it appears that a Gothic mode and a Gothic way of writing is the ideal opposite of *lagom*. Lindqvist's novels are full of ideas of excess, evil powers and extreme actions; his characters are perverted and haunted by their dreadful environment and by a careless and cynical society. They are Gothic, no doubt. But on the other hand, they once were *lagom*, their excess and evil are the offsprings of something that started as *lagom*.

Lindqvist's work has been widely successful, not only in Sweden but all over the world. There already exist two film versions of *Let the Right One In*; *Handling the Undead* is being turned into a film right now. On the other hand, Lindqvist's Gothic writing is extremely Swedish. He deals with national dreams and national nightmares, he appears to know the sanctuaries of his country so well that he is able to deconstruct them in every novel, every story. Blackeberg stands for the dying Folkhem, the numerous violent or perverted children deconstruct the idyllic *Bullerby* world, and the cruel sea or the absent nature in *Let the Right One In* destroys the idyllic *locus amoenus* of Sweden as a natural paradise.

It is difficult to predict if Lindqvist is going to start a new Swedish Gothic tradition. His topics are national; his style of writing is, however, unique. Still, it is clear that he has already enriched Swedish literature and Gothic literature with his stories, settings and protagonists and will probably continue to do so – because he has found the perfect balance between *lagom* and excess. He managed to unite these two forms of expression that at first glance seem to be incompatible. Indeed, John Ajvide Lindqvist is the master of *lagom* Gothic.

Works Cited

Berggren, Henrik and Trägårdh, Lars. *Är svensken människa?* Stockholm: Norstedts, 2006.

Botting, Fred. *Gothic.* London and New York: Routledge, 1996.

Forshaw, Barry. *Death in a Cold Climate.* London: Palgrave Macmillan, 2012.

Foucault, Michel. "Language to Infinity." Trans. Donald F. Bouchard and Sherry Simon. *Language, Counter-Memory, Practice.* Ed. Donald F. Bouchard. Oxford: Blackwell, 1977.

Georgieva, Margarita. *The Gothic Child.* London: Palgrave Macmillan, 2013.

Johannesson, Eric. *The Novels of August Strindberg: A Study in Theme and Structure.* Berkeley: University of California Press, 1968.

Låt den rätte komma in. Dir. Tomas Alfredson. Perf. Kåre Hedebrant, Lina Leandersson, Per Ragnar. 2008. DVD. Ascot Elite, 2009.

Leffler, Yvonne. "The Gothic Topography in Scandinavian Horror Fiction." *Domination of Fear.* Ed. Mikko Cannini. Amsterdam and New York: Rodopi, 2010.

Let me in. Dir. Matt Reeves. Perf. Chloe Grace Moretz, Kodi Smit-McPhee, Richard Jenkins. 2010. DVD. Universal, 2012.

Lindqvist, John Ajvide. *Handling the Undead.* Trans. Ebba Segerberg. London: Quercus, 2009.

---. *Harbor.* Trans. Marlaine Delargy. London: Quercus, 2010.

--- *Let the Right One In.* Trans. Ebba Segerberg. New York: Thomas Dunne, 2007.

---. *Little Star.* Trans. Marlaine Delargy. London: Quercus, 2012.

Parkvall, Mikael. *Lagom finns bara i Sverige och andra myter om språk.* Stockholm: Schibsted, 2009.

Redvall, Eva. "Skräckmästaren förvånad över framgången." *Sydsvenskan.* 19 Oct. 2005. Web. 15 Nov. 2014.

Andreas Schardt

Terror in the Garden: The Gothic as (Anti-)Pastoral in H.P. Lovecraft's "The Colour out of Space"

At first glance, the title of this article looks partly contradictory. Whereas the equation of terms like 'Gothic'and 'anti-pastoral' still seems somehow plausible, that of 'Gothic' and 'pastoral' appears to constitute a combination of literary forms that are diametrically opposed to each other. This corresponds to the views often found in the current usage of these terms. Whereas the pastoral is frequently associated with aspects like an idyllic nature, the Golden Age and nostalgia, the Gothic is connected to a dark age of superstition and anarchy threatening any type of idyllic and enlightened order. According to the recent edition of the *Oxford English Dictionary*, for example, "pastoral" is among other things defined as "a literary work portraying rural life or the life of shepherds, esp. in an idealized or romantic form" (Simpson s.v. "pastoral").[1] The term "Gothic", on the other hand, is characterized as designating anything "barbarous, rude, uncouth, unpolished, in bad taste, [or] savage" (Simpson s.v. "Gothic").

Despite this seeming incompatibility of the Gothic and the pastoral, there are instances in English and American literature where both forms co-occur.[2] A striking example is H.P. Lovecraft's short story "The Colour out of Space" from 1927. The Gardner farm and its environment, on which the narration focuses, exhibit idyllic features typical of a *locus amoenus*. After the impact of a meteorite, they are also characterized by Gothic elements, which gradually increase until eventually the landscape is totally devastated and all its living inhabitants are dead.

This article aims at analyzing the question why such a seemingly paradoxical coexistence of Gothic and pastoral elements is possible. I want to demonstrate that, already at the beginning of the pastoral in

---

[1] See also the definition in the *Penguin Dictionary of Literary Terms and Literary Theory*: "For the most part pastoral tends to be an idealization of shepherd life, and, by so being, creates an image of a peaceful and uncorrupted existence; a kind of prelapsarian world" (Cuddon s.v. "pastoral").

[2] For a more comprehensive analysis of Gothic-pastoral texts, most of which can be found from the late nineteenth century onwards, see my dissertation (Schardt).

ancient times, this mode exhibits particular features which allow for its simultaneous occurrence with the Gothic. Moreover, I will show that not only a co-existence of stock features usually assigned to these modes is possible but that they even overlap in certain areas. Thus, I will argue that the Gothic may not only be regarded as anti-pastoral but paradoxically even as partly pastoral.

In order to achieve this, I will first outline two features typical of one of the most influential ancient texts pertaining to the European pastoral tradition, Virgil's *Eclogue* I. The main focus will then be on the application of these traits to "The Colour out of Space". Having analyzed its overlap with such a seemingly different form as the pastoral, I will finally investigate what general conclusions can be drawn for the definition of the Gothic and the pastoral as modes.

The aforementioned OED definition of the pastoral as an overall sentimentalist form mainly portraying an artificial idyll can often be found in critical writings on this mode. Many scholars have argued that its main function since ancient times has been to offer a retreat from the city's depravity into the unspoilt nature of a *locus amoenus*, where man can regain his former unity with the natural world. Particularly important to them is the notion of the Golden Age, a mythical existence during which humanity lived in complete happiness and which preceded the atrocities of a harsh present. At times, there are even definitions of this mode as a purely escapist form, which leaves behind all the problems of the world outside. Renato Poggioli, for instance, argues that "the psychological root of the pastoral is a double longing after innocence and happiness, to be recovered not through conversion or regeneration, but merely through retreat" (1). According to him, the pastoral impulse is the consequence of the desire for the escape from the troubling realities associated with urban life into an imaginary and dream-like existence based solely on wishful thinking.[3]

---

[3] Such views of the pastoral as offering an escapist idyll have often been influenced by Friedrich Schiller's *On Naïve and Sentimental Poetry*. Defining the character of the sentimental idyll in the works of several eighteenth-century German poets, Schiller regards their main aim to be "the poetic representation of innocence and contented mankind" (Schiller 146). He argues that with such a background, poets logically seek settings which are far from tumult, education, and refinement. Moreover, he links the state of idyllicism in the Golden Age not

The longing for the flight into an unspoilt nature, resulting from the dissatisfaction with a fast-moving, urbanized world, is certainly an important feature of this kind of writing. Nevertheless, the idea that it *merely* concentrates on these idyllic aspects or that it is completely escapist is an oversimplification. From the beginnings of pastoral literature, there have been doubts about the possibility and permanence of such an existence; these have been included in the form of anti-pastoral features. This can be already demonstrated for one of the earliest texts of this tradition, Virgil's *Eclogue* I.

The poem contrasts the fate of two shepherds, Tityrus and Meliboeus, whose farms were originally confiscated for the settlement of veterans. However, unlike Meliboeus, who has to leave his lands, which will soon be devastated by intruding soldiers, Tityrus can stay in his idyll, since he has found an unnamed protector in Rome, who restores his rural possessions to him. The poem starts *in medias res* with this contrast (Virgil, I 1-5):

> M. Tityre, tu patulae recubans sub tegmine fagi
> silvestrem tenui Musam meditaris avena;
> nos patriae finis et dulcia linquimus arva.
> nos patriam fugimus; tu, Tityre, lentus in umbra
> formosam resonare doces Amaryllida silvas.

> [Meliboeus: Here you, Tityrus, lying beneath the shade of a spreading beech, practise silvestric poetry on your slim pipe; I have to leave the borders of my native country and my dear lands. I'm fleeing from my home land; you, Tityrus, can linger in the shade and teach the woods to resound 'fair Amaryllis'.][4]

Whereas Tityrus will be able to live in a kind of Golden Age on his idyllic lands, Meliboeus can only bemoan the loss of his rural enclave; the pastoral ideal is contrasted with an opposite view that longs for a time when it was still attainable (Lindenbaum 4). This contrast gains particular emphasis when Meliboeus opposes Tityrus' tranquil *locus amoenus* to the external *loca horribilia* which await him (Albrecht 16): while the former

---

only to a spatial but also to a temporal retreat with regard to the life stages of humanity: Apart from their idealized surroundings, he notes, these texts portray "the period before the beginnings of civilization in the childlike age of man" (146).

[4] The translations in this chapter are mine unless otherwise stated.

will lie in the shade among "hallowed springs" and "familiar streams", where the "sally hedge" will hum him "gently to sleep" (Virgil, I 51-55), the latter will have to leave the comfortable Italian countryside and go to "bone-dry Africa, Scythia, the chalky spate of the Oxus, even to Britain – that place which is completely removed from the whole world" (Virgil, I 64-66). His own *locus amoenus* will be lost to him after the intrusion of forces from outside: a "wicked soldier" will soon take possession of his land (Virgil, I 70), and he will never be able to see his once-happy flocks and green meadows again (Virgil, I 74-78).

Landscape descriptions are not the focus of the poem, which centres on the antithetical fates of the shepherds; nevertheless, the dual quality of the setting, reflecting the emotional conditions of the two protagonists, provides a suitable background for their respective situations. As pointed out before, Tityrus' blissful state is underlined by images of an idyllic nature. The intrinsic connection of the landscape that reflects the individual's emotional state is also highlighted when Meliboeus empathizes with Amaryllis, who missed Tityrus during his journey to Rome together with the local trees, bushes and fountains (Virgil, I 36). Such a portrayal of human beings as a part of a natural context that reveals their inner life is a typical feature of the ancient pastoral in general.[5] By contrast, Meliboeus' state of unhappiness is emphasized by images of an anti-pastoral nature, where a peaceful life in harmony with the environment is impossible. Here, the poem depicts how the harmony between man and the idyllic Roman countryside is disturbed due to his expulsion and the subsequent intrusion of soldiers from outside.[6]

In *Eclogue* I, the pastoral ideal is therefore established only to be at the same time questioned by being opposed to the restrictive urban sphere of contemporary Rome, which impinges upon the lives of humble figures. The poem contains an oscillation between the pastoral or idealized

---

[5] See for example, the natural environment that laments the death of Daphnis in Theocritus' *Idyll* I, which was the model for Virgil's fifth *Eclogue*, where the personified bushes cry: "Daphnis is a god!" ("ipsa sonant arbusta: 'deus ille, Menalca!'" [V 64]).

[6] Such a disruption of the rural environment by expropriations will again be mentioned in *Eclogue* IX; this time, however, these events will not occur in the future but have already taken place – Moeris tells Lycidas that he has lost his land and is now on his way to Rome (IX 2-6).

elements often associated with this mode and an anti-pastoral component which works against this harmony.

In fact, such a dichotomous incorporation of idyllic and disturbing traits as revealed in Virgil's *Eclogues* is a typical feature of the pastoral mode in general. Peter Lindenbaum argues that this kind of literature posits the pastoral ideal as a preliminary working hypothesis, which is used as a basis for further discussion; he therefore comes to the conclusion that there is "considerable criticism and questioning of the pastoral ideal in all pastoral writing" (ix). According to Peter Marinelli, "the pastoral is not by the widest stretch of the imagination an escapist literature in the vulgar sense", since "a note of criticism is inherent in all pastoral from the beginning of its existence" (11-12). Likewise, Leo Marx argues that

> [...] most literary works called pastorals – at least those substantial enough to retain our interest – do not finally permit us to come away with anything like the simple, affirmative attitude we adopt toward pleasing rural scenery. In one way or another [...] these works manage to qualify, or call into question, or bring irony to bear against the illusion of peace and harmony in a green pasture.[7] (25)

Against the simple vision of the pastoral ideal, he states, this mode brings up a counterforce which is more real. This force may impinge upon the green landscapes not only from the side of civilization but also from the surrounding wilderness (Marx 25).

The depiction of a shepherd and his land which become the victims of the more powerful world of politics and war also shows that the pastoral is not a purely escapist form. In fact, the situation as outlined in *Eclogue* I corresponds to the real historical situation: after the battle of Philippi in 42 BC, Antony and Octavian, who had emerged victorious, agreed that

---

[7] However, he also states that this questioning of the sentimentalist image associated with the pastoral ideal does not apply to all pastoral works. In fact, he distinguishes between the "complex and the sentimental kinds of pastoralism" (Marx 25). Whereas the former refers to the definition of pastoral as an escapist mode portraying a simple idyll, the latter requires "an effort of mind and spirit" (Marx 70). Since Virgil's *Eclogues*, however, on which the following analysis is grounded, are an example of the complex use of pastoral, this paper will neglect the sentimentalist forms of this mode (whose occurrence is much rarer in any case).

land in Northern Italy be confiscated for the settlement of veterans (Eck 11). In Virgil's poem, the exploration of the current political conditions is done with the help of the two shepherds. A particular strategy it uses in this respect is the insistence on the characters' vulnerability, which is conceived of as representing both current issues and human weakness in general. After all, many people at that time could read their own situation into the fate of Tityrus and Meliboeus, one of whom has become the victim of the aftermath of civil war, the other fortunate because he has found a protector. Besides, the general feeling of being oppressed by or dependent on more powerful forces one cannot control can be regarded as an integral part of being human. Accordingly, Paul Alpers argues that the weakness of the shepherd figure represents everyone's weakness in relation to their environment:

> In their simplicity and vulnerability, shepherds fittingly represent those whose lives are determined by the actions of powerful men or by events and circumstances over which they have no control. Even though they are among the least powerful members of society, they are far from alone in experiencing the dependency and victimization presented in this eclogue. (24)

He further notes that the powerlessness of simple characters, who are unable to change their situation and must accept their lot, is characteristic of the human condition in general: "The figure of the shepherd is felt to be representative precisely in figuring every or any man's strength relative to the world" (50).[8]

The situation described in Virgil's first *Eclogue*, in particular the use of a dichotomy between pastoral and anti-pastoral elements and the insistence on representative vulnerability, can also be applied to a Gothic text like H.P. Lovecraft's "The Colour out of Space". In this case, the anti-pastoral component which threatens an idealized existence has been Gothicized. The result is an extreme contrast of idyllic and terrible features. Moreover, the countrymen's weakness seems aggravated, since it is now regarded within a wider, 'cosmic' perspective.

At the beginning of the story, a surveyor is sent into the rural area of Massachusetts, which is supposed to serve as a new water reservoir for the fictional town of Arkham. The text portrays the countryside west of

---

[8] See also William Empson's view that the main function of pastoral writing is the process of "putting the complex into the simple" (22).

Arkham as a spot of untouched nature with "valleys with deep woods that no axe has ever cut" and "dark narrow glens where the trees slope fantastically, and where thin brooklets trickle without ever having caught the glint of sunlight" (Lovecraft, "Colour out of Space" 193). However, instead of conveying an atmosphere of bucolic peacefulness and tranquillity, there is something wrong with this place, which "is not good for imagination, and does not bring restful dreams at night" (Lovecraft, "Colour out of Space" 193). The landscape is also characterized by oddness, since "the trees grew too thickly, and their trunks were too big for any New England wood" (Lovecraft, "Colour out of Space" 194). The "blasted heath" constitutes the climactic centre of this anti-pastoral setting, since there is no living vegetation at all and only a "fine grey dust or ash" between sickly trees and dead trunks (Lovecraft, "Colour out of Space" 194).

Similarly to Virgil's first *Eclogue*, the text describes a landscape that has been devastated by the intrusion of more powerful forces from a larger world against which the inhabitants of the country are completely helpless. In Lovecraft's story, these forces are no human intruders from the city anymore but extraterrestrial beings; this results in an unearthly and surrealistic quality of the anti-pastoral elements: "Upon everything was a haze of restlessness and oppression; a touch of the unreal and the grotesque, as if some vital element of perspective or chiaroscuro were awry" (Lovecraft, "Colour out of Space" 194). Indeed, as the narrator learns from Amni Pierce, an old and supposedly demented man living in Arkham, the impact of a meteorite is responsible for the atrocious state of the natural environment, which gradually deteriorated in the aftermath until everything was dead.

At the beginning of Amni's story, the surrounding area of the Gardner farm, which will turn into a Gothic environment, is still described as a kind of *locus amoenus*: "That was the house which stood where the blasted heath was to come – the trim white Gardner house amidst its fertile gardens and orchards" (Lovecraft, "Colour out of Space" 196). This portrayal of an idealized setting conveys an image of a simple, pastoral life in close proximity to an original nature. After the meteorite's impact, however, the idyllicism and harmony associated with this spot are quickly subverted. The anti-pastoral/Gothic component in this setting by and large increases, eventually replacing all elements representing this ideal lifestyle. Not only is the harvest poisoned but the condition of all animals and plants worsens. For the Gardner family, their life in close proximity to nature leads to a deterioration in terms of their physical and mental health. The hostile being which arrives with this rock quickly turns their farm into a dangerous place, at whose centre, the well, it hides.

The 'monster figure' has an alluring quality for the human characters and gains more and more influence over them. Despite the obvious bad effects the Gothicized surroundings have on the family, its members nevertheless exhibit a "stolid resignation" and cannot leave the place anymore (Lovecraft, "Colour out of Space" 204); even worse, they keep drinking water from the poisoned well and eat the sickly food from the harvests. The monstrous being even makes the sons of Nahum Gardner, the farm's owner, jump into the well in order to suck their lives out. As their father remarks shortly before his death: "It beats down your mind an' then gets ye … […] draws ye … ye know summ'at's comin' but tain't no use …" (208). As the story progresses, everything organic – be it the plants, animals, or even humans – dies.

The portrayal of a rural context and its disturbance by a force from without is representative of specific anxieties in Alpers' sense. In fact, it can be linked to fears associated particularly with the history of early American settlement. Marx states that the natural environment of the New World provoked ambivalent feelings: on the one hand, it was associated with the freedom of being able to live a harmonious existence in unison with the fertility and seemingly infinite resources of an untouched nature; on the other hand, life on the frontier was also dangerous, as it was connected with an untamed wilderness, extreme temperatures and the encounter with the indigenous people, who were often perceived as a 'savage' threat:

> In a sense, America was *both* Eden and a howling desert […]. The infinite resources of the virgin land really did make credible […] the ancient dream of an abundant and harmonious life for all. Yet, at the same time, the savages, the limitless space, and the violent climate of the country did threaten to engulf the new civilisation. (Marx 43-44; emphasis in the original)

Thus, in Marx's view, the dichotomy between idyllic elements and their opposite was often employed to express the discrepancies between the image of America as a pastoral idyll and the anti-pastoral reality of the frontier experience (43-44). In Lovecraft's text, these images associated with the dangers and harshness of the American wilderness are Gothicized in order to give shape to the fears regarding the human inability to cope with it. As Oakes states, the deterioration of the natural environment as depicted in "The Colour out of Space" not only reflects contrary feelings towards life in the supposedly idyllic New World but eventually even subverts the pastoral ideal completely; in the end, the Gardner family's dream to lead a simple existence away from the life in the city is revealed to be impossible in the face of their extremely malevolent and hostile surroundings (Oakes 40).

However, the author severely intensifies this long-established contrast between idyll and disturbance. As mentioned before, the increasing decay of the land, which will eventually result in the 'blasted heath', is not attributed to the forces lurking within the wilderness or the city but to an invasion from outer space. Therefore, in the description of the meteorite and the consequences of its impact for the environment, specific emphasis is placed on the unearthliness or, in Lovecraft's terms, the "externality" of the threat.[9] The rock, whose material cannot be found on earth (Lovecraft, "Colour out of Space" 198), quickly turns the rural context into an unearthly setting: apart from the local animals' outer appearance, which has a bizarre quality, something seems to be wrong with the plants, which by and large attain the same strange colour as the meteorite (Lovecraft, "Colour out of Space" 199-201). Besides, the monster is also defined by a high degree of indistinctness. As Nahum says, "the way it's made an' the way it works ain't like no way o' God's world. It's some'at from beyond" (211). Therefore, even when the family notices the apparent menace lurking underneath their soil, they are unable to describe its exact characteristics. Mrs Gardner, for instance, has the feeling that "something was taken away – she was being drained of something – something was fastening itself on her that ought not be" (Lovecraft, "Colour out of Space" 202-203), but cannot account for its

---

[9] This is a central concept in Lovecraft's fiction, which he described as follows: "Now all my tales are based on the fundamental premise that common human laws and interests and emotions have no validity or significance in the cosmos-at-large. [...] To achieve the essence of real *externality*, whether of time or space or dimension, one must forget that such things as organic life, good and evil, love and hate, and all such local attributes of *a negligible and temporary race called mankind*, have any essence at all" (Lovecraft, *Selected Letters* 150; emphasis added).

origins. In fact, one of the few traits that still link it to earlier Gothic monster figures like Dracula is its vampiric quality, as it sucks the life out of the vegetation and the humans (Lovecraft, "Colour out of Space" 208-209). The only aspect by which it is actually visible is its colour, which comes out of the well and spreads throughout the farm during the night (Lovecraft, "Colour out of Space" 208). Still, even this quality is linked to the unspeakable, since it is not of the chromatic spectrum known to humanity.

In the face of such powerful forces, the simple countryman, like Virgil's Tityrus or Meliboeus, is presented as absolutely powerless. Accordingly, the Gardner farm, together with its surroundings, eventually perishes until nothing is left but the 'blasted heath'. However, it is not only the country-dweller who is conceived of as helpless and unable to change his dreadful destiny; it is also the city-dweller and, by implication, the civilized world of scientific progress which are unable to confront this monstrous invasion. During the first signs of damage after the meteorite impact, the city-dwellers are still represented within a traditional city-country opposition as more 'sophisticated' urbanites, who look down on the 'superstitious' peasants. When Nahum Gardner presents the unearthly blossoms of saxifrage grown at his farm to the editor of the *Gazette*, the latter writes a "humorous article about [...] the dark fears of rustics" (201). Immediately afterwards, however, the narrator concludes that "it was a mistake of Nahum's to tell a stolid city man about the way the great, overgrown mourning-cloak butterflies behaved in connection with the saxifrages", which hints at the real nature of this cosmic terror (Lovecraft, "Colour out of Space" 201). Moreover, when the situation at the farm finally escalates and the signs of an extraterrestrial threat cannot be negated anymore, Nahum sadly realizes that it is no use "telling the city people in Arkham who laughed at everything" (Lovecraft, "Colour out of Space" 206). The self-perception of the city-dweller as more superior and refined turns out to be a state of mere ignorance after the 'truth' has been disclosed which can be found in the rural context.

Lovecraft's text predominantly highlights the ineffectiveness of the urbanite's tools, in particular such as relate to the field of science, which is revealed during his encounter with the malignant being. Indeed, specific emphasis is placed on the association of the city-dweller with the academic world of scientific progress: after all, the only people from the city who take an interest in the strange occurrences at the Gardner farm are the professors from Miskatonic University. Their inability to provide a rational explanation for the consistency of the meteorite's material or its devastating effects for the environment (Lovecraft, "Colour out of Space" 196-198) and the fact that they eventually flee from the life-sucking colour themselves (Lovecraft, "Colour out of Space" 210-215) must be seen against the background of Lovecraft's sceptical view of the sciences; according to him, these would be totally useless when confronted with the forces of cosmic terror (Plaschka 71; Callois 80). This pessimism is also underlined by the story's end: although the extraterrestrial threat is gone, it nevertheless seems to have left some of its essence behind, which is why the land has never recovered properly. Even worse, at the time the narrator hears this narration, the local inhabitants keep telling the story that the blasted heath still grows each year. The people in the city, on the other hand, have returned to their former state of ignorance, discarding the strange events told by the country people as "queer" tales (Lovecraft, "Colour out of Space" 216).

In "The Colour out of Space", all human beings – whether from the city or the country – are therefore revealed to be totally weak in comparison to the monsters of the cosmos. One could even argue that humanity as a whole is put into the traditional position of the feeble country-dweller, who, being not confronted with a human but an omnipotent extraterrestrial threat, appears to be absolutely unimportant. Whereas the city-dweller is presented as being in a blissful condition of unawareness and the peasant as the one who at times comes closer to the 'truth', the menace posed by the cosmic terror is constantly present for both.

After investigating the overlap of the Gothic with the pastoral mode in Lovecraft's short story, some conclusions can be drawn on a theoretical level. As has become obvious, the Gothic and the pastoral, in terms of their use of stock features, do not insist on portraying *either* only the dark side *or* an idyllic state of the world and human nature respectively. Instead, both are flexible forms that are able to include aspects standing in contrast to these features. Therefore, it can be argued that an oscillation between order and disturbance is central to the pastoral as well as the Gothic. Both modes create a transgressive space, where an order is established, which is then put under scrutiny by being measured against a disruptive counterforce. In the pastoral, this order is represented by the 'pastoral ideal', which is disturbed by an anti-pastoral element; during this process, the question is put forward whether life in an original harmony and innocence is possible at all. Similarly, the Gothic features not only aspects that are disturbing and give rise to fear – it also includes an anti-Gothic element, an order of a kind that is established and subverted. If both modes are combined, the result is a paradoxical form, where an extreme state of harmony and innocence coexists with a world of terror and chaos.

Another conclusion can be drawn for the Gothic's and the pastoral's state as a literary mode. Usually, this term is understood by critics as a bundle of loose features, whose appearance in a certain number indicates the presence of a specific mode (Spooner 26; Cohen 32). As has been initially pointed out, features like medieval castles, terror, wicked counts etc. are usually perceived as part of the Gothic, while aspects like the Golden Age, idyllic nature and nostalgia are seen as integral to the pastoral. This is undoubtedly true, but there is also another aspect relevant to their definitions as mode. During the analysis of Lovecraft's text, it was demonstrated that both the Gothic and the pastoral employ their various stock features in order to explore the weakness of humanity in relation to its environment, which is often seen as embodying specific fears and uncertainties.

In fact, the idea that one of the major functions of the two modes lies in the exploration of human weakness is also supported by other texts which focus on this issue. In dystopian literature, for instance, emphasis is usually placed on the inescapable doom of the protagonist and his weakness in relation to the larger forces of a hostile system threatening him. In George Orwell's *Nineteen-Eighty-Four*, Winston Smith's temporary freedom he can enjoy in the idyllic countryside with his lover Julia turns out to be highly deceptive; after all, he cannot escape the extreme vigilance and violence as represented by the contemporary system in the long run. A more recent example would be Cormac McCarthy's *The Road*; depicting a barren landscape of a postapocalyptic world, where due to an unknown ecological catastrophe all vegetation has died, the novel emphasizes humanity's dependence on a functioning ecological system.

The Gothic and the pastoral may each have undergone an extreme modification in recent times, which makes it indeed questionable whether one can still use these terms at all or if it rather makes sense to speak of 'post-pastoral' and 'post-Gothic' forms (Botting; Gifford 148-173). However, the fact that there are still instances which preserve the typical

Gothic-pastoral insistence on representative vulnerability shows that both modes at times still live on by the preservation of this basic mechanism.

Works Cited

Albrecht, Michael von. *Vergil: Bucolica – Georgica – Aeneis. Eine Einführung*. 2nd ed. Heidelberg: Winter, 2007.

Alpers, Paul J. *What is Pastoral?* Chicago: University of Chicago Press, 1996.

Botting, Fred. "Candygothic." *The Gothic*. Ed. Fred Botting. Cambridge: Brewer, 2001. 133-151.

Caillois, Roger. "Das Bild des Phantastischen: Vom Märchen bis zur Science Fiction." *Phaïcon 1*. Ed. Rein A. Zondergeld. Frankfurt a.M.: Insel Verlag, 1974. 44-83.

Cohen, Ralph. "The Augustan Mode in English Poetry." *Eighteenth-Century Studies* 1 (1967): 32.

Cuddon, J.A., ed. *Penguin Dictionary of Literary Terms and Literary Theory*. 4th ed. Oxford: Blackwell, 1998.

Eck, Werner. "Augustus." Trans. Ruth Tubbesing. *Lives of the Caesars*. Ed. Anthony A. Barrett. Malden, MA: Blackwell, 2008. 7-37.

Empson, William. *Some Versions of Pastoral*. New York: New Directions, 1974.

Gifford, Terry. *Pastoral*. London: Routledge, 1999.

Lindenbaum, Peter. *Changing Landscapes. Anti-pastoral Sentiment in the English Renaissance*. Athens, GA: University of Georgia Press, 1986.

Lovecraft, H.P. *Selected Letters*. Vol. 2. Eds. August Derleth and Donald Wandrei. Sauk City: Arkham House, 1965.

---. "The Colour out of Space." *The Best of H.P. Lovecraft: Blood-curdling Tales of Horror and the Macabre*. New York: Ballantine, 1982. 193-217.

Marinelli, Peter V. *Pastoral*. London: Methuen, 1971.

Marx, Leo. *The Machine in the Garden: Technology and the Pastoral Ideal in America*. Oxford: Oxford University Press, 1964.

McCarthy, Cormac. *The Road*. London: Picador, 2006.

Oakes, David A. *Science and Destabilization in the Modern American Gothic: Lovecraft, Matheson and King*. Westport, CT: Greenwood Press, 2000.

Plaschka, Oliver. *Verlorene Arkadien: Das pastorale Motiv in der englischen und amerikanischen fantastischen Literatur – H.P. Lovecraft, James Branch Cabell, Mervyn Peake, William Gibson*. Dissertation: Universität Heidelberg: 2009. Web. 15 April 2014.

Poggioli, Renato. *The Oaten Flute: Essays on Pastoral Poetry and the Pastoral Ideal*. Cambridge, MA: Harvard University Press, 1975.

Schardt, Andreas. *Gothic Pastoral: Terrible Idylls in Late Nineteenth- and Twentieth-Century Literature*. Dissertation: Universität Heidelberg, 2013. Web. 15 April 2014.

Schiller, Friedrich von. *Naïve and Sentimental Poetry*, along with *On the Sublime* [1795-6]. Trans. Julius A. Elias. New York: Ungar, 1966.

Simpson, John, ed. *Oxford English Dictionary (OED). OED Online*. Oxford: Oxford University Press, 2011.

Spooner, Catherine. *Contemporary Gothic*. London: Reaktion, 2006.

Virgil. *Opera*. Ed. R.A.B. Mynors. Oxford Classical Texts. Oxford: Oxford University Press, 1969.

Susan J. Tyburski

Seduced by the Wild: Audrey Schulman's EcoGothic Romance

"Without wilderness, the world is a cage" (David Brower)

In her first novel, *The Cage*, published in 1994, Audrey Schulman explores the transfiguring power of wilderness as experienced by her heroine, Beryl Findham. In the process, a wilderness adventure tale is transformed into an ecoGothic romance. Northrop Frye, in his seminal study on the structure of romance entitled *The Secular Scripture* explains that, in a classic romance tale, the hero travels through other, alien worlds, and his adventures lead to a liberation or transformation of personal identity (129-157). In contrast, Gothic tales often serve as cultural arenas for social conflict, allowing audiences to explore their deepest fears and anxieties (Smith and Hughes 3). A key fear is the loss of personal identity and agency when immersed in the natural world, lending the Gothic tale an ecological dimension (Hughes 3). This essay will discuss key attributes of the romantic structure reflected in *The Cage*, and explore how Schulman employs this mode with an ecoGothic twist.

The 'ecoGothic' merges Gothic tropes with an ecocritical sensibility to create a tale in which the natural world plays a crucial role. As ecoGothic novelist Hilary Scharper explains, nature is not treated "as merely a backdrop or setting, but rather as an active and indeed central player in the narrative" (qtd. in Dawson). In Scharper's view, the ecoGothic "recognizes and engages with the fact that we are indeed at a moment of great ecological change and transition, and that some of our biggest challenges are in the area of human relationships with nature" (Dawson). Matthew Offenbacher emphatically states, "[i]n gothic stories landscape is destiny". Like Scharper, Schulman wrestles with these ecocritical issues in *The Cage*, as her characters encounter a natural environment that is alternately hostile and indifferent to their survival. Their reactions to that environment determine their destinies.

Despite the recent emergence of ecoGothic narratives from writers like Scharper and Schulman, the origins of the ecoGothic can be found much farther back in literary history. In their introduction to the recently published essay collection *Ecogothic*, Andrew Smith and William

Hughes describe the ecoGothic as "an ecologically aware Gothic that has its roots within the Romantic, and not just within recent environmental concerns" (1). Smith and Hughes acknowledge a "shared critical language" between Romantic and Gothic literature; however, while the Romantic vision emphasizes unity with nature, the Gothic sensibility explores "estrangement rather than belonging" (2). This conflict between the Romantic and Gothic visions of nature are played out in Schulman's novel, through her characters' various interactions with the arctic landscape and through the conflict within her heroine, who idealistically longs for union with the Wild but learns that the Wild can be a cruelly destructive force.

The Cage begins with Beryl's acceptance of an assignment to photograph polar bears in their arctic habitat from within the confines of a special bear-proof cage (Schulman 8-10). Schulman's heroine has been selected for the job because her small stature renders her one of the few nature photographers capable of working within the claustrophobic confines of this cage. In the opening lines of the novel, we find Beryl sitting in her tiny closet, preparing for this assignment by conjuring the frozen wilderness and her anticipated meeting with the bears:

> The wind blows. All sound echoes close and loud. Snow shivers across the ground. She sits, her legs crossed. The only warmth for miles around is contained in the heavy arms of the white bears that mill about her cage, curious, strong and hungry. The snow squeaks beneath their feet. Pale mist blows at her from their black mouths. The bears push their wide white faces forward, against the cage. They suck in her smell, snort out. Steam touches her skin. Her face, like their beards, is covered with frost – it's moisture from their breath, from her breath. (1-2)

From the outset, the bears hold a sensual fascination for Schulman's heroine. She imagines that the cage will allow her to immerse herself in their world, protected by the thinnest of boundaries, and still survive. The cage is permeable, to an extent; it allows steam from the bears to caress her skin; it allows their breaths to mingle, and a mutual frost to form on their faces. However, these tantalizing sensations quickly turn dark. Beryl imagines, in graphic detail, the resulting horror if the cage fails, eliminating the fragile boundary between her and the bears:

She understands that if the cage fails in any way, they will kill her. They'll reach in, rip the biceps from her flailing arms, the bowels from her belly, the tendons from her neck. They'll bite and tear, swallow. Her body will jerk at first beneath their strength, then slowly slacken. Her neck will roll back for their touch as though for a kiss.

Her eyes watch, dark and small, like theirs. (Schulman 1-2)

This shocking scene works like a classic horror film, warning the reader at the outset that similar terrors could lie just around any corner. The image of Beryl's neck rolling "back for [the bears'] touch like a kiss" lends a hint of eroticism to this gruesome scene. The description of her eyes watching, "small and dark" (1-2), like the eyes of the bears, suggests a shared animal essence. These unsettling details, with their disturbing sensuality, provide a distinctive Gothic flavour to this scene. They also embody the central conflict at the heart of this novel between the Romantic and Gothic visions of the Wild: desiring union with the natural world and fearing the destructive power of that alien world.

The seductive power of the bears hums like an underground current throughout Schulman's novel. Like a lover, Beryl longs for some kind of union, to know the ultimately unknowable essence of the Wild that courses beneath the bears' white fur. This 'fatal attraction' suggests a Gothic sensibility. According to *The Cambridge Guide to Literature in English*, when Gothic novels and romances arose in the late eighteenth and early nineteenth centuries, "[t]he word 'Gothic' had come to mean 'wild', 'barbarous' and 'crude'" (Ousby 405). Gothic fiction was often set in isolated locations, including "mountainous landscapes", and employed plots centered on "suspense and mystery, involving the fantastic and the supernatural" (Ousby 405). All of these Gothic elements – the remote arctic landscape, the mysterious dreams and fantasies the heroine experiences, and the suspense and terror created by the characters' immersion in the bears' hostile environment – exist in *The Cage*.

As David Mogen, Scott Sanders and Joanne Karpinski explain in their introduction to *Frontier Gothic*, "Gothicism must abide on a frontier [...]. American frontier gothic literature derives from [the] conflict between the inscripted history of civilization and the history of the other, somehow immanent in the landscape of the frontier" (17). Shoshannah Ganz describes a "nascent mutation of the Gothic" (87) that she calls "Canadian ecoGothic" (87); Canadian ecoGothic narratives "advocate environmental awareness and change" (Ganz 88). This genre emerges from a long Canadian tradition of narratives that advance a Gothic view of nature as "the threat, the ever present and fearful monster seeking to swallow human beings whole" (Ganz 88). Schulman, a Canadian writer, engages this Gothic tradition with a heroine irresistibly drawn to a remote arctic landscape and encounters with a mysterious 'Other', seduced by erotic dreams and magical visions of polar bears. The heroine is plunged into a threatening wilderness that ultimately leads to her transformation and a new appreciation of the Wild, embracing an ecocritical perspective that emphasizes our need to develop a realistic, respectful relationship with the natural world.

Initially, Schulman's heroine is seeking liberation from her sheltered life. Her parents are each portrayed as overly protective, although they manifest their worry in different ways. Beryl's father finds comfort in specific facts and figures, wanting to know the "likelihood of danger" resulting from the expedition expressed as a solid statistic (Schulman 5). Before she departs, her father obsessively photographs his daughter in a series of staged scenes. Beryl observes: "He wanted to hold the facts in his hand like a flat package of Polaroids" (5). Schulman crafts this revealing sentence like a poet, using not only a bit of alliteration, but also the echoes of assonance between "facts", "hand", and "flat package", like an incantation. This technique further emphasizes the sole adjective, "flat", connoting the artificiality of, and the futility of keeping his daughter safe through, "posed" photographs.

In contrast, Beryl's mother's reaction to the news of her daughter's latest assignment is more visceral. She touches her stomach, "as though the organs that had borne Beryl had twitched at the news" (4). Schulman explains that her heroine watched for similar nervous gestures from her mother throughout her childhood, "with the same fear that a person on a dark night feels when she peers at the handle of her door" (4). These details suggest an oppressive domestic environment in which the heroine is trapped. As Kate Ferguson Ellis explains in *The Contested Castle: Gothic Novels and the Subversion of Domestic Ideology*, Gothic tales traditionally subvert the notion of home as a safe refuge and instead transform it into a prison for young women (xii-xiii).

Schulman's heroine longs for liberation and seeks escape from her domestic prison through encounters with the Wild, mediated through photography. Unlike her father, Beryl found a larger, more "magical" world revealed through the lens of her camera (Schulman 8). She first recognized the alien essence of animals when she photographed the pregnant family cat, Minsie. Through her lens, "Minsie became the size of a jungle creature [...]. The stomach, covered in black fur, stretched tight as a drum, became magical, secretive and strong [...]. Beryl had focused and shot quickly, filled with awe" (8). She quickly discovered a preference and a talent for photographing animals, but, as Schulman writes, "[h]er pictures were never cute. They were somehow speculative and awed" (15). These attempts to capture the wild essence of the family pet are also an attempt to touch the Sublime, defined by Edmund Burke as that which "excite[s] the ideas of pain and terror" (51). The heroine's liberation could be achieved, at least temporarily, through this experience of the Sublime – a classically Romantic ideal (Greenblatt A54).

As her career progressed, Schulman's heroine pursued increasingly authentic photographs of wild animals. Prior to the arctic expedition, Beryl tried "to photograph whales while swimming with them in the wild", but was unprepared for their overpowering presence:

> The water darkened, stilled and then moved forward so that it carried her slightly forward too, and she looked up to see passing above her – between her and the boat, blocking the shimmering plane of the surface entirely – a gray smooth body bigger than her apartment, bigger than her life. Her first thought was that it would fall, crushing her. That the whale didn't fall made her understand she was in a foreign world where all the things she had grown up with didn't exist: arms and legs, hair and gravity, clear light, sharp edges, distinct sound. (Schulman 15)

During this encounter, Beryl begins to apprehend, in the presence of the wild 'Other', her relatively inconsequential place in the universe. She is literally 'bewildered', as her former perspective is destroyed, and she begins to open to the transformative possibilities of wilderness. She also gets closer to actual immersion in wilderness, as she enters the whales' natural domain.

Schulman's heroine is similarly disoriented when she attends a pre-expedition lecture on polar bears. She attempts to comprehend their enormous mass – "standing up to eleven feet tall on their hind legs" and weighing "almost two thousand pounds" (18). Schulman conveys the improbable, alien nature of the bears with a technological metaphor: "She could no more understand that much dangerous mass in motion than she could imagine a truck shaking itself into life, its metal skin rippling" (18). Beryl decides to accept the polar bear assignment because "[s]he simply wanted to have taken photographs of a creature awful and strange. A creature who even when caged would be outside of all human containers" (31-32). Ironically, she pursues the goal of capturing the Wild incarnate on film while placing herself in a cage. In the course of Schulman's narrative, the barriers between the heroine and the wilderness are progressively eliminated, and she ultimately finds herself roaming the wild arctic tundra, terrifyingly vulnerable to the natural forces that surround her.

The heroine's longing for an encounter with a wild 'Other' is also a desire to escape the confines of her body, with all of its unsatisfactory limitations. Schulman details how Beryl suffered from anorexia in college, when she attempted to reduce herself to her bare essence, "something elegant and elemental" (24). As she learns more about polar bears, she fantasizes "flipping a four-hundred pound seal up into the air with one hand", and hunting her overweight, hairy neighbour:

> She imagined herself stalking her neighbor, the breath in her chest coming as a distinct wind, her shoulders wide as a door. She lowered her head and felt the fur grow thick and warm across her back, her head become wider and flatter. (Schulman 25-26)

This fantasy foreshadows the heroine's ultimate transformation into a more elemental, animal version of herself as she travels further into the wild. The end of the novel finds the heroine emerging from the arctic tundra, having lost most of her male companions and suffering serious frostbite. Her experience is thus not one of Romantic union with the Wild, as she imagined, but a more brutal encounter with the horrific realities of the natural environment. Nevertheless, this encounter does prove liberating, as Beryl is permanently altered, both physically and spiritually; she emerges with a new respect for the realities of the wilderness.

Like other Romantic heroes and heroines, Beryl travels to a strange, alien land. Her first encounter with the arctic wilderness is through the window of a small airplane:

> She felt she'd traveled to a different planet. At three in the after-noon they left behind the trees. The land swept on below, flat, gray-green, covered with twisting rivers and lakes of a crystal blue untouched by even dirt, for the Arctic has no substance as complex as dirt, only rock and sand like a newborn world [...]. Time passes differently. A single day can last two months, the sun making slow circles at the top of the sky, round and round like a hawk hunting. (Schulman 52)

The predatory image of the sun circling like a hungry hawk foreshadows the danger that lurks in this desolate landscape. As they fly further north, Beryl notices "a lightening in the air" (54) and suddenly sees with greater "clarity" (54) due to the lack of dust and moisture. Schulman writes that her heroine's clearer vision contrasts with her former civilized existence, "as if she'd been living in a fog all her life" (54). The further she ventures into the wilderness, the "clearer" her vision becomes.

When the magazine crew arrives at the small airport in Churchill, they are met by a mysterious guide named Jean-Claude. Beryl is drawn to Jean-Claude in the same way she is drawn to the polar bears and to the arctic landscape. He is "an unknown" (77). She imagines "him doing almost anything. Baying suddenly deep and wild as a wolf, or leaving them two weeks into the expedition, simply walking off across the snow heading due north" (79). Later, the other men convince Jean-Claude "to do some calls of arctic animals"; Schulman writes: "Space and cold echoed in his calls as physical as a touch on Beryl's face" (125).

Beryl studies Jean-Claude, observing how he moves, and trying to fathom how he relates to the Wild and how he survives in the arctic landscape. Jean-Claude gives her a gift of an Inuit suit made of caribou skin and wolf hide, and advises her to wear it next to her skin, without any other clothes (118). When the heroine puts it on, she breathes in the musky odour of the suit, and suddenly feels empowered:

> It seems she had always waited for this feeling, the soft skin of a caribou brushing up between her legs. She felt strong and big [...]. She was surprised at her new mass, the smells she encom-

passed. She wondered if this was how the bears felt. (Schulman 119)

In donning this suit – and later when she makes love with Jean-Claude – Beryl begins to merge with the Wild. This physical union foreshadows a more spiritual union Schulman's heroine experiences with the Wild as she moves further into the arctic landscape.

Beryl also has strange dreams of the bears she has come to photograph. After her arrival in Churchill, she dreams of "the white arms of a gigantic bear who waltzed her gently across the rolling flat plains of the tundra" (59). She also dreams of a formal dinner date with the bear, who spills over the sides of his chair and under their table, while plates of food await under silver covers. In her dream, she instinctively wishes to "[remove] her plate from the table and [eat] her food from the ground" (67). These romantic visions suggest her longing for a relationship with the Wild, and are a stark contrast to the raw, brutal reality of the arctic wilderness she ultimately encounters.

The *Natural Photography* crew is forced to spend a few weeks in the small town of Churchill, awaiting a special fortified bus to take them into the arctic wilderness. Shortly after her arrival, Beryl decides to take a walk through town. She finds it odd that she is the only pedestrian. Other residents pass her in cars, staring. Suddenly, a patrol car stops and the officer, Margie, orders her to get in immediately, stating, "It's behind you". When Beryl looks over her shoulder, she sees a large polar bear about thirty feet away (82-83). After this close call, Schulman's heroine sits by her hotel window, looking out at where "[t]he vast white prairie extended to the horizon beneath a solid blue sky" (95) and thinking about how she is trapped behind windows or camera lenses, unable to experience this amazing wilderness directly. The reader is reminded of the emotional barriers she erected to protect herself from overbearing men, as she begins to realize how her entire life, up to this point, has been lived in a type of cage (95).

While waiting for the expedition to begin, the *Natural Photography* crew spends days at the town dump, watching and photographing the polar bears searching for food. On one occasion, a polar bear catches fire when it lands on a burning mattress and is consumed by flame as it runs away. The magazine crew can only look on in horror (99). This gruesome scene illustrates the conflicts that arise as humans encroach on the bears' wild territory, injecting an ecocritical awareness into this Gothic tale. It also suggests the arbitrary violence of the arctic environment, and foreshadows the crew's ultimate encounter with this indifferent force.

Schulman's heroine finds a kindred spirit in Margie. She begins spending evenings in the bear patrol car as Margie roams the town, searching for bears so she can chase them away from human dwellings. In response to a question about why she tries to protect the bears, Margie explains, "[T]hey're beyond most animals because they're unpredictable. They don't react the same way every time [...]. I have great respect for the bears. They truly scare me" (92-93). Margie shares a fascination with this unfathomable 'Otherness'. When Beryl describes her dreams of romantic dinners and dancing with the bears, she asks Margie, "Isn't that weird?" Margie responds, "No. I dream like that all the time" (94). These shared dreams are like ecoGothic spectres that haunt the women, attempting to seduce them into crossing over into another realm in which humans and bears co-exist as equals, and humans are able to have authentic relationships with wild creatures.

Ian Duncan discusses this Gothic sensibility in *Modern Romance and Transformations of the Novel*, focusing on "the transformative dynamics" (3) of Ann Radcliffe's work. According to Duncan, Radcliffe's novels allowed nineteenth-century readers to escape the constrictions of existing social norms and enter a magical world – "a cultural uncanny" (9). Similarly, Schulman's dreaming women enter a magical 'uncanny' world where they are able to interact with the wild bears without consequence. At the heart of the transformation Duncan describes is a "heroine's romance subjectivity, an ethical-aesthetic compound of sensibility and stoicism [...] represented as [...] spiritual integrity, a warrant of grace" (37). We see such 'sensibility and stoicism', 'spiritual integrity' and 'grace' displayed by Beryl Findham as she encounters various challenges in the arctic wilderness, and is able to survive this brutal environment through her discovery of her inner resilience and appreciation for the Wild.

The crew travels into the arctic wilderness on a fortified bus (Schulman 143). Beryl and another photographer take turns photographing hungry polar bears from within the specially constructed cage (Schulman 164-174; 177-179). During her first session in the cage, Schulman's heroine reaches out and touches the fur of a bear pressing against the bars. The bear "cough[s] in shock at her touch", and turns to look "at Beryl straight

on, eye to eye" (168). She becomes mesmerized by the raw physicality of
the nearby bear:

> The bear's nose moved, wet, gleaming ebony skin, the curled
> inner tunnel shimmering a dark red. The black drawn-in smile of
> her mouth pulled back, opened, the inside dark as velvet, wet.
> Beryl realized she'd been moving her hand toward the nose. To
> touch it, to stroke the small slit openings for eyes. (Schulman
> 169)

During this encounter with the bear, Schulman's heroine seems to have
crossed over to some 'Wild' dimension. When she looks back at the
crew's civilized haven, the bus, it stands out, "all wrong" (171). When
she fails to respond to the men on the walkie-talkie, they chase the bears
away and run out to remove her from the cage. Beryl emerges as though
from another world. The men suddenly seem alien to her (171). For the
first time, Schulman's heroine has come close to actual contact with one
of the bears – and through it, with the Wild.

In an essay entitled "The Erotic Landscape", Terry Tempest Williams
writes of eroticism as a "bridge" to such an authentic experience of the
natural world. She wonders:

> [...] what walls we have constructed to keep our true erotic nature
> tamed. And I am curious why we continue to distance ourselves
> from natural sources.
>
> [...]
>
> We can choose to photograph a tree or can sit in its arms, where
> we are participating in wild nature, even our own. (Williams 106;
> 111)

Like the "walls" Williams describes, the cage used by Beryl to
photograph the bears becomes a metaphor for the trappings of civilization
that protect us from encounters with the wild. As the novel progresses,
civilized barriers are stripped away, until Beryl and her fellow adventur-
ers are left completely exposed to the raw terror of the wild. One by one,
the other crew members succumb to various gruesome deaths, until Beryl
and Jean-Claude are left to walk across the frozen tundra, alone, towards
the safety of the distant town. Schulman injects a feminist perspective in
her adventure tale, as the female protagonist is not waiting for rescue by a
male hero, but instead braves the wilderness herself, first through her

encounters with the bears through the bars of a protective cage, and later as she engineers her own survival when most of the men in her party are killed or lost.

The wilderness encountered by Beryl is not an idyllic Arcadia, the fairytale wilderness of Walt Disney, a predictable mechanistic wilderness, the transcendent wilderness of Emerson, or the benevolent source of 'natural resources'. Once the barriers of the civilized world are stripped away, Beryl encounters the dark, brutal heart of wilderness – an ecoGothic world. The arctic environment burns away skin, toes and fingers – as well as Beryl's Romantic notions about this barren land of ice, snow and bears. Her fantasies come face to face with the savage reality of wilderness. At the same time, Beryl discovers that wilderness – bereft of familiar landmarks and cultural icons – offers the exhilarating freedom to explore other identities, other realities, other modes of being.

David Mogen, Scott Sanders and Joanne Karpinski describe the origin of the "American Gothic" as "the most fundamental conflict shaping American experience, the battle between civilization and nature" (15). They quote Martin Buber in explaining that the wilderness destroys our safe havens through "strange lyric and dramatic episodes, seductive and magical, but tearing us away to dangerous extremes, loosening the well-tried context [...] shattering security" (qtd. in 15). This conflict between civilization and wilderness is the ecoGothic essence of Schulman's novel.

Beryl's stark and brutal encounter with the Wild is, literally, a transfiguring experience, as she loses toes to frostbite. At the end of the novel, she reaches the safety of the town, dressed in her Inuit suit. Like a triumphant Romantic hero, Beryl Findham returns to the 'cage' of civilization. She has come face to face with the Wild, and discovered that she possesses the inner strength of a survivor. As readers, we remain haunted by her encounters with the arctic heart of wilderness, and the realization of the fragile cages in which we all live. While the romance of this adventure tale is inspiring, its ecoGothic elements leave us with an unsettled feeling about our own relationships with the natural world.

Works Cited

Brower, David. "The Final Interview: David R. Brower." *Online! with David Kupfer*. 5 August 2000. Web. 1 November 2013.

Burke, Edmund. *A Philosophical Inquiry into the Origin of Our Ideas of the Sublime and Beautiful*. Trans. Abraham Mills. New York: Harper & Brothers Publishers, 1856.

Dawson, Jennifer. "'Perdita' by Hilary Scharper – Blog Tour." *Literal Life*. 12 April 2013. Web. 7 July 2014.

Duncan, Ian. *Modern Romance and Transformations of the Novel: the Gothic, Scott, Dickens*. Cambridge: Cambridge University Press, 1992.

Ellis, Kate Ferguson. *The Contested Castle: Gothic Novels and the Subversion of Domestic Ideology*. Chicago: University of Illinois Press, 1989.

Frye, Northrop. *The Secular Scripture: A Study of the Structure of Romance*. Cambridge, MA: Harvard University Press, 1976.

Ganz, Shoshannah. "Margaret Atwood's Monsters in the Canadian EcoGothic." *EcoGothic*. Eds. Andrew Smith and William Hughes. Manchester: Manchester University Press, 2013. 87-102.

Greenblatt, Stephen, ed. *The Norton Anthology of English Poetry*. New York: Norton, 2006.

Moers, Ellen. "Travelling Heroinism: Gothic for Heroines." *Literary Women: The Great Writers*. Garden City, NY: Doubleday, 1976. 122-140.

Mogen, David, Scott Sanders, and Joanne Karpinski, eds. *Frontier Gothic*. Rutherford: Associated University Presses, 1993.

Offenbacher, Matthew. "Green Gothic." *La Especial Norte* #4. June 2009. Republished at *helloari.com*. Web. 7 July 2014.

Ousby, Ian. *The Cambridge Guide to Literature in English*. Cambridge: Cambridge University Press, 1988.

Schulman, Audrey. *The Cage*. Chapel Hill: Algonquin, 1994.

Smith, Andrew and William Hughes, eds. *Ecogothic*. Manchester: Manchester University Press, 2013.

Williams, Terry Tempest. "The Erotic Landscape." *Red: Passion and Patience in the Desert.* New York: Pantheon, 2001. 104-111.

Erik Redling

Monstrous Woodcuts: Experiments with Scary Word-Image Relations in Lynd Ward's Gothic Work

The 1990s saw the emergence of 'visual culture' and, concomitantly, a 'visual turn' in academia, especially in cultural studies, when scholars began to develop a strong interest in the role of the visual in culture, i.e. images, perception, and technologies.[1] Unsurprisingly, the rise in importance of vision also had an impact on the field of Gothic studies. No longer solely confined to Gothic writings from the eighteenth century to the present, academics in this area of expertise extended their focus to include 'Gothic' paintings, photographs, films, TV series, comics or graphic novels, and computer games as well.[2] In the wake of the 'visual turn' in Gothic studies, I want to examine the pictorial narratives made by the American artist, wood engraver, and visual storyteller Lynd Ward, who lived from 1905 to 1985. Ward discovered the art of woodcut novels in Leipzig where he came across a copy of *Die Sonne* (Engl. *The Sun*), an expressionistic version of the Icarus myth, by the originator of the woodcut novel, the Flemish painter and graphic artist Frans Masereel. This 'wordless novel' inspired him to develop his own image narratives such as *Gods' Man* in 1929.

Art Spiegelman and other critics have pointed out that Ward used dramatic light-and-dark contrasts to create, like Masereel, works of art informed by an Expressionist style that indicate different moods – e.g., a happy mood is evoked through white images of parties of the rich while a bleak mood is triggered by black images of factory workers. But Ward

---

[1] In *Visual Studies: A Skeptical Introduction*, James Elkins claims that "visual culture" is predominantly "an American movement and it is younger than cultural studies by several decades" (2). "The term", he continues, "was used – perhaps for the first time in an art-historical text – in 1972 in Michael Baxandall's *Painting and Experience in Fifteenth-Century Italy*, but visual culture did not appear as a discipline until the 1990s" (2).

[2] Cf. Christoph Grunenberg, ed., *Gothic: Transmutations of Horror in Late-Twentieth-Century Art* (Cambridge, MA: MIT Press, 1997), Gilda Williams, ed., *The Gothic: Documents of Contemporary Art* (Cambridge, MA: MIT Press, 2007), and Catherine Spooner and Emma McEvoy, eds., *The Routledge Companion to Gothic* (London: Routledge, 2007) 193-279.

also utilized black-and-white effects to establish a decidedly Gothic dimension in some of his pictorial novels. In this article, several Gothic elements in Ward's work will be highlighted in three steps: first, his pictorial narratives will be situated within the context of early American comic strips and cartoons in order to demonstrate that he not only perceived his work as art, but also enriched his woodcut art with additional meaning, symbolic and iconic, in order to heighten its aesthetic quality; second, the focus will be on Ward's use of black-and-white imagery and other Gothic aspects in his first novel *Gods' Man* which, I claim, is deeply informed by German Dark Romanticism and the urban Gothic tradition; and, finally, close attention will be paid to scary or gloomy word-image relations – and here again: Ward's use of black-and-white contrasts – in his special illustrated edition of Mary Shelley's *Frankenstein*.

I. Art vs. Popular Culture: The Rise of Woodcut Novels in the 1920s

Ward's – and Masereel's – woodcut novels differed decidedly from the newspaper strips that were so popular in the US in the late 1920s and early 1930s. Typically, American daily newspapers of this period featured horizontal, black-and-white comic strips – see, for instance, the extremely popular "Mutt and Jeff" cartoon series – and a special Sunday 'comic supplement' which consisted of several coloured comic strips such as "The Gumps" series, published in the *Chicago Sunday Tribune*. These comic strips usually relied on domestic comedy and, if successful enough, they appeared as book collections on the newsstands as well. The short sequences of interrelated images with humorous intent strictly speaking did not constitute 'comic books' or 'graphic novels'. In fact, the first actual comic books emerged in the mid-1930s.

In contrast to the newspaper strips and reprint-books, Ward's pictorial narratives consist of long sequences of woodcut images that convey a story in a single or even in multiple narrative strands, e.g. *Wild Pilgrimage* and *Vertigo*. Each page displays only one centre justified image, which adds what Spiegelman calls "gravitas" (xxiv) to Ward's works of art, instead of an always changing arrangement of several interconnected images which underlines the light and playful character of the comic strips. Also, Ward's pictorial images are black-and-white prints of wood engravings, rather than the pen-and-ink images favoured by the comic strip artists. Finally, Ward's novels are 'wordless novels', that is, they do not feature bubbles with text or text passages as the newspaper strips do. They are solely made up of images and invite the reader to slowly flip through them.

Ward purposefully abandoned the woodcut-technique employed by Masereel in favour of the wood engraving method because the latter permitted him to create a more refined spectrum of dark and light effects. A brief comparison of woodcuts made by Masereel (Fig. 1: image from Masereel's *The City*, 1925; "woodcut" – with the grain) and wood engravings made by Ward (Fig. 2: image from Ward's *Vertigo*, 1937; "wood engraving" – against the grain)[3] will illustrate the hitherto unsurpassed mastery which Ward achieved:

Fig. 1   Fig. 2

[3] All images from Lynd Ward's novels included in this essay are used with the permission of the Library of America.

Both depictions of an urban amusement park manifest incredible craftsmanship, but Ward's image displays much finer lines and much more complex black-and-white effects as, for instance, his rendering of the lights on top of the rollercoaster and the rain pouring down on the visitors of the amusement park show (Fig. 2). The latter print also evokes a dizzying effect and thus illustrates the title of Ward's woodcut novel *Vertigo*.

In order to elevate the fledgling genre of woodcut novels to the higher echelons of art, Ward adopted several elements from the motion pictures of the 'silent era' such as the dark mood of German Expressionist films – e.g., Fritz Lang's *Metropolis* and *M* – and the 'intertitles' or 'title cards'. However, he does not merely copy the latter but transforms the filmic device into a literary one. Figure 3 and especially Figure 4 (from D. W. Griffith's film *Intolerance*, 1916) show typical intertitles used in the era of silent films which help viewers to interpret the prior or subsequent action depicted in the film:

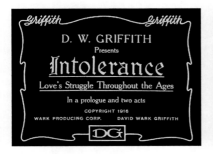

Fig. 3   Fig. 4

Ward employs intertitles as chapter headings rendered in an Art Deco style and the five chapter headings point to a drama or, in this case, a tragedy in five acts (see Figs. 5-9). All five 'vignettes' are similarly designed and yet they convey additional information to the readers: the ornament, which looks like a stylized tip of a paintbrush, remains unchanged in the first and last vignette and, as such, indicates a circular structure; whereas the other three 'brushes' in-between display symbols that foreshadow the story of the subsequent section. For example, the rosebud shaped like a snakehead in the second vignette (Fig. 6) – together with the onomatopoetic hissing sound of the consonant 's' in 'mistress' – point to temptation and sin; the rose in the fourth vignette (Fig. 8), the romantic interlude or 'ritardando', symbolizes the love between the protagonist and his wife:

Fig. 5   Fig. 6   Fig. 7

Fig. 8   Fig. 9

Apart from such elements borrowed from the silent films, Ward translates literary devices such as 'intertextuality', that is, a series of relationships between texts, into the field of vision. One example taken from Ward's wordless novel *Gods' Man* (Fig. 10) will illustrate his 'intervisual' or 'intericonic' references:

Fig. 10   Fig. 11

The wave depicted in the second print of Ward's pictorial narrative (Fig. 10) evinces an intericonic reference to Masereel's *The Sun*, in particular to the image of a huge wave on which the male figure tries to reach the sun (Fig. 11). The same image of the wave also probably refers to a famous coloured woodcut print made by the *ukiyo-e* artist Hokusai, "The Great Wave off Kanagawa" – the first print in Hokusai's well-known series *Thirty-six Views of Mount Fuji*. In this print the image of a landscape foregrounds a gigantic 'wave whipped up by a storm' that threatens the three boats (Jap. *oshiokuri-bune*) and the lives of the rowers while the snow-capped Mount Fuji resides majestically in the background. Likewise the storm has stirred up the big wave in Ward's picture, which in turn threatens the boat and the life of the young artist. Such intericonic references to other woodcut artists make manifest Ward's deliberate effort of situating his woodcut novels not only in the Western but also in the Eastern history of woodcut art and demonstrate his various ways of enriching his woodcut novels with additional aesthetic-visual meaning.[4] Ward's wordless novel *Gods' Man* in particular is steeped in the tradition of Dark Romantic art and literature, thus augmenting his graphic novel with further layers of meaning.

---

[4] Other intericonic references include the image of a kiss between the young protagonist and his wife in Ward's *Gods' Man*, which resembles the renowned painting "The Kiss" by the Austrian Symbolist artist Gustav Klimt.

II. Dark Romanticism and Urban Gothic: The Gothic Dimension of Lynd Ward's *Gods' Man*

Ward's first novel *Gods' Man* not only relies on Art Deco and Expressionist styles, but also draws heavily on Dark Romantic themes, that is, themes such as 'night', 'nature', 'magic', 'monster', and 'death', that were favoured by the dark side of the Romantic movement, and aspects of urban Gothic.[5] In fact, I contend that Ward's woodcut novel *Gods' Man* is the first Dark Romantic and urban Gothic wordless novel, and I will underpin my argument with a brief discussion of four aspects: the Gothic city, the pact with the mysterious masked man, a Cerberus-like spider, and the death of the young artist in a dark romantic setting, the 'black' mountains.

a. The Gothic City

The modern city that mercilessly crushes its inhabitants has been a popular theme in Modernist art: for instance, John Dos Passos portrayed New York City as a city that "steamrolls" (see the chapter entitled "Steamroller", 579-591) its characters in his masterpiece *Manhattan Transfer* from 1925, and Fritz Lang shows how the M-Machine metamorphoses into a Moloch and devours its workers in his famous silent film *Metropolis* from 1927. In an interesting twist, Ward gives this popular Modernist *topos* his own Dark Romantic spin in *Gods' Man*, creating a Gothic metropolis that follows the urban Gothic tradition of representing modern cities as Gothic spaces.[6]

Picking up the theme of 'Wanderlust' so popular in Romantic and Dark Romantic art and literature, Ward begins his graphic narrative with the journey-motif: a young artist sits in a boat, survives a furious storm (see

---

[5] On Dark Romanticism and the urban Gothic tradition, see, for instance, G. R. Thompson, ed., *The Gothic Imagination: Essays in Dark Romanticism* (Pullman, WA: Washington State University Press, 1974) as well as Emma McEvoy's essay "Gothic and the Romantics" and Robert Mighall's "Gothic Cities", which are both collected in Catherine Spooner and Emma McEvoy, eds., *The Routledge Companion to Gothic* (London: Routledge, 2007) 19-28, 54-62.

[6] See, for example, Linda Dryden's exploration of nineteenth-century London as an urban Gothic space in her volume *The Modern Gothic and Literary Doubles: Stevenson, Wilde and Wells* (Houndmills: Palgrave Macmillan, 2003).

the huge wave depicted in Fig. 10 above), and sails towards an island he notices on the horizon. After he has arrived at the island, he steps out of his boat and discovers a modern city located on top of a hill in the not too far distance (Fig. 12):

Fig. 12

The white colour of the city and in particular its site allude to a famous key concept in American culture: the "City upon a Hill" (Winthrop 10). The Puritans hoped that they would found a new community – a City upon a Hill – that would serve as a beacon of light to the whole world, including Old Europe. Against this backdrop, the young artist represents a pilgrim who discovers a white modern city that symbolizes his hope of artistic (and financial) success. In short: he dreams the American Dream.[7]

---

[7] The scene also points to a biographical dimension: In 1927, Lynd Ward returned from his fruitful stay in Old Europe to New York City where he tried to become a successful artist by introducing the American audience to his experimental woodcut novels that would serve as his beacon of light, his 'sun', to the world.

This dream turns into a Gothic nightmare as the shift from a white to a dark city forebodes. The young artist wanders to the city and reaches it at night (Fig. 13):

Fig. 13

The massive black city introduces a dark mood and, to be more precise, the Romantic *topos* of the "sublime" which Edmund Burke defined in his essay "A Philosophical Enquiry into the Origin of Our Ideas of the Sublime and Beautiful" as the feeling of awe and terror aroused by "great objects" that are "vast in their dimensions" and "ought to be dark and gloomy" (Burke 306). According to Burke, "whatever is in any sort terrible [...] is the source of the sublime" (305). Ward transfers the concept of the "sublime" from nature to the modern city and depicts it as a black mountain massif that excites awe and the feeling of what can be called "dark terror".

b. The Pact with the Masked Man

An additional Dark Romantic feature is the protagonist's pact with the masked man. Art Spiegelman and other critics label the young man's contract with the masked man as a "Faustian theme" (Spiegelman, "Reading Pictures" xii) and, to be sure, the pact echoes the pact Faust makes with Mephistopheles in Wolfgang Goethe's *Faust*. Yet the narrative includes further Dark Romantic themes such as the sublime nature and the young man's desire for success.

The young protagonist of *Gods' Man* tries to pay his room and board at an inn with a painting, but the owner merely laughs at the young man's idea and refuses to accept the painting of the sun (intra-iconic reference) as payment (Fig. 14). A black masked man, however, shows interest in the young artist's work, buys his paintings, and offers him a magic paintbrush (Fig. 15). The subsequent story-within-the-story (indicated by the series of small pictures: Figs. 16-21) insinuates that the magic paintbrush has actually made painters from ancient Egypt to the Modernist Era (Fig. 19 probably alludes to Albrecht Dürer and Fig. 21 possibly to Vincent van Gogh) successful:

Fig. 14   Fig. 15

Fig. 16   Fig. 17   Fig. 18

Fig. 19   Fig. 20   Fig. 21

Lured by the masked man's story – it is the narrative that endows the brush with the aura of magic – the protagonist signs the pact with the masked man (Fig. 24):

Fig. 22   Fig. 23   Fig. 24

Rather than having a Faustian thirst for knowledge, the young artist paints images of the sublime nature – e.g. a big wave – and yearns for artistic success. These are typical *topoi* of the Romantic movement. The dark turn happens when the young man signs the contract with the masked man, who represents Death, in order to become successful with the help of a magic paintbrush.

c. The Cerberus-like Spider: A Visual Blend

A further Dark Romantic feature of his work is the depiction of a monster, a Cerberus-like spider. After the young man has signed the contract, he experiences a stellar rise: his paintings of modern buildings secure him fame and success, and he falls in love with a beautiful woman who turns out to be a "mistress" – her right shoulder shows a branded Dollar-sign – and laughs at his naiveté. The young artist beats up the mistress' new lover, a police officer, and is imprisoned. After his release from prison, a group of men chase him out of the city (Fig. 25). The final print of this sequence shows an image of the men that hints at a supernatural or fantastic creature: a visual blend of Cerberus and a gigantic spider (Fig. 26):

Fig. 25   Fig. 26

Ward's visual allusion to the multiple-headed hound of Greek and Roman mythology, which guards the Underworld and blocks the path of people who, having crossed the Styx, want to return to Earth, underscores the Dark Romantic dimension of the wordless novel: the image of the Cerberus-like spider turns the city retrospectively into a modern underworld which is guarded by the monstrous creature. The young protagonist barely manages to escape from the sentinels of the Gothic Underworld, which in classical mythology represents the realm of the dead, to an Edenic place in the countryside.

d. The Young Artist's Fall into an Abyss

The young artist's fall into an abyss constitutes a final Dark Romantic element of the wordless novel. After his escape from the fantastic monster, a romantic interlude or *ritardando* – i.e., the delay of the final part – follows: the young artist falls in love with a woman in a natural, Edenic setting, not in the sinful city; they gaze together at the starry night, they kiss – a visual reference to Gustav Klimt's "Der Kuss" – and have a child. However, the blissful time is interrupted when the shadow of the masked man announces his arrival (Fig. 27). He points at the young man's signature on the contract (Fig. 28) and then shows the artist the place where he wants to have his portrait painted: at the top of the highest mountain (Fig. 29):

Fig. 27   Fig. 28   Fig. 29

Waving goodbye to his wife and child (Fig. 30), the young man follows the lead of the masked men as they walk up a narrow path in the mountains (Fig. 31). Having reached the top of the mountain, the young man starts to paint the masked man under threatening dark clouds (Fig. 32). When the black man takes off his mask (Fig. 33), the young man realizes that he has made a pact with Death (Fig. 34) and subsequently falls into a deep and dark abyss (Fig. 36):

Fig. 30 Fig. 31 Fig. 32

Fig. 33 Fig. 34

Fig. 35   Fig. 36   Fig. 37

The *topos* of a young artist who paints in a mountain setting, the black mountain range, the personified Death, and the young man's fall into an abyss are all classic Dark Romantic themes. For instance, the Gothic novel *The Devil's Elixirs* (Ger. *Die Elixiere des Teufels*), written by E. T. A. Hoffmann, a major German Dark Romantic author, tells the story of the monk Menardus, who drank from the devil's elixir and, on his wanderings, sees a person sleeping dangerously close to the edge of a steep canyon called "Teufelssitz" or "Devil's Perch". As Menardus tries to awaken the person – a prince, his "Doppelgänger"? –, the man, terrified by the sight of Menardus, falls into the chasm. The pact with Death clearly echoes Faust's pact with Mephistopheles, but, as I have shown, the dominant dimension of the work is Dark Romanticism.

III. Gothic Paratexts: The Illustrated Lynd Ward Edition of Mary Shelley's *Frankenstein*

Lynd Ward's leanings toward Gothic tales are made explicit by his decision to illustrate the quintessential Gothic novel, Mary Shelley's *Frankenstein or The Modern Prometheus* from 1818, in 1934. However, Ward would not be Ward if he did not devise clever interactions between the text and his black-and-white images, which, to use a term coined by

Gérard Genette, constitute "paratexts" (Genette 1).[8] Three 'scary' word-image relations, which enhance the overall gloomy mood of Shelley's Gothic masterpiece, will be briefly discussed in the last part of the essay: the hand as a *leitmotif*, the contrastive pair 'the romantic white landscape' vs. 'the dark romantic landscape', and the monster as 'Narcissus'.

The very first woodcut image is positioned below the title of the Gothic novel and depicts the dark skeletal hand of the monster (Fig. 38). As part of Victor Frankenstein's creation, the hand darkens the sun and thus foreshadows the gruesome ending of the tale. The image of the next hand (Fig. 39) and its visual references to Prometheus' creation of man from clay and his theft of fire introduces the theme of Frankenstein as *The Modern Prometheus*:

FRANKENSTEIN

PREFACE

THE event on which this fiction is founded has been supposed, by Dr. Darwin, and some of the physiological writers of Germany, as not of impossible occurrence. I shall not be supposed as according the remotest degree of serious faith to such an imagination; yet, in assuming it as the basis of a work of fancy, I have not considered myself as merely weaving a series of supernatural terrors. The event on which the interest of the story depends is exempt from the disadvantages of a mere tale of spectres or enchantment. It was recommended by the novelty of the situations which it developes; and, however impossible as a physical fact, affords a point of view to the imagination for the delineating of human passions more comprehensive and commanding than any which the ordinary relations of existing events can yield.

I have thus endeavoured to preserve the truth of the elementary principles of human nature, while I have not scrupled to innovate upon their combinations. The *Iliad*, the tragic poetry of Greece — Shakspeare, in the *Tempest*

vii

Fig. 38   Fig. 39

---

[8] According to Genette, paratextual material accompanies written or printed texts, such as references to an author's name, a title, preface, and illustrations (Genette 1). Ward's paratextual material is not merely constituted by the customary referential additions, but invites readers to connect Shelley's narrative with his illustrations that enrich the written text with visual-aesthetic meaning.

Thus Ward uses a black-and-white contrast to juxtapose the dark hand of the created monster with the unspecified – illuminated, white – hand of creators: Prometheus, Frankenstein, the author. Throughout the novel, further images of hands appear to reinforce the visual and thematic *leitmotif*; for instance, the monster kills only with his hands.

Ward's contrastive approach becomes apparent in his illustrations of Alpine landscapes (Fig. 40 and Fig. 41):

possession of my own. We called each other familiarly by the name of cousin. No word, no expression could body forth the kind of relation in which she stood to me — my more than sister, since till death she was to be mine only.

W CHAPTER II

E were brought up together; there was not quite a year difference in our ages. I need not say that we were strangers to any species of disunion or dispute. Harmony was the soul of our companionship, and the diversity and contrast that subsisted in our characters drew us nearer together. Elizabeth was of a calmer and more concentrated disposition; but, with all my ardour, I was capable of a more intense application, and was more deeply smitten with the thirst for knowledge. She busied herself with following the aerial creations of the poets; and in the majestic and wondrous scenes which surrounded our Swiss home — the sublime shapes of the mountains; the changes of the seasons; tempest and calm; the silence of winter, and the life and turbulence of our Alpine summers — she found ample scope

27

closer to the lake, and we approached the amphitheatre of mountains which forms its eastern boundary. The spire of Evian shone under the woods that surrounded it, and the range of mountain above mountain by which it was overhung.

The wind, which had hitherto carried us along with amazing rapidity, sunk at sunset to a light breeze; the soft air just ruffled the water, and caused a pleasant motion among the trees as we approached the shore, from which it wafted the most delightful scent of flowers and hay. The sun sunk beneath the horizon as we landed; and as I touched the shore, I felt those cares and fears revive which soon were to clasp me and cling to me for ever.

I CHAPTER XXIII

T was eight o'clock when we landed; we walked for a short time on the shore enjoying the transitory light, and then retired to the inn and contemplated the lovely scene of waters, woods, and mountains, obscured in darkness, yet still displaying their black outlines.

223

Fig. 40   Fig. 41

While the first image (Fig. 40) depicts a romantic episode and landscape at the beginning of the novel – Frankenstein and Elizabeth taking a walk along the shores of Lake Geneva and marvelling at the beautiful Alpine scenery in broad daylight – the second image (Fig. 40) is an illustration of the last meeting between him and Elizabeth and foreshadows her death. It shows the newlywed couple walking along the shores of Lake Geneva at night shortly before the monster kills Elizabeth.

Finally, Ward often uses full-page illustrations to suggest the gigantic size of the monster (Fig. 42 and Fig. 43) and, in the woodcut print of the monster gazing at his reflection in a pool (Fig. 44), 'engraves' himself in the long tradition of illustrating the myth of Narcissus, however, in black-and-white woodblock prints:[9]

Fig. 42   Fig. 43   Fig. 44

In all three examples, Ward not only enhances the gloomy mood of Shelley's Gothic work with dramatic light-and-dark contrasts, but he also adds at times new visual meaning to the classic text and invites the reader to participate in a rich interaction between text and images.

In sum, Ward searched for ways to 'novelize' the genre of woodcut narratives and thus turn the fledgling genre into a new art form. Following in the footsteps of Masereel, he experimented with the visual syntax and iconicity of the pictorial narratives, and, drawing on elements and techniques prevalent in literary texts such as intertextuality, *leitmotif*, different narrative strands (stories-within-stories), symbols, and themes, he pushed the art form to unsurpassed heights. Ward's first woodcut novel *Gods' Man* demonstrates his creative use of elements taken from the Dark Romantic tradition in literature and art in order to generate a Gothic graphic novel. I hope to have shown that the contemporary

---

[9] See, for instance, the well-known *Narcissus* by Caravaggio – himself famous for his dramatic use of lighting.

'Gothic gaze' can no longer neglect this master of the wordless novel and should expand its horizon, its visual limits, to include the breathtaking work of Lynd Ward.

Works Cited

Burke, Edmund. "A Philosophical Enquiry into the Origin of Our Ideas of the Sublime and Beautiful." *Critical Theory Since Plato*. Ed. Hazard Adams. Rev. ed. Fort Worth: Harcourt Brace Jovanovich, 1992. 298-306.

Dos Passos, John. Manhattan Transfer. *John Dos Passos: Novels 1920-25*. Ed. Townsend Ludington. New York: Library of America, 2003. 477-837.

Dryden, Linda. *The Modern Gothic and Literary Doubles: Stevenson, Wilde and Wells*. Houndmills: Palgrave Macmillan, 2003.

Elkins, James. *Visual Studies: A Skeptical Introduction*. New York: Routledge, 2003.

Genette, Gérard. *Paratexts: Thresholds of Interpretation*. Trans. Jane E. Lewin. Cambridge: Cambridge University Press, 1997.

Grunenberg, Christoph, ed. *Gothic: Transmutations of Horror in Late-Twentieth-Century Art*. Boston: Institute of Contemporary Art; Cambridge, MA: MIT Press, 1997.

Masereel, Frans. *The City: A Vision in Woodcuts*. 1925. Mineola, NY: Dover, 2006.

---. *The Sun, The Idea & Story Without Words*. Mineola, NY: Dover, 2009.

McEvoy, Emma. "Gothic and the Romantics." *The Routledge Companion to Gothic*. Eds. Catherine Spooner and Emma McEvoy. London: Routledge, 2007. 19-28.

Mighall, Robert. "Gothic Cities." *The Routledge Companion to Gothic*. Eds. Catherine Spooner and Emma McEvoy. London: Routledge, 2007. 54-62.

Spiegelman, Art. "Reading Pictures." *Lynd Ward: Gods' Man, Madman's Drum, Wild Pilgrimage*. Ed. Art Spiegelman. Vol. 1. New York: Library of America, 2010. ix-xxv.

Spooner, Catherine, and Emma McEvoy, eds. *The Routledge Companion to Gothic.* London: Routledge, 2007.

Thompson, G. R., ed. *The Gothic Imagination: Essays in Dark Romanticism.* Pullman, WA: Washington State University Press, 1974.

Ward, Lynd. "On *'Madman's Drum.'*" *Lynd Ward: Gods' Man, Madman's Drum, Wild Pilgrimage.* Ed. Art Spiegelman. Vol. 1. New York: Library of America, 2010. 787-791.

---. "Gods' Man." *Lynd Ward: Gods' Man, Madman's Drum, Wild Pilgrimage.* Ed. Art. Spiegelman. Vol. 1. New York: Library of America, 2010.

Williams, Gilda, ed. *The Gothic: Documents of Contemporary Art.* Cambridge: MIT Press, 2007.

Winthrop, John. "A Model of Christian Charity." *The Journal of John Winthrop, 1630-1649.* Eds. Richard S. Dunn and Laetitia Yeandle. Cambridge, MA: John Harvard Library, 1996. 1-11.

Christian Schneider

"'It' forever": *Black Hole* as a Gothic Graphic Novel

The journey to darkness starts with brightness, with a jagged white crack on an all-black page (Burns, *Black Hole* [7]).[1] The crack widens and gains an unmistakeably organic quality: it becomes a repulsive gate for the reader, leading into a black and white world in which bodies in all their strange mutations reign (Burns, *Black Hole* [8]). Welcome to *Black Hole*. Charles Burns' graphic novel, first published in twelve instalments from 1995 to 2004, is not only regarded as a contemporary classic, but also commonly seen as a horror comic (Gravett 110-111) or at least as work which employs "elements of a horror novel" (Baker 62). At first glance, it seems perfectly straightforward to include it in this 'Gothic volume' if the Gothic is indeed an encompassing mode that surfaces in all kinds of texts, media and genres. However, a closer look reveals that the answer to the question of whether *Black Hole* is indeed a Gothic graphic novel is much more complex than one might think.

On the one hand, "gothic fiction need not be horrific and horror fiction need not be gothic" (Bloom 9); even if *Black Hole* is a horror graphic novel, it does not necessarily have to possess distinctly Gothic traits. On the other hand, it is also not a stereotypical horror text in the first place. The novel "denies any obvious generic identification with science-fiction/horror" (Smith 258). Especially considering the mainstream of traditional horror comics, Burns' work seems to stand alone. It neither follows the tongue-in-cheek "shock-logic formula" (Barker 122) of the incredibly influential 1950s horror comics, nor does it emulate the highly literate "dark fantasy and sophisticated suspense" (Round 16) of 1980s and 1990s Vertigo titles. *Black Hole* seems to present a dark vision that is as unique as it is eclectic.

---

[1] Since both single issues and collected edition lack any kind of pagination, *Black Hole* is a difficult case for citation, as John Lowther notes (13n3). I will partly follow his compromise and reference the chapters from the serial issues, with page numbers counted from the recto title page of the respective chapter; only in exceptional cases will I reference the collected edition or a serial issue as a whole.

Nonetheless, I will argue that *Black Hole* represents a distinctly Gothic vision, chronicling a perilous coming-of-age process typical of many other Gothic texts (see Oppolzer, *Failed Rites*). What is more, Burns' text is part of a larger tradition within US comics that can be characterized as an alternative Gothic vision. Indeed, *"Black Hole* didn't come out of nowhere; artists like Burns need to develop in a community of peers" (Wolk 341). His creative origins lie in the alternative comics titles that in turn "were rooted in the underground comix" (Duncan 654). These underground connections of Burns' work are worth examining in greater detail: we can find an astounding tradition of Gothic horror within the comix of the 1960s and 1970s, which is usually not associated with their image of sex, drugs and politicized critique (see e.g. Rosenkranz; Sabin). The underground titles had a special transgressive status from the beginning, since "they had nothing to do with the mainstream – in fact in many ways they were antithetical to it" (Sabin 92). This applies to both the mainstream within the medium of comics and the socio-cultural mainstream of the USA. The dominating ethical and aesthetic standards are subverted in all possible respects.

Within the medium of comics, these standards especially manifested themselves in the so-called 'Comics Code', the industry's self-regulatory set of conventions that was established in 1954 in order to curb the excesses of horror comics and their purported influence on young readers (Nyberg). By the 1960s, the Code was increasingly viewed as a restrictive regime limiting artistic expression. Thus, "the comics medium offered a particularly fruitful ground for iconoclasm. [...] To celebrate sex and drugs, as the counterculture did, was offensive to Middle America; to do it in the supposedly simon-pure comic-book form made the violation doubly piquant" (Witek, *Comic Books as History* 51). Fuelled by an "anti-Comics Code reaction" (Sabin 92), breaking its rules became a *raison d'être* for the underground:

> Where the Code-approved comics observed a rigid set of content guidelines that articulated a bourgeois ideology, the underground comix appeared to obey a single maxim: anything goes. The Code prohibited sexual innuendos; the comix wallowed in sex of the most bizarre kind. The Code banned violence; the comix routinely presented death, dismemberment, and mayhem beyond the wildest fantasies of the gory EC comics. The Code forbade any mention of drug use; the comix celebrated marijuana and LSD in

their stories, and many comix artists undertook their careers in the undergrounds after mind-expanding conversion experiences with peyote and LSD. For readers accustomed to the wholesome goings-on in the Code-approved comic books, the first sight of comix [...] seemed like appalling glimpses into some alien and rather disturbingly unhygienic dimension. (Witek, "Imagetext" 8)

This reaction to 'the first sight of comix' was not purely destructive. Sabin maintains: "If the Code meant, essentially, that a comic was prevented from saying anything meaningful about the real world, then by defying it this possibility was reawakened" (92). Yet, in their transgressive extremity, the subversive comics of the underground "were not only beyond the limits of the Code but exceeded every boundary of acceptable human expression" (Witek, "Imagetext" 10) at the time. If these titles represented a kind of maturity for comics, it was always a rebellious and almost adolescent maturity.

The comix' constant challenge to the Code makes it scarcely surprising that many underground artists were influenced by EC Comics, the most famous as well as infamous horror titles of the 1950s. EC's output was stylized as a last bastion of freedom of expression against the tyranny of censorship. Recognizing the influence, many underground titles emulate EC's cover layout explicitly (see e.g. Rosenkranz 169; 93; 97). Since the comix were self-published and thus did not necessarily have to meet any kind of financial demands, they were able to take the subversive impetus of horror to its extreme: "although they acknowledged their debt to the EC Comics [...], they took explicitness to levels that even these gory frontrunners could not have hoped to aspire to" (Sabin 106).

This strand within the underground soon led to the development of horror stories as a "major sub-genre" (Sabin 106) of comix. Titles like *Skull Comics* or *Slow Death* collected tales in the vein of the 1950s, together with other magazines with titles like *Bogeyman* or *Deviant Slice* (Sabin 106). On the cover of *Skull Comics*' first issue, EC's logo is featured, re-interpreteted as "Exorpsychic Comic". The foreword makes the continuity even more explicit; a host who emulates the Cryptkeeper in EC's *Tales from the Crypt* welcomes the readers and asks them:

> *Ever wonder what happened to those great old horror* comix that used to scare the shit out of ya way back in the 50's? Remember? Well, they all disappeared, an' it wasn't *black magic* what done

'em in, either! Those comix are *gone*! Until *now*, that is! Things bein' as they are these days, a few of us ol' characters decided it was time to revive th' *horror* comix ... in keepin' with th' *times*, y' understand! (Irons 1)

If "the suppression of comic books by the Comics Code is implicitly equated with contemporary political oppression" (Witek, *Comic Books as History* 54), the Gothic can be interpreted as a liberating means of resisting said oppression.

Various comix in this vein display an obvious "fascination with horror, cosmic retribution, sexual power, and the lure of evil" (Rosenkranz 166), often to the point that they were ostracized by other cartoonists, who asked "what's 'underground' about rotting corpses" (Bill Griffiths, qtd. in Rosenkranz 186). Furthermore, many horror stories are overshadowed by palpable sexism (Sabin 106) and dominated by crudity: "Nothing was suggested anymore, everything was shown" (Sabin 107). Still, some tales are surprisingly experimental and mature, as Sabin observes: "Horror also brought out the best in certain writers. After all, any story based in such a genre framework demanded more than abstract psychedelia or dumb scatology, and the EC comics had always made plot a priority" (106-107). The underground horror titles range from vulgarity to sophistication, opening up a distinctly subversive variety of the Gothic in comics.

Quite obviously, *Black Hole* is not a carbon copy of these comics, neither in style nor in theme. Yet, Burns acknowledges the underground's influence on his work in general, including the horror titles in particular (Hignite 128). A closer look reveals noticeable parallels, especially a similar relevance of graphic design. Many comix' riotous style gave their horror its cutting edge and its taboo-breaking effect. Burns' drawings are much more subdued than the manic psychedelia of artists like S. Clay Wilson or Rory Hayes. Yet, they seem to embody an inherently ominous and psychotic quality. Various scholars have noted *Black Hole*'s visual distinctiveness and its disquieting atmosphere. Perna summarizes: "In analyses and reviews, critics tend to focus on Burns's trademark visual style and the themes of physical mutation and body horror to explain its hair-raising mood" (8). Some even argue that "Burns' narrative gifts are much more visual than verbal" (Wolk 336), deeming his graphic style to be more intricate than his plot and characters. Yet, it is almost impossible to separate them with regard to their narrative function.

The general quality of Burns' drawings might be one aspect of what makes his work specifically Gothic. His style is "hard-edged, Manichean" (Hignite 104) in its highly contrasted black-and-white tones. In *Black Hole*, "everything is made up of either pure white or jet black, and mostly the latter" (Arnold). The titular blackness of the world is thus obvious at first glance. This stylistic clarity is combined with a sense of "meticulous detail" (Arnold) in Burns' drawings. Nevertheless, they do not depict a similarly clear or ordered world view. The focus on ill-fitting or strange details is too prevalent to paint an entirely wholesome picture. Many features gain an uncanny aspect, as familiar things become wholly alien. Douglas Wolk puts it succinctly: "Burns specializes in drawing people and things that look like they're just beginning to curdle" (337). Emulating the visual style of 1950s romance comics, his "stark clarity belies the nebulous and conflicted clues lying just beneath. […] Burns doesn't mimic but rather isolates and foregrounds the inherent strangeness and alien power of slick artwork and flat authority of the printed image" (Hignite 104).

His style was already a striking feature in his earlier works, creating "meticulous 1950s-style horror and science fiction stories, […] both horrifying and hilariously funny" (Sabin 188). According to Wolk, however, these stories also have a "far shallower creepy/campy vibe" (341). One of them, "Teen Plague", published in *RAW*, planted the seed that grew into *Black Hole*. The creative influence of 1950s horror comics on Burns' work is more obvious here, as the main story is mirrored in the *mise en abyme* of such a horror title (Burns, "Teen Plague" 43). This extremely camp story depicts the sexually transmitted possession of teenagers by a grotesque eyeball-like alien, demanding "an army of … love-slaves!" (Burns, "Teen Plague" 47). Nevertheless, the actual main story features other fears, which are not connected to the comic's intertextual sensationalism: the titular plague infects teenagers without any rational explanation, giving them horrible nightmares (Burns, "Teen Plague" 51) and bleeding skin rashes (Burns, "Teen Plague" 52). The tone here is much less camp, taking teenagers' anxieties seriously. This is the story Burns revisits in *Black Hole*, also telling us about "the 'teen plague' or 'the bug'" (Burns, *Black Hole 1* [1]). The novel's tone is similarly non-sensationalist; its "tenor very rarely departs from what you'd see in a monster-free coming-of-age story" (Wolk 340). Apparently, the graphic novel has left most of its obvious intertextuality behind, as "outer space aliens are replaced by the much more sinister alienation of the teenager" (Hignite 106).

Despite the lack of explicit links to the horror tradition of US comics, the genre designation is still fitting: Burns clearly uses motifs from horror films.[2] There are, for instance, features of the typical setup of a 1970s teenage slasher film in the vein of *Halloween* or *Friday, the 13th*: teenagers in a suburban setting, freed from adult supervision, indulging in sex and drugs, and unaware of the danger they are in. Like these films, the graphic novel depicts a "loss of control" (Spooner 102) on the part of its teenage protagonists. Yet, "*Black Hole* has as much fun defying the teen horror conventions as working within them" (Arnold). The setup evokes an ominous atmosphere, but it never fulfils the generic expectations: there are no monsters or serial killers on the loose.

More apt is perhaps the classification as body horror, defined by Kelly Hurley as

> a hybrid genre that recombines the narrative and cinematic conventions of the science fiction, horror and suspense film in order to stage a spectacle of the human body defamiliarized, rendered other. Body horror seeks to inspire revulsion [...] through representations of quasi-human figures whose ef-fect/affect is produced by their abjection, their ambiguation, their impossible embodiment of multiple, incompatible forms. ("Reading" 203)

True to its name, body horror presents the horrifying aspects of our bodies, their transgressive, abject and ultimately Gothic aspects. Peter Hutchings affirms that "body horror describes the ultimate alienation – alienation from one's own body – but this has often been coupled with a fascination with the possibility of new identities that might emerge from this" (41). It can be seen as a direct postmodern continuation of what Hurley calls the "abhuman" (*Gothic Body* 3) bodies of Gothic fiction. In this tradition, "the human body collapses and is reshapen across an astonishing range of morphic possibilities" (Hurley, *Gothic Body* 4) that are both nauseating and fascinating.

---

[2] Interestingly, *Black Hole*'s single reference to an explicitly Gothic text is to a parody, *Abbott and Costello Meet Frankenstein* (Burns, "Dream Girl" [7]).

It is not difficult to find such a view on the body in *Black Hole*. The teenagers' mutations are portrayed as what Wolk calls "Cronenbergian grotesqueries" (340), which mentions the director most commonly associated with the genre of body horror (Hutchings 41). In general, *Black Hole*'s bodies are commonly reduced to "[t]he insistent presentation of the abject" (Lowther 14). The metamorphosis usually turns its victims into beings that are indeed 'abhuman': they resemble animals, like Dave and his "vaguely feline" (Zeigler) face, demonic creatures, sprouting insectoid horns (Burns, *Black Hole 2* [1]), or entirely inhuman monsters, like the teenager Keith encounters in the woods (Burns, "Planet Xeno" [10]). Faced with such abnormal changes, it is no wonder that Chris reacts to her infection by claiming "I'm a monster" (Burns, "Seeing Double" [3]). Indeed, witnessing her rip off her own skin (Burns, "Sssssssss" [9-11]) and seeing its ghostly husk in the woods (Burns, "Planet Xeno" [8-9]) is a shocking sight for the reader.

The teenage setting is something that links *Black Hole* not only to slasher films, but the Gothic tradition in general. Spooner observes that the "Gothic has always had a strong link with adolescence" (88). For one, its forms have often been assumed to speak mainly to an adolescent audience (Spooner 89-90), whether as eighteenth-century Gothic romance or as teenage horror slasher. Adolescence is also an important topic of the Gothic. With regard to early Gothic fiction, Markus Oppolzer notes

> the great number of young and inexperienced characters whose lives, though wildly differing in other respects, seemed to follow a similar pattern: at some stage in their development, dramatic – if not traumatic – events separate them from some system of order and hurl them into a world of confusion and indeterminacy. (*Failed Rites* 1)

He analyzes the role of these adolescents in socio-anthropological terms, focusing on their failed initiation depicted by the Gothic: "What most early gothic novels (and many modern ones) have in common is an accumulation of liminal experiences (birth, death, *puberty*, relocation, change in social status etc.) combined with a denial or perversion of rites of passage" ("Denied Rites" 177; emphasis added). According to his argument, the liminal status of the young adults is the perfect test case for the Gothic's sub- and perverted institutions: the teenagers are outsiders to them, yet are "frequently still at the mercy of, and vulnerable to, the exercise of institutional powers, or shown to be the products of such an

influence" (*Failed Rites* 2). Ultimately, "major bourgeois institutions [...]
fail to live up to their responsibilities and thus pave the way for deviance"
(Oppolzer, "Denied Rites" 178).

Oppolzer's reading appears to neglect another important aspect of Gothic
adolescence: its bodily abjection. As Spooner makes clear, "[t]he body at
the centre of many contemporary Gothic narratives is definitively an
adolescent one" (87). The problems of puberty are mapped out in

> a prevailing atmosphere of disgust which provides duplicate
> images for the adolescent's disgust with the changes in his or her
> own emerging body, from acne to menstruation. The body, we
> might say, is always rising up against the adolescent, a bloody,
> half-formed body. (Punter, *The Literature of Terror* 150)

This liminal state extends to the body. In puberty, "we exist on a terrain
where what is inside finds itself outside (acne, menstrual blood, rage) and
what we think should be visibly outside (heroic dreams, attractiveness,
sexual organs) remain resolutely inside and hidden" (Punter, *Gothic
Pathologies* 6).

The monstrous teenagers embody something that is wrong with the world
of *Black Hole*. Even more disturbing, however, is how they react to the
plague. The ones not afflicted shun the sick ones, who disappear into the
woods. A fatalistic tone of despair dominates the viewpoints of the
characters. The title in itself can be seen as a hint. The 'Black Hole' is a
markedly Gothic metaphor, "a locus of dissolution, a space of loss and
mystery in which all meanings are consumed, all thought loses itself, all
sense evaporates, and all boundaries collapse" (Botting, "Aftergothic"
295). In our postmodern era, in which all other Gothic locales have
already been dealt and played with (Cavallaro 27-28), a black hole seems
to constitute the ultimate Gothic space. It is the perfect representation of
the unrepresentable, where everything loses its meaning, shape and being:
"Nothing escapes from a black hole, not even light" (Botting,
"Aftergothic" 296). It is anti-matter, anti-being.

Such a sense of futility, of not being able to escape, dominates the minds
of Burns' teenagers, who are a far cry from adolescent optimism. Keith's
vision makes this clear from the novel's very beginning: "I felt like I was
looking into the future … and the future looked really messed up. [...] I
was looking at a hole … a *black* hole and as I looked, the hole opened
up" (Burns, "Biology 101" [3-4]). His vision is shared by other victims of

the plague, as the teenagers continually remind themselves of their own impotence and confinement: "I'll never do it" (Burns, "Racing Towards Something" [24]); "It'll never get better ... I'll *always* be like this" (Burns, "Cut" [8]); "[I]t was always impossible. I was stuck" (Burns, "Bag Action" [9]); "Can't do it. I'll never do it" (Burns, "A Dream Girl" [7]). This general feeling of pessimism is especially pronounced in the utterances of Rob's mutation, the little mouth on his neck. As a non-too-subtle representation of his repressed subconscious (Lowther 20), it declares: "It ... it won't work ... it can't last. It's impossible ... nnn ... never make it out alive. It won't work ..." (Burns, "Under Open Skies" [11]). The teenagers seem to experience what Sean Collins calls "the number-one effect of the story and the art here: claustrophobia". As with other comics, the panel layout works to create this effect. Collins notes its "uniform" pattern, with very straight lines that more often than not separate the characters. Hignite notes about Burns' style: "Each panel is dramatically composed, calling attention to the static artificiality" (104) of both dialogue and image.

The title of Burns' graphic novel has further negative connotations. Lowther summarizes its diverse meanings, also noting "the black holes of [...] bodily openings – vaginas, mouths, wounds" (11) that pervade the book. The gaping hole of "Biology 101" is programmatic: *Black Hole* "may be the most Freudian graphic novel you will every [sic] read" (Arnold), where "nearly every image is a sexual metaphor, with the distorted clarity and mutability of a nightmare" (Wolk 336). Phallic and vaginal symbolism pervades Burns' drawings, especially in the dream sequences, with their giant snakes (Burns, "Sssssssss" [2; 4]), sausages (Burns, "Cook Out" [2]) and tadpoles (Burns, "A Dream Girl" [17]), or wounds (Burns, "Sssssssss" [4]) and rock arches (Burns, "Sssssssss" [5]). These images are always connected with abjection rather than celebration. Wolk observes that "sex in *Black Hole* [...] means body-horror, sickening transformations, and loss" (336). In truly Gothic spirit, sex *is* death. The genital symbols also include wounds and cut-off arms (Burns, "Windowpane" [23]), and it is no surprise that Chris and Rob first have sex in a graveyard (Burns, "Racing Towards Something" [11]). Afterwards, his penis appears to her "like a ghost. ... like some dead thing had crept into me" (Burns, "Racing Towards Something" [15]).

The dangers of sex in *Black Hole* are obvious, as the mutating bug is spread via sexual intercourse – "of course", as Wolk comments sardonically (337). While the disease is obviously reminiscent of HIV, the potential metaphoric relation is far from straightforward: "The bug of *Black Hole* is not identical to AIDS. It strikes only teens and is not lethal in itself. [...] Still, at no point in the narrative proper does the disease just clear up like a bad case of acne and the sick teens believe the bug to be fatal" (Zeigler). Similarly, the bug, "like AIDS during its first years of discovery, has no known cause. The disease, like AIDS, is primarily a sexual-social disease" (2). Still, the infection is not deadly *per se*. Not even the mutations appear to last forever, as a quote from one of its survivors in the last published issue makes clear:

> It's like tryin' to explain sex to a nun – there's no way you'd ever understand it unless you *lived* it. I was *there*, okay? Half my fuckin' friends *died* out there, man. I never dreamed I'd get out of that shit-hole ... but one day I notice the stuff on my face is starting to heal and a couple of months later, I'm totally fuckin' *clean* ... out walking around with all the normal assholes. (Burns, *Black Hole 12* [3])

As Collins observes, this passage "directly contradicts" another quotation, comparing the plague to "a horrible game of tag [...] ... once you were tagged, you were 'it' forever" (Burns, *Black Hole 1* [1]). To its victims, the disease cannot be explained rationally. Its phantasmagorical mutations rather seem to belong in the various dreams and drug visions that conjure up the same demented distortions. The symptoms are psychological rather than purely physiological. Andrew Arnold notes in his review that the mutations are specific to each person's psyche, "like corporeal manifestations of their inner souls". As a symbolization of teenage alienation, "those infected become as outwardly repulsive and rejectable as they feel inside" (Arnold).

Overall, the plague has no explanation and cannot be understood or contained. It might be the main thing symbolized by the image of the black hole, where all explanations and meanings fail to hold true; no wonder it induces vertigo when one looks at it (Burns, "Biology 101" [5]). The hole might also signify the blackness of death, an interpretation illustrated by the dark bullet holes that bear witness to Dave's murder spree (Burns, "A Dream Girl" [27]). Seeing them traumatizes Keith so much that he refuses to acknowledge the massacre: "I'm not here. I'm not seeing this" (Burns, "A Dream Girl" [26]). In the face of death's meaninglessness, the human mind breaks down.

This failure of articulation, hindering perception and understanding, is also evident in *Black Hole*'s fragmented narrative. Critics have noted the novel's jumbled timeline, "riddled with flashbacks, flashforwards, and multiple perspectives" (Wolk 337), as the chapters do not follow a clear chronology. This "add[s] to the disorienting effects of the story" (Raney 29; see also Perna 9). Raney even identifies a truly Gothic "blurring of past and present" (29) in Burns' complex temporal construction, as certain events are revisited from different points of view. This structure is further complicated by the common graphic depiction of "visions, memories, fantasies, and dreams" (Perna 12) that was alluded to further above. Underlined by homodiegetic narrative inserts, the whole graphic novel is presented through the multiple perspectives of the teenage protagonists (Raney 25; Perna 11-12). Burns gives us constant insight into their interior lives. Frequently, he literally lets us share their point-of-view, with obvious cases of primary internal focalization, within dreams (e.g. "Biology 101" [7]; "Sssssssss" [3-7]; "Who's Chris?" [2]) as well as outside of them (e.g. "Cut" [15]; "Lizard Queen" [10]). The distinction between reality and imagination, which is often blurred, overlays the already unclear sequence of events, making it difficult for the reader to decide what has actually happened and what has not – and when. While there seems to be at least some guidance offered by the undulating panel borders that indicate a dream perspective, such borders are also used for memory flashbacks, thus creating even further confusion. At the same time, Keith's horror trip in the woods is drawn within straight borders (Burns, "Windowpane" [18-21]), giving it a status of perceived reality. The shifts between levels of reality are fluid and varying. Strikingly, Burns' style does not change between them, presenting – as remarked above – the monsters of a nightmare with the same abject corporeality as the 'real' mutations (Burns, "Who's Chris?" [2-3]). The plague's irrational status is thus further emphasized. Drugs dissolve the borders further: Chris gets drunk, which collapses the panel layout and lets wavy, snake-like lines invade her reality from the gutter, illustrating a mental breakdown that cannot be depicted straightforwardly: "Things turning. Seeing double, triple" (Burns, "Seeing Double" [12-13]). Correspondingly, under the influence of LSD, Keith looks at a picture and imagines Chris in it; this is a metaleptic merger of reality and fantasy which pulls both worlds into one single panel, where only the shifting panel margins mark their division (Burns, "Windowpane" [13]).

This encompassing surrealism adds to the disquieting atmosphere. Here, *Black Hole* is probably the closest to the unruly psychedelic spirit of the underground. However, whereas the comix presented and celebrated mind-expanding freedom, Burns' graphic novel shows protagonists who are victimized and trapped by chaotic circumstances: "No minds are expanded" (Collins) by the hallucinogenic offers presented. This atmosphere of psychedelia turned ominous and threatening, like a horror trip, is a common motif associated with the aftermath of the countercul- ture movement in the 1970s. The time and tone are often conceived as "the sixties gone toxic, a whole historical and countercultural 'bad trip'" (Jameson 117), a dark reversal of the positively carnivalesque hippie spirit which one might call 'Altamont Gothic' (Morgan 133). Incidentally or not, the same tone of disillusionment seems to have dominated the end of the comix movement, as "Things Started to Get Uglier" (Art Spiegelman, qtd. in Sabin 118). As Hatfield observes, the comix "succumbed to their own clichés – sex, drugs and hedonism" (19), embodying "the fecklessness and anomie of the fading counterculture" (20).

Another, maybe more obvious example of metafictional commentary can be found in yet another graphic depiction of this monstrous world: Eliza's artwork, tellingly kept in the cellar of the house she stays in (Burns, "Bag Action" [18-19]). Her portraits of demonic beings can be seen as a continuation of Burns' grotesque images; however, they lack his refined linework, displaying much rawer and more expressive lines. They foreground their status as drawings, their constructedness, and thus stand in contrast with and subvert the slick illustrations of the 'real' world. Here, the helplessness of the teenagers within the chaotic world becomes obvious in the mysterious drawing of a boy tied to the tree, who "might be Keith; it might be someone else; it might not be there at all" (Wolk 340).

Linking different levels of time and reality, this repetition of motifs and images is turned into something disturbing and even threatening. As Perna observes, *Black Hole* "operates through a logic of the uncanny, suspending the reader between familiarity and unfamiliarity, primarily via visual means", as it attempts to "evoke a sense of déjà vu" (9). This visual system "works to confine and oppress" (Collins) both characters and readers of Burns' comic. Perna also argues that the sense of déja vu has a metaleptic function, "blurring the position of the reader in relation to the story" (9), as they are confused by the images' ambiguous actuality.

Such a sense of repetition can be read as an extremely Gothic trait of *Black Hole*. On the one hand, it may be an expression of teenage trauma, which consists of recurring ambiguous images of real and imagined events from a time of emotional upheaval, "spiralling inward into that gravitational maw until that bad thing might as well be constant" (Collins). Burns' perspective on the 1970s would thus constitute a portrayal of one's past as an adolescent – which in his case is true – focused on the process of reliving the often horrific liminality of that period. On the other hand, Burns' repetition "creates doublings of his characters, events, and images" (Perna 9), evoking the uncanny duality so typical of Gothic fiction (Botting, *Gothic* 6; 13; 85). Even beyond a chapter titled "Seeing Double", *Black Hole* is suffused by a sense of doubling and mirroring.

Most obviously, this manifests itself in the doubling of the story's characters, who are often portrayed as *alter egos* of one another. Perna rightly observes that "[o]ne character may resemble another in appearance" (10; see also Raney 8). Indeed, most of Burns' characters share a similar appearance, as they "look like they come from his repertory company" (Collins and Hyacinth). The doublings also work across gender lines. There is sometimes a deliberately uncanny similarity between Keith and Chris (e.g. Burns, "Biology 101" [2]; "Cut" [14]), whose faces are also shown together as one (Burns, "The End" [8]), like a "split screen" (Perna 10). However, their faces do not match like those of Chris and Rob, which are portrayed as conjoined after their graveyard tryst (Burns, "Racing Towards Something" [14]), illustrating both the closeness of their sexual union and the uncanny contamination of the bug. This doubling across gender boundaries reminds one of the sexual uncertainties of the Gothic (see e.g. Haggerty). In the atmosphere of physiological mutations, this sexual doubling is also imbued with a sense of perversity. Indeed, sexualities become more fluid, as male and female traits merge graphically. Rob and Eliza have hermaphroditic reverse genitals: Rob's mouth mutation has vaginal connotations, while Eliza's tail might appear as a penis (Gravett 110-111; Collins and Hyacinth).

Returning to the bug's abject effects, the sexual connotations of the protruding horns and convex wounds it produces make Wolk's reading convincing. For him, the disease is arguably "not a metaphor for AIDS

[…] or for herpes, or even for pregnancy" but for "sex itself" (337), the first and often traumatic experiences with the transgressive aspects of sex and sexuality. However, I would even go further: *Black Hole* describes not just the 'bug' of sex, but the 'disease' of growing up. Even Wolk acknowledges that the "mutations stand in for the physical and emotional changes of adolescence" (340). This would make Burns' book a model case of the adolescent Gothic, from the pubescent body horror to "the startling absence of adults" (Collins and Hyacinth). The teenagers are left alone in a state of liminality and confusion, scaring and alienating them. The inherent horror of this reading is probably best illustrated by the collected edition's dust jacket. In the book's endpapers, we find the yearbook photographs that are also reproduced at the beginning of each serial issue: one picture showing an uninfected adolescent boy or girl, the next cruelly detailing a mutation. However, the dust jacket features probably the most poignant transformation of all: that of Charles Burns himself, who has no mutations, but is turned from an optimistic-looking young man into a bald middle-aged man with a sceptic frown. As Rob's mouth spouts pessimism in "a child's voice" ("Under Open Skies" [11]), it becomes clear that the innocence of childhood is irrevocably lost. Sex and drugs cannot provide an escape; they function rather as messengers of the terrifying future. In a sense, growing up inevitably leads to oppression and death.

Yet, if *Black Hole* and its distortions, transgressions and transformations are indeed manifestations of carnivalesque adolescence, one can view the graphic novel from another perspective as well; *Black Hole* can be read as promising liberation and new beginnings. If its effects are as temporary as the quote above reveals, "the teen plague [will] ultimately [be] like being a teenager itself: It sucks, but you grow out of it" (Collins). This idea also seems to lie behind Chris' transformation: she literally starts shedding her skin, growing and leaving her old self, her childhood, behind. Sexual awakening has not turned her into "a monster but a whole being" (Wolk 341).

Indeed, sexual activity may entail frightening consequences and wounds of its own, but it is not merely equated with death and horror. Rob and Chris' one-night stand in the graveyard represents sex leading to death, but it is also sex despite and against death: "*we* were alive … we were *so* alive and that's all that mattered" (Burns, "Racing Towards Something" [11]) is what Chris says about it. Ultimately, sex is portrayed as pleasurable and fulfilling. While negative experiences like Eliza's rape (Burns, "Driving South" [15]) are not ignored, "the sex scenes Burns actually chooses to depict [...] seem to be a lot of fun for the participants, and to bring them closer together emotionally" (Collins and Hyacinth).

In general, Wolk is right when he detects "final glints of hope" (337) in the ending of *Black Hole*. Keith and Eliza make a getaway, leaving the woods and their constant black shades behind, entering a landscape that is drawn with much lighter and less stark lines (Burns, "Driving South" [1-3]). The chapter's title page illustrates this by showing their car exiting a dark valley (Burns, "Driving South" [1]). Eliza in particular symbolizes the power of hope that lies in the transformation during adolescence. Her tail, which she does not hide shamefully, has the power to grow back and represents "Eliza's refusal to let the bug rob her of *jouissance*, pleasure and desire" (Lowther 22). It is the one mutation not connected with abjection, but with sexual allure (Burns, "Bag Action" [17]) and child-like play (Burns, "Driving South" [2]). Eliza also envisions Keith "escaping [...]. Flying away from all the messed up stuff" (Burns, "Driving South" [12]). In the final chapter, Burns presents Keith's last "dream sequence that reprises the structure of one of the book's first scenes, transformed from a vision of hellish squalor into an apparition of serenity and stark beauty" (Wolk 340). It ends with the programmatic words: "It doesn't always have to be bad. Sometimes things work out" (Burns, "The End" [9]). For the adolescents, it might be true that "maybe things *will* work out, that their grotesque fumblings have become something meaningful" (Wolk 340-341) and a new life awaits them. Still, the graphic novel ends on a highly ambivalent note; Burns does not offer us and his protagonists a definite happy ending. There is no guarantee that Keith and Eliza will actually make it, as the nightmare of the past may continue to haunt them (Burns, "The End" [10]) and their plans for the future are just as unreal, drawn within wavy panel borders (Burns, "The End" [12-13]).

Keith's last dream vision gives us yet another revelation concerning the novel's title. It starts with the same white slit that was mentioned at the start of this chapter: this time it proves to be the crack from which Keith is born in a bizarre nativity scene (Burns, "The End" [2-3]). The black hole is thus not only a gate to hell, but a gate to life, as Walton persuasively interprets it: "That sliver of light to which Keith is born is the black hole of the novel; it is the entirety of existence, the act of birth itself. [...] The 'blackness' of the black hole is, in actuality, the entirety of reality and light, where the desirable 'light' is the darkness and nothingness (absence of individual identity) within the womb" (532). This explains why the black hole in the beginning is paradoxically represented by a trace of white. From this perspective, the horror of the novel lies in the realm of life rather than in death, in being rather than in not-being, as one has to endure the growing pains of existence and "go through all this shit", as Keith puts it (Burns, "The End" [3]). Life presents us with torturing chaos and change, symbolized by the mutations as well as the constant garbage of broken things, another recurring image that also reappears in the dream and is already shown at the beginning of the chapter (Burns, "The End" [1 verso; 1]).

The nothingness of what is either death or the womb seems to promise the end of pain. In his first vision of things to come, Keith notices that "this totally black place [...] felt nice ... nice and safe" (Burns, "Biology 101" 6). The usual Gothic fear of darkness is inverted. A pervading ambivalence balances and mixes birth and death, darkness and light, innocence and experience. This ambiguity is even more pronounced in the second ending that Burns depicts, revealing Chris' fate. Whereas Keith and Eliza can face the trauma of growing up together, she is alone, mourning the loss of Rob. Her reaction seems to be regression (Collins and Hyacinth), swimming out into an ocean of blackness where "there's nothing left to be scared of" (Burns, "Summer Vacation" [27]), first in a dream, then in real life. She enjoys the feeling: "I'd stay out here forever if I could" (Burns, "The End" [41]). Yet, while her dream might indeed be regressive or escapist, its repetition in reality is "the beginning of her new life" (Wolk 341). While she contemplates putting an end to her pain – "I go through times when I just want to end it all. Be done with this life" – she immediately adds "... but then I look around and think, how could I give up all of this?" (Burns, "The End" [40]). It is the acceptance of life and adolescence, despite their frightful changes and the promise of further pain, with which Burns chooses to end his graphic novel. There is no certainty, granted, but the Gothic ambivalence appears less terrifying as new possibilities open up – for the Gothic adolescents as well as for the no longer adolescent Gothic graphic novel.

Works Cited

Arnold, Andrew D. "A Trip through a 'Black Hole.'" *Time Online*. 21 Oct. 2005. Web. 10 Nov. 2014.

Baker, Anthony D. "Black Hole." *Encyclopedia of Comic Books and Graphic Novels*. Ed. M. Keith Booker. Vol. 1. Santa Barbara, CA: Greenwood Press, 2010. 61-63.

Barker, Martin. *A Haunt of Fears: The Strange History of the British Horror Comics Campaign*. London: Pluto Press, 1984.

Bloom, Clive. "Introduction: Death's Own Backyard: The Nature of Modern Gothic and Horror Fiction." *Gothic Horror: A Guide for Students and Readers*. Ed. Clive Bloom. 2nd ed. Basingstoke: Palgrave Macmillan, 2007. 1-24.

Botting, Fred. "Aftergothic: Consumption, Machines, and Black Holes." *The Cambridge Companion to Gothic Fiction*. Ed. Jerrold E. Hogle. Cambridge: Cambridge University Press, 2002. 277-300.

---. *Gothic*. London: Routledge, 1996.

Burns, Charles. "Bag Action." *Black Hole* 4. Northampton, MA: Kitchen Sink Press, 1997.

---. "Biology 101." *Black Hole* 1. Northampton, MA: Kitchen Sink Press, 1995.

---. *Black Hole*. New York: Pantheon, 2005.

---. *Black Hole 1*. Northampton, MA: Kitchen Sink Press, 1995.

---. *Black Hole 2*. Northampton, MA: Kitchen Sink Press, 1995.

---. *Black Hole 12*. Seattle: Fantagraphics, 2004.

---. "Cook Out." *Black Hole* 5. Seattle: Fantagraphics, 1998.

---. "Cut." *Black Hole* 3. Northampton, MA: Kitchen Sink Press, 1996.

---. "A Dream Girl." *Black Hole* 10. Seattle: Fantagraphics, 2002.

---. "Driving South." *Black Hole* 11. Seattle: Fantagraphics, 2003.

---. "The End." *Black Hole* 12. Seattle: Fantagraphics, 2004.

---. "Lizard Queen." *Black Hole* 8. Seattle: Fantagraphics, 2000.

---. "Planet Xeno." *Black Hole* 1. Northampton, MA: Kitchen Sink Press, 1995.

---. "Racing Towards Something." *Black Hole* 2. Northampton, MA: Kitchen Sink Press, 1995.

---. "Seeing Double." *Black Hole* 5. Seattle: Fantagraphics, 1998.

---. "Sssssssss." *Black Hole* 1. Northampton, MA: Kitchen Sink Press, 1995.

---. "Summer Vacation." *Black Hole* 9. Seattle: Fantagraphics, 2001.

---. "Teen Plague." *Big Baby*. *RAW* 2.1. Ed. Kim Thompson. Seattle: Fantagraphics, 2010 [1989]. 41-62.

---. "Under Open Skies." *Black Hole* 7. Seattle: Fantagraphics, 2000.

---. "Who's Chris?" *Black Hole* 3. Northampton, MA: Kitchen Sink Press, 1996.

---. "Windowpane." *Black Hole* 6. Seattle: Fantagraphics, 1998.

Cavallaro, Dani. *The Gothic Vision: Three Centuries of Horror, Terror and Fear*. London: Continuum, 2002.

Collins, Sean. "Favorites: Black Hole." 23 February 2009. *The Savage Critic*. Web. 17 January 2011.

Collins, Sean, and Dick Hyacinth. "Best of the 00s/Favorites: Black Hole – a Discussion." 8 March 2009. *The Savage Critic*. Web. 17 January 2011.

Duncan, Randy. "Underground and Adult Comics." *Encyclopedia of Comic Books and Graphic Novels*. Ed. M. Keith Booker. Vol. 2. Santa Barbara, CA: Greenwood Press, 2010. 647-655.

Gravett, Paul. *Graphic Novels: Stories to Change Your Life*. London: Aurum, 2005.

Haggerty, George E. *Queer Gothic*. Urbana, IL: University of Illinois Press, 2006.

Hatfield, Charles. *Alternative Comics: An Emerging Literature*. Jackson: University Press of Mississippi, 2005.

Hignite, Todd. *In the Studio: Visits with Contemporary Cartoonists*. New Haven: Yale University Press, 2006.

Hurley, Kelly. *The Gothic Body: Sexuality, Materialism, and Degeneration at the Fin De Siècle*. Cambridge: Cambridge University Press, 1996.

---. "Reading Like an Alien: Posthuman Identity in Ridley Scott's *Alien* and David Cronenberg's *Rabid*." *Posthuman Bodies*. Eds. Judith Halberstam and Ira Livingston. Bloomington, IN: Indiana University Press, 1995. 203-224.

Hutchings, Peter. "Body Horror." *Historical Dictionary of Horror Cinema*. Lanham, MD: Scarecrow, 2008. 41.

Irons, Greg. "Introduction." *Skull* 1 (1970): 1.

Jameson, Fredric. *Postmodernism, or, the Cultural Logic of Late Capitalism*. London: Verso, 1991.

Lowther, John. "In *Black Hole*." *Zeitschrift für Anglistik und Amerikanistik* 59.1 (2011): 11-25.

Morgan, Jack. *The Biology of Horror: Gothic Literature and Film*. Carbondale, IL: Southern Illinois University Press, 2002.

Nyberg, Amy Kiste. *Seal of Approval: The History of the Comics Code*. Jackson: University Press of Mississippi, 1998.

Oppolzer, Markus. "Denied Rites of Passage: Social Puberty in the Gothic Novel." *Sozio-Kulturelle Metamorphosen*. Ed. Justin Stagl. Heidelberg: Winter, 2007. 175-186.

---. *Failed Rites of Passage in Early Gothic Fiction*. Frankfurt a.M.: Peter Lang, 2011.

Perna, Laura. "'There Was Something Screwy Going On …': The Uncanny in Charles Burns's Graphic Novel *Black Hole*." *The Birmingham Journal of Literature and Language* II (2009): 7-15.

Punter, David. *Gothic Pathologies: The Text, the Body, and the Law*. New York: St. Martin's Press, 1998.

---. *The Literature of Terror: A History of Gothic Fictions from 1765 to the Present Day*. 2nd ed. Vol. 2. New York: Longman, 1996.

Raney, Vanessa. Rev. of *Black Hole*. *ImageTexT: Interdisciplinary Comics Studies* 2.1 (2005). Web. 10 Nov. 2014.

Rosenkranz, Patrick. *Rebel Visions: The Underground Comix Revolution, 1963-1975*. Seattle: Fantagraphics, 2008.

Round, Julia. "'Is This a Book?': DC Vertigo and the Redefinition of Comics in the 1990s." *The Rise of the American Comics Artist: Creators and Contexts*. Eds. Paul Williams and James Lyons. Jackson: University Press of Mississippi, 2010. 14-30.

Sabin, Roger. *Comics, Comix & Graphic Novels*. London: Phaidon, 1996.

Smith, Andy W. "Gothic and the Graphic Novel." *The Routledge Companion to Gothic*. Eds. Catherine Spooner and Emma McEvoy. London: Routledge, 2007. 251-259.

Spooner, Catherine. *Contemporary Gothic*. London: Reaktion, 2006.

Walton, Peter. "The 'Archaic Mother' in Charles Burns' *Black Hole*: A Psychoanalytic Reading." *International Journal of Comic Art* 10.1 (2008): 522-534.

Witek, Joseph. *Comic Books as History: The Narrative Art of Jack Jackson, Art Spiegelman, and Harvey Pekar*. Jackson: University Press of Mississippi, 1989.

---. "Imagetext, or, Why Art Spiegelman Doesn't Draw Comics." *ImageTexT: Interdisciplinary Comics Studies* 1.1 (2004). Web. 10 Nov. 2014.

Wolk, Douglas. *Reading Comics: How Graphic Novels Work and What They Mean*. Cambridge, MA: Da Capo Press, 2007.

Zeigler, James. "Too Cruel: The Diseased Teens and Mean Bodies of Charles Burns's *Black Hole*." *SCAN: Journal of Media Arts Culture* 5.2 (2008). Web. 10 Nov. 2014.

Ellen Redling

Gothic Nightmares Then and Now: The Oneiric Descents in Edgar Allan Poe's Short Stories and Falling Dreams *ad extremum* in Christopher Nolan's Film *Inception*

The Gothic mode relies heavily on the evocation of primal and visceral fears in the recipients.[1] Gothic cinema can even augment such fears by bringing scary visions onto the screen, thus potentially rendering them more vivid and almost 'real'. As Kat Morris *et al.* make clear, at the beginning of American horror films in the 1930s, when many films "took their inspiration from gothic horror literature" a "new rating system was introduced [...] the 'H' rating for films labeled 'Horrific' for 'any films likely to frighten or horrify children under the age of 16 years'". Twenty-first century films keep to the idea of providing horrifying images and thus utilizing visuality in an effective way. Yet, they often seem to be less blunt, but rather more intricately psychological than the 1930s films, which in turn links them to deftly constructed older forms of the psychological Gothic.[2] For example, while the 1934 film *The Black Cat* bears the same title as Edgar Allan Poe's famous story, it really only superficially draws on it (Sova, *Edgar Allan Poe* 28), transforming Poe's subtle horror of 'interred' guilt haunting the protagonist into somewhat crude images of dead women openly displayed.

By contrast, recent films like Christopher Nolan's *Inception* from 2010 show a clearer indebtedness to older Gothic stories which are focused on the human psyche, despite the fact that there are no explicit intertextual

---

[1] As Fred Botting points out: "Through its presentations of supernatural, sensational and terrifying incidents, imagined or not, Gothic produced emotional effects on its readers rather than developing a rational or properly cultivated response. Exciting rather than informing, it chilled their blood, delighted their superstitious fancies and fed uncultivated appetites for marvellous and strange events [...]" (4).

[2] Gothic stories which display a major focus on psychological aspects in turn differ from yet earlier Gothic forms. As Dawn Sova makes clear, psychological Gothic is often thought to "depart from the usual gothic fare in its emphasis upon introspection rather than action and incident. The focus is placed on [...] perceptions and observations [...] rather than a crumbling castle or abbey" (*Critical Companion* 69).

references. *Inception* can, for instance, be compared to stories by Poe such as "A Descent into the Maelström" and "The Fall of the House of Usher" due to the various nightmarish falls and descents experienced by the protagonist Cobb in *Inception*, which point to a loss of control and breakdown of his mind.

Nevertheless, Nolan's methods do not represent carbon copies of older techniques; they rather transgress them and may thereby satisfy an ever growing "demand for more thrilling horrors" (Botting, "Candygothic" 135). As this article will demonstrate, Nolan's film increases the horror of the traditional psychological Gothic by employing various techniques. One of these is creating multiple levels of 'reality' rather than just two. Furthermore, Nolan uses the idea of a vivid nightmare *ad extremum*: the immense number of 'falling dreams' presented in his work go far beyond the instances of an oneiric fall or descent depicted in Poe's stories mentioned above. Nolan's work thereby has the ability to destabilize any potential feeling of security and clear vision on the part of the protagonist as well as the recipients to a much greater extent than traditional psychological Gothic did. As will be expounded, this ability is also due to *Inception*'s focus on *both* the psychological complexities of a human mind and the anxieties linked to an unstable modern-day business society; Poe's stories, by contrast, are predominately centred on a human psyche. Although Poe himself was indeed wary "of the corrupting influence of materialism" (Galloway xxiii) and may have inserted this wariness into his stories, he probably did not foresee the fearful heights – and downfalls – which materialism can reach in our current day and age.

I. Gothic Nightmares

To early critical readers of the Gothic in the 1930s, the mode in its entirety seemed to constitute what Herbert Read later described as "dream literature" (viii) or Elizabeth MacAndrew called "literature of nightmare" (3).[3] One look at Mary Shelley's introduction to her own

---

[3] In the early to mid-twentieth century some critics even regarded a vast majority of literary works – not just Gothic works – as closely resembling dreams. David Rein, for instance, not only states that "literary creations such as Poe's are essentially like dreams" (367), but also says – much more generally – that "storytelling, like dreams, may reflect the teller's deepest feelings" (368). Such a

Gothic novel *Frankenstein* might seem to substantiate Read's and MacAndrew's theses. She here describes having been inspired to write down her work by a vivid nightmare: "I saw – with shut eyes, but acute mental vision – I saw the pale student of unhallowed arts kneeling beside the thing he had put together [...]. I opened [my eyes] in terror" (9). She also states that she hopes to frighten the reader with her work just as she was scared by this vision (9). The work is therefore directly compared to a nightmare.

In the 1930s positing such a general oneiric quality of Gothic literature was aimed at clearly setting the mode off from both realism in a very broad sense and from materialistic rationalism. As Chris Baldick and Robert Mighall explain:

> Gothic Criticism emerged from the uneasy confluence of two antithetical strands of modern romanticism in the 1930s: on the one side the reactionary medievalism of the eccentric bibliophile and vampirologist Montague Summers, and on the other the revolutionary modernism of André Breton, leader of the surrealists. Although clearly situated at opposite ends of the political spectrum, they both inherit a certain common romantic assumption that 'dream' or fantasy is in itself the deadly enemy of bourgeois materialistic rationalism. (211)

The main problem that Baldick and Mighall perceive regarding such an emphasis on a dream-based essence of the mode is that it can obstruct an analysis of immediate "historical, cultural, and religious implications of the Gothic" (211). Indeed, if one examines MacAndrew's elaboration on Gothic fiction as a 'literature of nightmare' in greater detail, it becomes clear that both the establishment of a link to medieval literature and the critical interest in the subconscious and the surreal, which was due to the discoveries of Freud, can have the effect of blocking out anything that is particular as well as culturally relevant about the Gothic mode. MacAndrew writes:

> Among [the Gothic's] conventions are found dream landscapes and figures of the subconscious imagination. Its fictional world gives form to amorphous fears and impulses, common to all

---

type of interest in dreams, however, appears to merely serve to justify a biographical approach, since to Rein Poe's stories directly reflect the author's very own dreams (368-371).

mankind, using an amalgam of materials, some torn from the author's own subconscious mind and some the stuff of myth, folklore, fairy tale, and romance. It conjures up beings – mad monks, vampires, and demons – and settings – forbidding cliffs and glowering buildings, stormy seas and the dizzying abyss – that have literary significance and the properties of dream symbolism as well. (3)

However, rather than seeing the dream quality as all-encompassing and as hindering a historical or cultural analysis, one could examine Gothic works in which dreams or nightmares seem to play a special role and where they signal both timeless fears as well as time-bound ones.

A particular kind of nightmare, the so-called 'falling dream', in which the dreamer pictures himself or herself falling down in his or her dream and usually wakes up because of this frightening experience, seems to fit the label of a 'Gothic dream' through the ages very well since it is typically associated with vulnerability, loss of control and fear of dying. It can also be linked to the fall of Lucifer, Adam and Eve's fall from grace, the apocryphal story of Christ's 'Harrowing of Hell', Dante's *Inferno* and the numerous tales of journeys into the underworld that can be found in ancient mythology. Falls in Gothic works appear, for instance, in Matthew Lewis' *The Monk* and E. T. A. Hoffmann's *The Devil's Elixirs*, where they allude directly to the fall of Lucifer.[4] It is the connection to the underworld and to hell which renders the fall *per se* a particularly Gothic motif, which in turn seems to question any kind of delimitation of the Gothic in terms of temporal boundaries.

The fall as part of a nightmarish vision can be regarded as a special case of falling and will need to be looked at in more detail. Edgar Allan Poe makes extensive use of the falling nightmare – especially in his short stories "A Descent into the Maelström" and "The Fall of the House of Usher". Again it could be argued that the falling dream and the fall evoke timeless fears in the characters and readers which are due to a long tradition of Western religion, literature and culture. This tradition in turn may have led to changes in Western cognition – to the overall perception of a downward movement as being detrimental to a human being. The following contrastive list of conceptual metaphors which George Lakoff

---

[4] Concerning the fall as a general Gothic motif please also see Erik Redling's article in this volume.

and Mark Johnson establish in their seminal work *Metaphors We Live By* is insightful here:

HAPPY IS UP; SAD IS DOWN […]

CONSCIOUS IS UP; UNCONSCIOUS IS DOWN […]

HEALTH AND LIFE ARE UP; SICKNESS AND DEATH ARE DOWN […]

HAVING CONTROL or FORCE IS UP; BEING SUBJECT TO CONTROL or FORCE IS DOWN […]

[…]

GOOD IS UP; BAD IS DOWN […]

VIRTUE IS UP; DEPRAVITY IS DOWN. (15-16)

Despite this general cognitive framework it will be demonstrated that the potential scariness of Edgar Allan Poe's stories does not merely rely on timeless fears evoked by these falling nightmares, but is directly related to contemporary theories of the sublime and Poe's interest in madness.

Furthermore, I would like to suggest that the falling dream appears to especially touch the nerve of people living in twenty-first-century Western societies, since it can be linked to the famous 9/11-photograph by Associated Press photographer Richard Drew, the so-called 'Falling Man' photo, which depicts a man jumping from the World Trade Center.

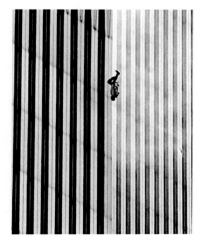

Fig. 1 World Trade Centre Jumper © 2001; Richard Drew/AP

What is more, with the image comes the knowledge that soon after this leap the entire World Trade Center was to fall down as well. In this photograph as well as in collective memory a nightmare is shown to be happening in real life. As Laura Frost writes, "this, of the many upsetting images from the day, had a lasting traumatic effect on some viewers" (180).

Present-day popular culture also utilizes the terrifying image of the 'Falling Man'. This can be seen, for instance, in the current American series *Mad Men*, which in its opening credits and on one of its posters presents a cartoonized version of the main protagonist, Don Draper, falling down from a high office building.[5] One could interpret this scene as signalling his psychological as well as professional descent, i.e. failures both in his personal life and in the modern business world which followed upon the heels of his enormous success. The series is set in the 1960s and not in the twenty-first century. However, it displays the growth of the world of big-money advertizing and thus the beginnings of extremely consumerist Western societies. This is a world in which success might not last long and jobs are highly insecure. The series as such is surely not 'Gothic', but it employs the image of a – living – nightmare that is often used in Gothic works and connects it to the vagaries of the modern world and to the terrifying 9/11 'Falling Man' photo.

As I will argue, the falling dreams displayed in Christopher Nolan's Gothic film *Inception* tap into similar fears of the current age. Thus, rather than standing for anti-materialism and an a-historical as well as a-cultural perspective that both Read's and MacAndrew's readings of Gothic literature might imply, the dreams in Nolan's work can be interpreted as directly reflecting contemporary cultural debates and anxieties. Through this link to current issues and its use of nightmares *ad extremum* Nolan's film goes beyond older Gothic works such as Poe's and thereby tests and transgresses Gothic strategies of the past. Nevertheless, Gothic falling dreams then and now do share some common ground, since the dreams portrayed in Poe's stories are also not completely a-historical, being closely connected to theoretical debates on the sublime, a thriving concept in eighteenth as well as early nineteenth-century Gothic.

---

[5] Regarding *Mad Men* and the 'Falling Man' photo please also confer Junod.

II. Descents and Falls in Poe's Nightmarish Gothic Works

Various critics have looked at the sublime in Poe's short stories such as "A Descent into the Maelström" and "The Fall of the House of Usher",[6] and madness seems to be an obvious topic in many of his works. Both stories present potentially insane characters and the former story creates a sublime image of a mountain and a thunderous whirl; the latter story even directly mentions the "sublime" (90). However, so far no link has been established between these two areas of research and the concept of a 'falling dream', which plays a particularly large role in these two stories.

The sublime can interestingly include the act of looking down at something – like the Maelström or the House of Usher – in awe. As the ancient Roman philosopher Lucretius, whose works immensely influenced notions of the sublime in the eighteenth and nineteenth centuries,[7] expounds, the danger can lurk *sub pedibus*, i.e. 'beneath [our] feet'. He paints a picture of a fearful abyss and the ruin of the world:

> […] let [common folk] believe as they will that heaven and earth will be indestructible, entrusted to everlasting safety; and yet from time to time the very present force of danger applies from somewhere this prick of fear, lest the earth should be snatched away suddenly from beneath their feet (*pedibus … subtracta*) and be borne into the abyss (*in barathrum*), and the sum of things, left utterly without foundation (*prodita … funditus*), should follow on, and the world should end in a confused ruin. (qtd. in Porter 171-172)

In a similar destructive vein, madness is often associated with a downward movement – a fall into madness. Thus, as will be shown, a falling dream in these stories can foreshadow and emblematize these sublime and mad falls.

In Edgar Allan Poe's short story "A Descent into the Maelström" a young man is led towards the edge of a high cliff on Mount Helseggen in Norway by an old-looking man, who is a fisherman. From a distance they gaze down upon the sea, which is beginning to show signs of the formation of a large whirl, the Maelström. The old man calls the place on which they are standing a "little cliff" (177), while the young man is

---

[6] Confer, for example, Hobby and Ljungquist.
[7] See, for instance, Janowitz.

terrified of approaching its edge any further and of the idea of losing his ground. Shortly after, however, the young man agrees to taking a closer look and watches dizzily how "[i]n five minutes the whole sea [...] was lashed into ungovernable fury" (179). The sea becomes a roaring monster, "heaving, boiling, hissing" (179) and displaying "streaks of foam" (179), which is reminiscent of a rabid animal. The young man's terror increases. He feels the mountain "tremble [...]" (180) and holds on to the herbage surrounding him, afraid of falling down into the "mouth of the terrific funnel" (180).

Later in the story it can be inferred that the old fisherman took the young man to this precise spot in order to let the latter relive the fear that he himself had felt while actually being drawn into the Maelström three years earlier and to thus enable him to give credit to the older man's tale. Convincing the young man is crucial to the old fisherman since he had already told his story once before and was not believed then (193). Throughout his tale the older man, who only looks old because of what he has lived through (177), draws attention to the similarity of their situation on top of the cliff at this particular moment and his own fear while being sucked into the whirl. For example, he explains: "*as you saw yourself*, the belt of surf is considerably lower than the general bed of the ocean, and this latter now towered above us, a high, black, mountainous ridge" (188; emphasis added). The older man wants the younger one to see what he saw, and to experience what he experienced. Naturally, this cannot be fully realized since the danger the older man was in "three years past" (177) was much greater; this is probably why he refers to the cliff as "little" earlier on. On the other hand, the distance from the Maelström and therefore comparative safety of the young man can add pleasure to this dangerous situation. As the eighteenth-century French writer Jean-Baptiste Dubos explains in his *Critical Reflections on Poetry, Painting and Music*, which had a great influence on the aesthetic theories of emotion by Shaftesbury, Francis Hutcheson and Edmund Burke:

> `Tis this very attractive which makes us fond of the disquiets and alarms, occasioned by the perils which we see other men exposed to, whilst we are exempt ourselves from danger. `Tis pleasant, says Lucretius, to behold from the seashore, a vessel struggling with the waves which are just ready to swallow it up. (11)

A certain distance from immediate danger may render it pleasurable. The *readers* of Poe's story are, however, *twice* removed from the older man's experience. They neither were present "three years past" (Poe, "Descent" 177) nor are they there now, standing on top of the cliff like the young man, watching the monstrous sea. The trick which is therefore employed is to connect the old man's feelings while being sucked into the Maelström as well as the young man's sensations with the general human experience of a frightening falling dream. The older man relates: "And then down we came with a sweep, a slide, and a plunge, that made me feel sick and dizzy, *as if I was falling from some lofty mountain-top in a dream*" (187; emphasis added). Since they are standing on a mountain-top, the older man is implicitly linking the actual situation of the younger man with the well-known nightmare and vice versa – as the young man finds himself in a living nightmare. Reality and dream thereby become interchangeable and the readers – by being reminded of this well-known, terrifying nightmare – can be transported in their imagination into the situation of the younger man. Thus, they can get closer to the older man's experience, while yet retaining the same distance that the young man has.

Instead of suggesting an opposition to reality, the falling dream – the beginning of which is acted out by the young man standing on the cliff – is thereby meant to give the readers access to direct and real emotions. It serves to convey a feeling of the sublime, a tension of the fibres which Edmund Burke describes as a sensation of both "terrors" and "curiosity" (191) in the face of something of "terrific grandeur" that takes you on the "pathway between Time and Eternity" (190).[8] This is a feeling which – as the young man in Poe's story puts it – no rational explanation, no book or "school-master" (Poe, "Descent" 192) can completely evoke or clarify.[9]

---

[8] Confer Edmund Burke's linking of "the modes of astonishment or admiration and those of terror" (54) as well as his analysis of the sublime and infinity: "But let it be considered that hardly any thing can strike the mind with its greatness, which does not make some sort of approach towards infinity; which nothing can do whilst we are able to perceive its bounds" (58).

[9] Interestingly, the narrator in another of Poe's short stories, "The Imp of the Perverse", reflects on a fall, connects desire and fear – Burke's astonishment/admiration and terror – to it, and also argues that these feelings are opposed to reason: "We stand upon the brink of a precipice. […]. And because our reason violently deters us from the brink, *therefore* do we the most impetuously approach it. There is no passion in nature so demoniacally impatient, as that of him who, shuddering upon the edge of a precipice, thus meditates a plunge" (273-274; emphasis in the original). However, here the narrator does not link this

The crucial idea which the young man elaborates on twice is that you actually have to be there, i.e. close to the Maelström, to know what it looks and feels like. He points out that

> [t]he ordinary accounts of this vortex had by no means prepared me for what I saw. That of Jonas Ramus [...] cannot impart the faintest conception either of the magnificence, or of the horror of the scene – or of the wild bewildering sense of *the novel* which confounds the beholder. I am not sure from what point of view the writer in question surveyed it, nor at what time; but it could neither have been from the summit of Helseggen, nor during a storm. (180; emphasis in the original)

The definitions which the *Encyclopædia Britannica* offers are similarly "unintelligible, and even absurd, amid the thunder of the abyss" (Poe, "Descent" 182). A greater vision or emotional insight – rather than literal understanding – therefore only works via the 'real' sublime experience or – in the absence of this direct access to the Maelström – via the falling nightmare. To the readers, the dream thus interestingly opens the door to the old man's terrifying reality.

With the falling dream, Poe's story draws on a nightmare which many humans can relate to in some way or another. Either they have already experienced it themselves or they have heard about it. In contrast to mere bad dreams that do not awaken the sleeper, nightmares are usually "characterized by powerful emotion" (Hartmann 64) and defined as "long, frightening dreams leading to an awakening that generally turn out to come from long REM periods late in the night" (Hartmann 64). Recent empirical evidence suggests that the specific falling nightmare might not appear often in a person's life, but if it does it constitutes one of the most "particularly intense, unusual, or otherwise salient nightmares" (Robert and Zadra 410). This is why the theme of falling is "among the most frequently reported themes in studies based on questionnaire or interview data" (Robert and Zadra 410). As popular dream websites such as *dreammoods.com* point out, falling dreams are commonly associated with "an indication of insecurities, instabilities, and anxieties. You are feeling overwhelmed and out of control in some situation in your waking life".[10]

---

fall to a dream but uses this example of a 'perversity' of sensation – he feels both desire and fear – to excuse the crime of murder which he committed.

[10] Sigmund Freud, of course, had his own, narrow explanation regarding falling

The falling nightmare in "A Descent into the Maelström" is not really used to point to a general sense of loss of control. It is rather employed to emotionally involve the reader in an experience of the sublime in the face of a potential fall into infinity. However, the descent could also signal a metaphorical 'fall' into madness on the part of the old fisherman. As the readers learn early on, the fisherman has aged significantly during the three years after the incident. Furthermore, other fishermen did not believe that he actually survived the Maelström. Thus, the old man might in fact be a madman and thus a so-called 'unreliable narrator'.[11] However, the readers will never find out for certain. This topic of a metaphorical 'descent' of the mind is only touched upon in this story, as the sensations of fear and wonder *per se* seem more important than other features that are potentially connected to them. However, in Poe's short story "The Fall of the House of Usher", the crumbling of the mind actually becomes the main theme.

"The Fall of the House of Usher", unlike "A Descent into the Maelström", does not explicitly reference the 'falling dream'. However, dreaming can be regarded as one of the major topics of this story. As David Saliba has pointed out, the main setting of the story as such can be seen to represent a "dreaming mind" (165); the crumbling "House of Usher", which belongs to the narrator's friend Roderick Usher, can stand for a psyche falling apart.[12] However, the fall does not just begin at the point when the narrator enters the house of his friend, that is when he is confronted with the problematic psyche of Roderick, who summoned him

---

dreams and a loss of control, linking such dreams to the act of giving in to an erotic temptation – predominantly on the part of women (386). He also connected them to childhood games like see-saw, which according to him reappear in darker and more frightening forms in the dreams of adults and also have sexual connotations (275-276).

[11] An 'unreliable narrator' is a narrator who, generally speaking, loses credibility either because of his/her lying, madness, downright immorality or mere naïvety. For an overview of the concept, please see Nünning's article "Unreliable Narration zur Einführung: Grundzüge einer kognitiv-narratologischen Theorie und Analyse unglaubwürdigen Erzählens". The most well-known example of unreliable narration in Poe can be found in his story "The Tell-Tale Heart" (see Nünning 5). Regarding paradoxical narrative authority in "A Descent into the Maelström" please also confer Person.

[12] See, for example, Martindale, who argues that "the house symbolizes a psyche in the process of disintegration" (10).

there because he needed his help. It begins earlier on – with a frightening vision which the narrator himself has while standing *outside* the house. When he looks at the "bleak walls" and the "vacant eye-like windows" (Poe, "Fall" 90) of the house, he becomes afflicted with "an utter depression of soul which I can compare to no earthly sensation more properly than to the *afterdream* of the reveller upon opium – the bitter *lapse into everyday life* – the hideous dropping off of the veil" (Poe, "Fall" 90; emphasis added). Interestingly, his use of the words "afterdream" and "lapse into everyday life" could signal that he is currently in a state of dreaming, but afraid of being confronted with reality – scared of waking up into the terrible afterdream of everyday life. The gloom of the house seems too bitterly real to him and its closeness oppresses him. He seeks relief by looking for a higher position, that is a place from which he arguably has a more sublime view:[13] "I reined my horse to the precipitous brink of a black and lurid tarn that lay in unruffled lustre by the dwelling, and gazed down – but with a shudder even more thrilling than before – upon the remodelled and inverted images of the grey sedge, and the ghastly tree-stems, and the vacant and eye-like windows" (Poe, "Fall" 91). To his dismay, he subsequently has to leave this position of "thrilling" distance, descend and enter the house – a fall which leads him closer to bitter reality again. Thus, one could argue that from the beginning of the story, the setting is indeed that of a 'dreaming mind', but that it is really the narrator who is dreaming and that he is in effect having a falling nightmare;[14] he is afraid of the fall since this would mean waking up and being confronted with his own madness in real life. His own fear of falling or descending into madness finds its window-like reflection in the descent of Usher's mind – which he is now about to witness in his nightmare. However, the narrator most likely wishes the recipient to believe that only Usher is mad in order to not have to deal with his own problems.

---

[13] He notices earlier that there is nothing sublime about his initial impression of the house: "There was an iciness, a sinking, a sickening of the heart – an unredeemed dreariness of thought which no goading of the imagination could torture into aught of the sublime" (90). This is why he then seeks to gain another perspective on the house.

[14] John Hammond has pointed out that "[t]his tale [...] is in a sense a dream of the narrator's" (73), but does not go into much detail and does not link this observation to a falling dream.

Just before entering Usher's house, the narrator shifts the focus away from his personal feelings to his friend's illness. He is there, as he reminds himself, to help his friend through the "cheerfulness of [his] society" (91). The narrator emphatically busies himself with "[s]haking off from my spirit what *must* have been a dream" (92; emphasis in the original) in order to get a clearer impression of the house. The readers are thereby most likely led to believe that the narrator – upon stepping inside the house – is perfectly awake and sane, while Usher is the one who is benighted. Through the use of rational language (Sova, *Critical Companion* 69), the narrator gives himself the air of a trustworthy scientist or doctor coming to the aid of his suffering friend. He even describes the appearance of his friend down to the tiniest details.

However, the narrator's fall into madness is inevitable, and due to the concomitant discrepancy of this development with his supposed role as an objective, "scrutinising observer" (Poe, "Fall" 93) he can also be regarded as an 'unreliable narrator'. In fact, in the course of the story he comes 'closer and closer' to Usher,[15] which marks his own descent. He turns from witnessing Usher's madness to experiencing it directly together with him. The increased blending of the two minds becomes palpable when the narrator suddenly sees Usher's sister Madeline at the precise moment in which his friend starts speaking about her. As Usher explains, Madeline is severely ill and he is terribly afraid of losing her since she is his "'sole companion'" (96). For a while her name is not mentioned – i.e. one can say that she is only latently there – and Usher has a surge of creativity, painting, reading and writing wildly.[16] Again, the narrator is convinced that this situation resembles a dream, but is not itself a dream – "I listened, *as if in a dream*, to the wild improvisations of

---

[15] See the narrator's comment: "And thus, a closer and closer intimacy admitted me more unreservedly into the recesses of his spirit […]" (97).

[16] Lynne P. Shackelford explains that the comparison which the narrator makes between Usher and the eighteenth-century painter John Henry Fuseli is of great importance here, since "[t]he work upon which Fuseli's fame rests and the work which Poe evokes in his tale is *The Nightmare*" (19), in which the artist "depict[s] a general rather than an individual experience of the bad dream" (19). Shackelford suggests that the narrator has a nightmare at the end of the story which resembles the painting. However, as I show in this article, the narrator can be said to have a nightmare – to be precise, a falling nightmare – from the beginning onwards.

his speaking guitar" (97; emphasis added) – and thereby most likely deludes himself. Shortly afterwards, the narrator finds out that Madeline has died and helps his friend bury her in a vault. What he is not aware of is that they buried her alive; she comes back to haunt them by making "low and indefinite sounds" (104). The narrator, who cannot decipher the meaning of this, once more tries to "[s]hake off" (103) this "incubus" (103). He aims to calm his extremely "agitated" (105) friend down by reading a story to him. However, the noises appearing within the tale are eerily echoed by sounds created by Madeline and the tale is broken off. By now the narrator has himself become "[c]ompletely unnerved" (107) and Usher reveals, screaming wildly: "'*We have put her living in the tomb!* [...] MADMAN! I TELL YOU THAT SHE NOW STANDS WITHOUT THE DOOR!'" (108; emphasis in the original). Importantly, the exclamation "MADMAN!" is ambiguous – Usher is either referring to himself or to the narrator. Madeline's ghost, who now appears and could represent not just a guilt that lies in the past but the disease of the madness *per se* which both he and Usher tried in vain to get rid of, now quite literally befalls her brother and kills him – "she [...] *fell* heavily inward *upon* the person of her brother [...] and [...] *bore him to the floor* a corpse" (108; emphasis added) – thereby carrying the fall of Usher out in front of the narrator's eyes. The narrator, who now takes to flight, then witnesses the complete downfall of the house of Usher.

Due to the final unity established by the word "MADMAN" and its double point of reference, the narrator has seen both Usher's and his own descent – despite the fact that he himself still links all the events to Usher only. Those readers who also merely focus on Usher could feel relieved that the latter has died and that this mad occurrence is now over. But this sense of security might be deceptive,[17] as the ending leaves the narrator in the state of a nightmarish vision – "the deep and dank tarn at my feet closed sullenly and silently over the fragments of the 'HOUSE OF USHER'" (109). One could argue that the narrator has still not realized that *he* is the one who is mad and who has just had a falling dream but has not awoken from it. The both pleasurable and terrifying sublime has been replaced by an endless nightmare, as the tarn at whose brink he stood at the beginning of the story is now "at [his] feet".

---

[17] Confer Sova: "The end of the standard gothic tale brings resolution [...]. The end of 'The Fall of the House of Usher' serves no such purpose. Instead, it raises questions that can never be answered [...]" (*Critical Companion* 69).

III. Falling Dreams on Multiple Levels of 'Reality' in Christopher Nolan's *Inception*

In terms of the usage and meaning of a falling dream, "The Fall of the House of Usher" displays a greater intricacy than "A Descent into the Maelström". However, both stories serve as fruitful points of comparison for Christopher Nolan's *Inception*, which yet again increases the psychological complexity through its large number of falling dreams and the great multitude of levels of 'reality'. Other Gothic films dealing with falling nightmares and a crumbling psyche – such as the famous Hitchcock film *Vertigo* from 1958 and Martin Scorsese's 2010 movie *Shutter Island* – do not portray such a large number of dreams and levels, which is why they were not chosen for this analysis of the transgression of the limits of older Gothic methods. It is most likely that it is *Inception*'s emphasis on both a human mind *and* the modern unstable business world which complicates and transgresses the strategies employed by other works that almost solely focus on a person's mind. In *Inception* the world of finance and corporate spying becomes directly intertwined with the dream world(s), which also adds action to traditional psychological strategies.

The most important fall in Nolan's film is that of Cobb's, the protagonist's, wife Mal to her death, which, as the viewer learns towards the latter part of the film, occurred in the recent past and was witnessed by him. He recalls finding himself in a hotel room, prepared to celebrate their anniversary there together just as they had done for years, only to look out across the street to see his wife about to jump from the opposite window. She is convinced that the world in which they are living is not real and that she needs to kill herself in order to end up in real life. Cobb is unable to convince her that she is currently in the real world and that she would actually die were she to leap, leaving him and their two children behind. In this scene he even climbs out of the window himself, sits on the window sill just like she is doing across the street and tries to prevent her from jumping, while she insists that they need to take the leap together. The perilous situation high up in the air is reminiscent of the location of the two men in "A Descent into the Maelström" and can in a like manner create both fear and awe in the viewer of the film. With every leap in the film, which to some extent resembles Mal's fatal leap on various dream levels, this feeling can be evoked again and again.

The reason Mal's belief in the world's illusory nature is so strong is that some time ago Cobb implanted an idea in her subconscious – namely that the world which she is living in is not real – while they were indeed living in a dream world and she was initially unwilling to return to reality. What he did not foresee was that Mal could never get rid of this idea, no matter which world they inhabited – whether it was a dream sphere or the real world. It became an *idée fixe*.

Mal's fall initiates a trauma of grief and guilt that heavily influences Cobb's life and his work. As an 'extractor' of secret corporate infor- mation from a person's mind it is his job to go down into the subcon- scious of this person while he or she is sedated. Parallel to this invasion of another person's mind, however, he is inadvertently also moving further into his own. This parallel movement brings to mind that the narrator in "The Fall of the House of Usher" thinks it is his task to discover what is wrong with his friend, while he is really delving into his own psyche. In both cases one could argue that this task is similar to that of a psychiatrist 'invading' the subconscious of a patient– with Poe and Nolan, however, there is an additional twist as the psychiatrist turns out to be the patient.[18]

The dream world in which Cobb operates becomes peopled not only with subjects thought up by the dreamer, but also with Cobb's own visions, 'projections', of his wife and children. As in "The Fall of the House of Usher" the two minds – i.e. the target mind and the protagonist's mind – become blended. The 'projection' of the wife is similar to Madeline's sudden appearance in Poe's story. Cobb's task does not divert his attention away from his trauma, but rather aggravates it, which is reminiscent of the failure of Poe's narrator to concentrate solely on his friend's troubles. However, Cobb's situation seems even worse than that of his earlier counterpart since he knows that he is in a dream world and is aware that in order to wake up from a dream, a fall is needed within this subconscious world. Cobb thus constantly needs to 'consciously' enact versions of his own wife's death himself, i.e. initiate and carry out

---

[18] As Graham Clarke clarifies regarding *Inception*, "In many ways these processes, of 'extraction' and 'inception', are paranoid fears long associated with psychoanalysis. You can have your best-kept secrets, or your creativity, stolen by the analyst, or the analyst can coerce you into thinking something that you did not think before, by operating directly on your unconscious mind" (203).

falling nightmares, in order to return to 'reality'. Poe's narrator, by contrast, becomes only partially aware of the need for the fall and its implications. He knows he will be confronted with gloom if he leaves his elevated, sublime position and enters the house of Usher, but he is not conscious of the fact that it is his own depression he is faced with.

Cobb's psychological situation becomes even more difficult when he is on a new mission. The businessman Saito puts pressure on him to implant – instead of extract – an idea in the mind of Saito's major rival, Robert Fischer, a thought which will lead to the loss of the rival company's monopoly on the energy market. Although the viewer is not aware of this at the beginning of the film, Cobb's act of implanting an idea in Fischer's mind is the exact replica of what he – Cobb – did to his wife years ago. The protagonist is thereby getting closer and closer to his original guilt. However, only by completing this mission will Cobb be able to buy back his status of legal innocence regarding the murder of his wife, for which he is being charged, and only thereby will he see his children again. But while he has the goal of a cleared legal file in sight, his own sense of guilt is still very much present, and the implantation process sets in motion multiple falling dreams on numerous dream levels.

In order to place the idea very deep into Fischer's subconscious and thereby make him believe that it is really his own thought and not an artificial one, Cobb will need to go down three dream levels. Another level will be added to this later on – dream level 4, also known as 'limbo'. Voicing his disappointment, Blogger Carl Neville describes the four levels as follows: "Level one dream is basically The Bourne Identity [...] rainy, grey, urban. Level two is the Matrix, zero gravity fistfights in a modernist hotel, level three, depressingly turns out to be a Seventies Bond film while the raw Id is basically just a collapsing cityscape". In a similar vein, Mark Fisher has lamented the fact that the dream levels merely resemble the levels found in videogames. However, these findings could also be read differently. To me, the allusions to other films and videogames seem to be deftly chosen to show the way popular culture and materialism have become so closely intertwined with the psyche that they cannot be torn apart anymore. What it all comes down to is the modern business world represented by the cityscape on level 4, which has disturbingly invaded the core of the psyche and – through its own collapse – is connected to the downfall of the psyche. Furthermore, the crumbling skyscrapers may eerily call to mind the terrorist attacks of 9/11.

This introduction of the viewer to the levels constitutes the point at which the experience of following the plot can start to get ever more complicated for the spectators. While the readers of Poe's "The Fall of the House of Usher" are only confronted with the problem of deciding if what is happening is part of a dream or belongs to 'reality', the viewers of *Inception* are faced with four dream levels and – perhaps – one 'real' one, that is five levels in total. Cobb puts together a team to help him navigate Fischer's mind. His main assistant is the dream architect Ariadne, who designs the dream spaces.

The difficulty with these spaces is that even after they have been laid out, they can constantly and unexpectedly change. For example, they are subject to ripple effects from dream spaces that are further up. When Yusuf, the driver of a van that transports the sleepers including Cobb on dream level 1, initiates the fall of the van which is needed to wake them by driving it off a bridge, gravity is lost on level 2, leaving Arthur, another member of the team, wonder how to make the sleepers on *this* level fall.[19] As the critic Ian Paul argues, such interconnections can be read according to Gilles Deleuze and Felix Guattari's theory of the rhizome, "with multiple beginnings and ends and without clear separation".[20] To complicate the navigation among the spaces even more, they are either destroyed or self-destruct shortly before a return to a dream level that is further up or to the 'real' world. They thereby become increasingly hostile to the dreamer, threatening to push him out. The sudden eerie changes occurring on the various dream levels are similar to what happens in "The Fall of the House of Usher" – for example, when Madeline echoes sounds that belong to the story the narrator is reading out loud to Usher. However, Poe does not establish numerous levels

---

[19] Only simultaneous falls on all dream levels supposedly lead back to the level of 'reality'.

[20] Ian Paul does not go into any further detail, but the reference to Deleuze and Guattari's theory of the rhizome is crucial since this theory entails a departure from older, orderly and hierarchical systems of reality towards a rhizomatic undoing of such an order: "unlike trees or their roots, the rhizome connects any point to any other point, and its traits are not necessarily linked to traits of the same nature" (Deleuze and Guattari 1605). The dream levels in *Inception* become similarly interlinked, which destabilizes their seemingly strict hierarchy.

between which ripple effects could take place. As the story is written, these effects most likely occur on one and the same dream level, while Nolan orchestrates a complex 'Cob(b)web'[21] of intersecting levels.

Importantly, Nolan did not adapt his film from any previously existing novel but instead wrote directly for the screen, having all the filmic means, particularly the visual effects, in mind.[22] He thus creates impressive dream spaces in which the laws of gravity are frequently suspended – such as a vision of Paris, "where the city literally rolls back on itself like a roll of linoleum tile" (Ebert). Mark Fisher uses this scene to criticize that the dreams in *Inception* are *"undreamlike"* (emphasis in the original) and fail to be "uncanny" since Ariadne is "behaving more like the CGI engineer who's creating the scene than any dreamer". It is true that *Inception* does not present the dreams as blurry images as one would find in Hitchcock's *Vertigo*; nor does it use surreal effects like the ones employed in Hitchcock's *Spellbound*, which were designed by Salvador Dalí. However, I would argue that uncanniness in *Inception* is precisely evoked by linking the modern business world or even film industry to the dreams themselves and thus destabilizing any potential opposition between business – or outer world – on the one hand and the human psyche – or inner world – on the other.

Another extraordinary image is that of the protagonist and Ariadne "standing between two large mirrors where they see their reflections echo into infinity on either side. The mirrors then shatter and vanish only to

---

[21] Cobb, the name of the protagonist, might refer to a spider, which in a now obsolete English form was called "cob" (see *OED*), since he originally also worked as a dream architect alongside being a dream extractor and thus built complex dream labyrinths or webs in order to catch his prey – i.e. to discover corporate secrets. One could argue that he increasingly gets caught up himself in these webs.

[22] Other recent films such as Martin Scorsese's *Shutter Island* from 2010 similarly focus on the eerie psyche of the protagonist and also depict the breakdown of the latter's mind, blurring the boundaries between 'reality' and imagination or dreams. However, Scorsese's film does not make as much use of immense visual effects and an extreme number of elaborately drawn levels. In terms of eeriness it arguably outdoes the eponymous novel by Dennis Lehane which it is based on through its frightening music score and film-noir effects, but it does not reach the visual complexity of *Inception* – perhaps because the story was not first and foremost conceived to be viewed rather than read.

reveal a street that they begin to traverse" (Paul). To Paul, this image depicts the "idea of the multiple and layered reality" presented in the film, and he connects it to Jean Baudrillard's metaphor in *Simulacra and Simulation* of the actual world and a map of it becoming indistinguishable from each other. This metaphor points to a state of 'hyperreality', i.e. a "model [...] of a real without origin or reality" (Baudrillard 365). However, the mirrors might also signal the fusion of various minds and identities depicted in the film and can be compared to the eye-windows in "The Fall of the House of Usher", which have a both outward – mirror-like reflection – and inward quality – seeing what is inside – to them. Again, the sense of infinity conveyed in *Inception* exceeds the two-sidedness of "The Fall of the House of Usher".

The destruction of the dream spaces before awakening – for instance, the above-mentioned roll-back of 'Paris' – is reminiscent of the downfall of the house of Usher, signalling in each case the disintegration of the protagonist's psyche. However, Nolan includes numerous destructions and comes up with ever new ideas of how they take place. For instance, on dream level 3 an avalanche comes down and on level 4 skyscrapers fall apart.

As the film progresses, Cobb and his team are intruding further and further into Fischer's mind. However, since Cobb himself is preoccupied by his own subconscious, his own imaginations of his wife and children crowd in on the scene, which also alters the dream space. As has been mentioned further above, Fischer's and Cobb's subconscious thus eerily flow together. Mal – or rather the projection of Mal created by Cobb's psyche – sabotages her husband's endeavours to focus on Fischer by killing the latter on level 3. As in "The Fall of the House of Usher" the female role, i.e. Mal/Madeline, is not only that of a victim but also that of an aggressor. Interestingly, Mal can be read as the French word *mal*, meaning evil, while Madeline could be shortened to Mad and directly linked to the narrator's – and Usher's – madness. However, unlike Madeline, Mal does not only personify female evil and a distressing reminder of guilt, but also is a major factor distracting him from his modern-day work. By appearing in Fischer's dreams, Mal keeps Cobb from getting his job in the world of corporate spying done. This could indicate the growing pressures of today's world, where work often takes priority over private life, and the concomitant pernicious neglect of the powers of the psyche that in turn can come back to haunt the worker.

Since Cobb and his helpers are so deep down in Fischer's mind, the latter does not wake from his death on level 3 but instead falls into level 4, 'limbo'. Mal, Cobb and Ariadne also end up on this level. 'Limbo' turns out to be the decisive dream space since it is the one that is furthest down both in Fischer's and in Cobb's psyche. As in "The Fall of the House of Usher" a dream space is mostly imagined as being spread out horizontally like a labyrinth,[23] while a movement towards the core of the psychological problems is signalled by a descent. However, as has been discussed, the large number of and intricate interconnections between the levels point to a higher complexity of the rhizomatic labyrinths found in *Inception*.

In 'limbo' Mal and Cobb once spent decades growing old together before Cobb implanted the idea that 'this world is not real' in his wife's mind. Ariadne accompanies Cobb to this level and acts as a kind of psychiatrist there, helping him to face his monster, Mal – just as the mythological Ariadne aided Theseus in his fight against the Minotaur. But she needs to leave level 4 together with Fischer – so Cobb has to go the last step on his own, which means letting Mal go. This saying goodbye can be read on a psychological level as well as on religious and mythological levels. On the one hand, Cobb is now finally facing up to both his guilt and grief, by apologizing to Mal for the 'inception' of the idea and by choosing to part with her. On the other hand, he to some extent resembles Christ in the 'Harrowing of Hell', where he liberates the souls trapped in limbo, and Theseus as well as Orpheus in their travels to the underworld. The effect of such a blending of various readings can be that Cobb's singular psychological experience is to some extent rendered timeless and given an elevating quasi-religious and mythological aura. Establishing a link to Orpheus seems particularly fitting in this case since Orpheus famously looks for his deceased wife in Hades, finds her but in the end returns to the real world alone. In fact, Cobb tells Mal that she is just a 'shade', which is reminiscent of the Greek underworld, the world of shades.

A crucial intertext of *Inception* might also be Dante's *Inferno*, which presents nine Circles of Hell that resemble *Inception*'s various dream

---

[23] Early on in *Inception*, Cobb asks the aspiring dream architect Ariadne to conceive of the dream levels as types of labyrinths. Similarly, the narrator of "The Fall of the House of Usher" makes his way "through many dark and intricate passages" (93) to get to the centre of the house/psyche.

levels. It is particularly *Inception*'s level of 'limbo' and its parallels as well as contrasts to Dante's work that evoke this connection. In *Inferno*, 'Limbo' is the First Circle of Hell (27), which is located behind the 'Gate of Hell' but at the same time hovers on the brim of the proper beginning of Hell (31), while in *Inception* 'limbo' is the fourth dream level, the seemingly last one. This fourth level in *Inception* could on the other hand be compared to the Fourth Circle in *Inferno*, where prodigality and avarice are denounced (40). In *Inception*, it is similarly on the fourth level that the skyscrapers crumble, which could mark the downfall of materialism and of an exaggeratedly business-oriented, consumerist society. By linking Nolan's film to Dante's *Inferno*, *Inception* thus can be seen as bringing together the concept of an impending hell with that of materialism. Moreover, in this context it is only fitting that the term "level" can be polysemous – calling to mind both Dante's Circles of Hell and the levels of videogames and thus both the literary past as well as the technological present.

After his multiple falls, Cobb seemingly returns to the 'real' world. He has bought back his liberty and apparently his sanity. He is reunited with his father-in-law and his children. But there are some things wrong with this pretty fairy-tale ending. His children, whom he allegedly has not seen for years, have not aged. They look exactly like his 'projections' of them in his former dreams. Moreover, the top that he usually spins in order to find out whether or not he is in a dream, continues spinning and does not fall down, which is a signal to Cobb that he is still in a dream world.

The standing top may be an allusion to Boethius' concept of *nunc stans* or *nunc permanens*, an "eternal now", a moment which remains and produces eternity.[24] It is a transcendental, Godly 'now'. However, since the top is spinning as well as standing, it might be more precise to speak about a fusion between a human or moving 'now' and a transcendental eternal 'now', a mixture of *nunc fluens* and *nunc stans* which can evoke dizziness.[25] The viewers may therefore be left wondering not only if 'reality' exists at all,[26] but also whether or not the protagonist will need to continue living in dream worlds and will have to go on falling and

---

[24] Confer Boethius' *De Trinitate* c. 4: PL 64, col. 1253. He there uses the terms *nunc permanens* and *nunc currens* instead of *nunc stans* and *nunc fluens*.
[25] Compare Hick's analysis of Thomas Mann's *Zauberberg*.
[26] See Calvert.

thereby reliving his nightmare over and over again, trapped somewhere between a human world and a transcendental one. Cobb's worlds of innumerous falls thus seem both time-bound and timeless, which ties in with the blending of particular psychological readings and generalizing religious-mythological interpretations that was mentioned above.

Just as in "The Fall of the House of Usher", there might not be an awakening at the end, but a ceaseless nightmare, but here this idea is taken to the extreme. The ending of Nolan's film seems to be only the beginning, the 'inception', of the nightmare. Alpha and Omega merge – just as the final dream level becomes 'limbo', Dante's impending Hell.

Far from being merely immaterial, a-historical and a-cultural, the dreams in both Poe's tales and Nolan's film *Inception* reflect contemporary theoretical and cultural contexts in each case. However, Nolan's film transgresses older forms of the psychological Gothic in various ways – firstly, by means of its focus on *both* the human psyche and twenty-first-century materialism; secondly, through its fusion of psychological, mythological and religious contexts and, thirdly, through the immense number of falling dreams it presents, which may even call to mind the terrifying image of the 9/11 'Falling Man'. Furthermore, since Cobb is more 'consciously' involved in his own dreams and since his subconscious consists of a confusing number of dream levels, his endless falling nightmare can appear even more frightening, even more unstable, than the nightmarish visions the readers are confronted with in Poe's short stories.

A crucial question that remains is whether or not we will soon witness filmic transgressions of Nolan's techniques; in other words, will the Gothic films of the future contain even more levels of 'reality' and evoke even greater feelings of destabilization and insecurity? The history of film, which shows that the movies became faster and more complex, and the growing visual-processing capabilities of the modern-day 'digital natives'[27] suggest that this will be the case and that the transgressor Nolan will in turn be transgressed.

---

[27] 'Digital natives' are young people who have been exposed to electronic resources already from their birth onwards (Morgan 20). Hani Morgan, for example, discusses the heightened visual faculties of modern-day pupils (21).

Works Cited

Baldick, Chris, and Robert Mighall. "Gothic Criticism." *A Companion to the Gothic*. Ed. David Punter. Oxford: Blackwell, 2001. 209-228.

Baudrillard, Jean. "Simulacra and Simulations." *Literary Theory: An Anthology*. Eds. Julie Rivkin and Michael Ryan. Malden, MA: Blackwell, 2004. 365-377.

Boethius. *De Trinitate. Anicius Manlius Severinus Boethius: The Theological Tractates*. Trans. H. F. Stewart, E. K. Rand and S. J. Tester. London: Loeb Classical Library, 1973. 1-31.

Botting, Fred. *The Gothic*. New York: Routledge, 1996.

---. "Candygothic." *The Gothic*. Ed. Fred Botting. Cambridge: Brewer, 2001. 133-151.

Burke, Edmund. *A Philosophical Enquiry into the Origin of our Ideas of the Sublime and Beautiful*. Ed. Adam Phillips. Oxford: Oxford University Press, 1990.

Calvert, Leon Saunders. "*Inception*: Film, Dreams and Freud." *Offscreen* 31 May 2011. Web. 29 June 2014.

Clarke, Graham. "Failures of the 'Moral Defence' in the Films *Shutter Island, Inception* and *Memento*: Narcissism or Schizoid Personality Disorder?" *The International Journal of Psychoanalysis* 93 (2012): 203-218.

"Cob." Def. 4. *Oxford English Dictionary Online*. Oxford English Dictionary, n.d. Web. 30 June 2014.

Dante. *The Divine Comedy*. Trans. John Aitken Carlyle, Thomas Okey and Philip H. Wicksteed. New York: Random House, 1944.

Deleuze, Gilles, and Felix Guattari. "A Thousand Plateaus." *Literary Theory: An Anthology*. Eds. Julie Rivkin, and Michael Ryan. Malden, MA: Blackwell, 2004. 378-386.

Dreammoods.com. 2014. Dream Moods, Inc. Web. 27 June 2014.

Drew, Richard. *Falling Man*. 2001. Photograph. AP.

Dubos, Jean-Baptiste. *Critical Reflections on Poetry, Painting and Music*. London: Nourse, 1748.

Ebert, Roger. Rev. of *Inception*, dir. Christopher Nolan. *Roger Ebert* 14 July 2010. Web. 29 June 2014.

Fisher, Mark. "The Lost Unconscious: Delusions and Dreams in *Inception*." *Film Quarterly* 64.3 (2011): 37-45.

Freud, Sigmund. *Die Traumdeutung*. Frankfurt am Main: Fischer, 1972.

Frost, Laura. "Still Life: 9/11's Falling Bodies." *Literature after 9/11*. Eds. Ann Keniston and Jeanne Follansbee Quinn. New York: Routledge, 2008. 180-206.

Galloway, David. "Introduction." *Edgar Allan Poe: The Fall of the House of Usher and Other Writings*. Ed. David Galloway. London: Penguin, 2003. xvii-lv.

Hammond, John R. *An Edgar Allan Poe Companion: A Guide to the Short Stories, Romances and Essays*. London: Palgrave Macmillan, 1981.

Hartmann, Ernest. *Dreams and Nightmares: The New Theory on the Origin and Meaning of Dreams*. New York: Plenum, 1998.

Hick, Christian. "Vom Schwindel ewiger Gegenwart: Zur Pathologie der Zeit in Thomas Manns *Zauberberg*." *Der Zauberberg: Die Welt der Wissenschaften in Thomas Manns Roman*. Eds. Dietrich von Engelhardt and Hans Wißkirchen. Stuttgart: Schattauer, 2003. 71-106.

Hobby, Blake. "The Sublime in Edgar Allan Poe's 'The Fall of the House of Usher.'" *The Sublime*. Eds. Harold Bloom, and Blake Hobby. New York: Bloom's Literary Criticism, 2010. 45-54.

Hoffmann, E. T. A. *The Devil's Elixirs*. Trans. Ronald Taylor. Richmond: Oneworld Classics, 2011.

Inception. Dir. Christopher Nolan. Perf. Leonardo DiCaprio, Ken Watanabe, Joseph Gordon-Levitt, Ellen Page, Marion Cotillard, Tom Hardy, Cillian Murphy, Tom Berenger and Michael Caine. Warner Bros., 2010. Film.

Janowitz, Anne. "The Sublime Plurality of Worlds: Lucretius in the Eighteenth Century." *Tate Papers* 13. 1 April 2010. Web. 20 Jan 2015.

Junod, Tom. "Falling (Mad) Man: Is the Poster for the New Season of *Mad Men* a Desecration? Or Just How We Continue to Reckon with 9/11?" *Esquire* 30 Jan 2012. Web. 5 Nov 2014.

Lakoff, George, and Mark Johnson. *Metaphors We Live By*. Chicago: University of Chicago Press, 2003.

Lehane, Dennis. *Shutter Island*. New York: Harper, 2011.

Lewis, Matthew. *The Monk*. London: Penguin, 1998.

Ljungquist, Kent. "Poe and the Sublime: His Two Short Sea Tales in the Context of an Aesthetic Tradition." *Criticism* 17.2 (1975): 131-151.

MacAndrew, Elizabeth. *The Gothic Tradition in Fiction*. New York: Columbia University Press, 1979.

Mad Men. Writ. Matthew Weiner *et al*. Dir. Matthew Weiner *et al*. Lionsgate, 2007-present. DVD.

Martindale, Colin. "Archetype and Reality in 'The Fall of the House of Usher.'" *Poe Studies* 5 (1972): 9-11.

Morgan, Hani. "Using Digital Story Projects to Help Students Improve in Reading and Writing." *Reading Improvement* 51.1 (2014): 20-26.

Morris, Kat *et al*. "Hollywood Horror History: Classic Horror of the 1930's." *The Horror Honeys*, Web. 27 June 2014.

Neville, Carl. "Neither Here Nor There." 17 July 2010. Web. 5 Nov 2014.

Nünning, Ansgar. "Unreliable Narration zur Einführung: Grundzüge einer kognitiv-narratologischen Theorie und Analyse unglaubwürdigen Erzählens." *Unreliable Narration: Studien zur Theorie und Praxis unglaubwürdigen Erzählens in der englischsprachigen Erzählliteratur*. Ed. Ansgar Nünning. Trier: Wissenschaftlicher Verlag, 1998. 3-39.

Paul, Ian. "Desiring-Machines in American Cinema: What *Inception* Tells Us about Our Experience of Reality and Film." *Senses of Cinema* Oct. 2010. Web. 27 June 2014.

Person, Leland S. "Trusting the Tellers: Paradoxes of Narrative Authority in Poe's 'A Descent into the Maelström.'" *The Journal of Narrative Technique* 23.1 (1993): 46-56.

Poe, Edgar Allan. "The Fall of the House of Usher." *Edgar Allan Poe: The Fall of the House of Usher and Other Writings*. Ed. David Galloway. London: Penguin, 2003. 90-109.

---. "A Descent into the Maelström." *Edgar Allan Poe: The Fall of the House of Usher and Other Writings*. Ed. David Galloway. London: Penguin, 2003. 177-193.

---. "The Imp of the Perverse." *Complete Stories and Poems of Edgar Allan Poe*. New York: Doubleday, 2012. 271-275.

Porter, James I. "Lucretius and the Sublime." *The Cambridge Companion to Lucretius*. Eds. Stuart Gillespie, and Philip Hardie. New York: Cambridge University Press, 2007. 167-184.

Read, Herbert. "Foreword." *The Gothic Flame*. Devendra P. Varma. London: Barker, 1957. vii-viii.

Rein, David M. "Poe's Dreams." *American Quarterly* 10.3 (1958): 367-371.

Robert, Geneviève, and Antonio Zadra. "Thematic and Content Analysis of Idiopathic Nightmares and Bad Dreams." *Sleep* 37.2 (2014): 409-417.

Saliba, David R. *A Psychology of Fear: The Nightmare Formula of Edgar Allan Poe*. Washington: University Press of America, 1980.

Shackelford, Lynne P. "Poe's *The Fall of the House of Usher*." *Explicator* 45.1 (1986): 18-19.

Shelley, Mary. *Frankenstein*. Ed. Maurice Hindle. London: Penguin, 2003.

Shutter Island. Dir. Martin Scorsese. Perf. Leonardo DiCaprio, Mark Ruffalo, Ben Kingsley, Michelle Williams, Patricia Clarkson and Max von Sydow. Paramount, 2010. Film.

Sova, Dawn B. *Edgar Allan Poe, A to Z: The Essential Reference to his Life and Work*. New York City: Facts On File, 2001.

---. *Critical Companion to Edgar Allan Poe: A Literary Reference to His Life and Work*. New York: Facts on File, 2007.

Spellbound. Dir. Alfred Hitchcock. Perf. Ingrid Bergman, Gregory Peck, Michael Chekhov, Leo G. Carroll and Rhonda Fleming. United Artists, 1945. Film.

The Black Cat. Dir. Edgar G. Ulmer. Perf. Boris Karloff, Béla Lugosi and David Manners. Universal, 1934. Film.

Vertigo. Dir. Alfred Hitchcock. Perf. James Stewart, Kim Novak and Barbara Bel Geddes. Paramount, 1958. Film.

Simone Broders

"No Sex Please, We're Vegetarians": Marketing the Vampire and Sexual Curiosity in *Twilight, True Blood* and the *Sookie Stackhouse* Novels

> We rather chuse to suffer the smart pang of a violent emotion than the uneasy craving of an unsatisfied desire. (Aikin 123)

This is how Anna Letitia Barbauld describes the emotional effects of the horror story as early as 1773, when the very beginnings of Anglophone vampire literature, such as Coleridge's "Christabel" from 1797 to 1800 had not been written yet and Lord Byron's "The Giaour" and Polidori's "The Vampyre" still lay 40 years in the future. Yet Barbauld's sentiment describes precisely what makes the vampire so successful as a Gothic stock character, as vampires offer both violent emotions and the craving of unsatisfied desires.

The vampire has long since moved on from the ghastly monster of folklore and early literary versions, and has been transformed into the popular imagination of the vampire, described by Carol Senf as "dark, brooding, powerful, and generally sensual, [...] far more attractive than his human adversaries" (2). As Senf has shown, the sexual initiation of the heroine by the vampire has become both a traditional plot device bridging the gap between Gothic and Romance, and a successful marketing strategy. Vampires are as easily recognized by their good looks and their brazen eroticism as by their sharp fangs and their pallor. Like Venus traps, they lure their victims into mortal danger. At the same time, the vampire's bite also constitutes the ultimate fantasy of acting upon one's sexual curiosity without fear of unwanted consequences or moral judgment. Whereas Victorian Gothic literature in Britain reveals the ambivalences of nineteenth-century power relations in a sexually repressed society, contemporary US vampire novels hitting international shelves illustrate a different kind of paradox. The US American self-fashioning as the 'land of the free', encouraging civil liberties, personal initiative, and economic independence, is diametrically opposed to the strong influence of right-wing religious factions attempting to advance evangelical positions on political topics such as diversity, education, bioethics, homosexuality, and abortion. The conflict between the credoes of liberty and equality and the restrictive doctrines of the conservative portion of the population is negotiated in various current vampire narratives and becomes particularly evident in the marketing strategy of the country's current most successful vampire bestseller.

I. *Twilight*

In Stephenie Meyer's *Twilight* saga, beginning in 2005, the vampire-turned-superhero does not only abstain from human blood, which is why he calls himself a 'vegetarian', but also from sexual relations since he regards them as being too dangerous. Edward claims that he might end up killing his fragile human partner: "It's just that you are so soft, so fragile. [...] I could kill you quite easily, Bella, simply by accident [...]. I could reach out and crush your skull by mistake. You don't realize how incredibly breakable you are. I can never, never afford to lose any kind of control when I'm with you" (*T* 271).[1] Meyer's novel, in spite of elaborating on Edward's physical beauty, does not present any sexual contact until Edward and Bella exchange their marriage vows. Sexual curiosity is a sin to be avoided.

This has frequently been attributed to Meyer's religious views, sparking off an ongoing debate on whether or not *Twilight* is basically Mormon propaganda; an assumption based on the emphasis on family and traditional gender roles, Edward's angelic appearance, Bella's strict health code, and the ban on premarital sexual intercourse (Aleiss). Despite the sexual connotations of the vampire motif itself, Meyer uses vampires as a marketing tool for right-wing evangelical propaganda. Meyer denies weaving any ideas concerning her faith into the novels, although she admits that the Bible did provide her with inspiration regarding the apple on the original book cover.[2] The apple as the Biblical forbidden fruit appears in the text itself:

> 'I'm curious,' I said as I picked up an apple, turning it around in my hands, 'What would you do if someone dared you to eat food?'

---

[1] Individual volumes will be abbreviated as follows: *Twilight* (*T*), *New Moon* (*NM*), *Eclipse* (*E*), and *Breaking Dawn* (*BD*).

[2] "The apple on the cover of *Twilight* represents 'forbidden fruit'. [...] In the end, I love the beautiful simplicity of the picture. To me it says: *choice*" (Meyer, "Twilight: FAQ"; emphasis in the original).

'You're always curious.' He grimaced, shaking his head. He glared at me, holding my eyes as he lifted the slice of pizza off his tray, and deliberately bit off a mouthful, chewed quickly, and then swallowed. I watched, eyes wide.

'If someone dared you to eat dirt, you could, couldn't you?' he asked condescendingly. (*T* 181)

Edward does not accept the highly symbolic apple from Bella. His choice of words is also significant, echoing Genesis 3:19, after the Fall: "In the sweat of thy face shalt thou eat bread, till thou return unto the ground; for out of it wast thou taken: for dust thou art, and unto dust shalt thou return". The meadow in the mountains where Edward reveals his true nature to Bella becomes their version of Eden, a *locus amoenus* where "the lion fell in love with the lamb" (*T* 240).[3]

Edward's 'vegetarianism' is a contradiction in terms, as the vampire per definition needs human blood to survive. Sustenance by the blood of animals is not only against his nature, but it also deprives vampires of their sensuality. From the early Victorian vampires to Anne Rice's hedonistic creature Lestat,[4] the vampire's bite has been a code for suppressed sexual curiosity; the vampire, both dead and alive and thus a walking paradox, was allowed to break the taboos of orthodoxy (Senf 7-8). Edward, however, constantly battles his desire for both Bella's blood and body and adheres to an obsolete code of conduct. Bella remains a virgin until her marriage, a fact that is stressed several times in the novels and their movie versions; she calms her worried father's fears during an embarrassing birds-and-bees talk (*E* 53), Bella's astrological sign is Virgo (*E* 116); in the movie version of *New Moon*, she travels to Italy with Virgin Airlines.

To Bella, Edward is as remote and cold as the marble statue of a Greek god. Bella repeatedly compares him to Michelangelo's David (*E* 389) and talks about his "marble-hard lips" (*E* 238), "stone chest" (*E* 39), "a perfect statue, carved in some unknown stone, smooth like marble" (*T* 228). Like a statue in a museum, Edward is physically beautiful, but may not be touched. It is not a coincidence that unlike their sexualized cousins, Meyer's immaculate vampires are not destroyed by sunlight, but

---

[3] This is an allusion to Isaiah 11:6, in which an age of paradise on earth is described.

[4] Lestat appears in Anne Rice's 1976 novel *Interview with the Vampire*.

sparkle like diamonds.[5] This characteristic of Meyer's vampires is not a novelty. It matches the description of the sun god Apollo in Alice and Claude Askew's *Ghost Seer*, first published in 1914. In their tale "The Stranger", the teenage girl Daphne falls in love with the sun god, who appears to her in a forest clearing:

> He is glorious – so glorious that I cannot believe him to be a mortal man. He frightens me a little [...]. He is as bright as a flame is bright, his shining flesh gleams like marble through the green bushes. His eyes draw me – compel me –, and yet they are fierce eyes – very fierce. [...] He [...] seemed to shoot down from the branches of a high fir tree, and he was white and shining and nude. A fierce brightness seemed to diffuse from him. (7; 32)

Apollo's kiss eventually kills her, so she can be with him forever. Like Daphne, Bella has to die to be with Edward. The association of the vampire with the sun god is paradoxical on the surface, given that vampires as creatures of darkness can traditionally be killed by exposure to sunlight, yet it connects Edward to the Apollinian principle. According to Nietzsche, the Apollinian represents reason and order while the Dionysian principle is ecstasy and creative chaos (Koopmann 260-276; Nietzsche 27-38). The vampires of *True Blood* and the *Sookie Stackhouse* novels are Dionysian, with ritualistic sexuality taking place in the television adaptation. Apollinian self-restraint, however, is a fitting concept to describe the self-control of Meyer's chaste vampires, who constantly fight the temptations of both body and blood. Despite Meyer's protestations that romance and erotica were not her preferred genres, the *Twilight* saga and its adaptations draw much of their appeal from their subtle eroticism.[6] Edward is frequently shown with an open shirt, even in the crucial scene in *New Moon* when he attempts to kill himself. The werewolves strip down to their underwear before shifting to their animal form. Edward watches Bella secretly in her bedroom, and there is a lot of physical contact between the couple.

---

[5] "Edward in the sunlight was shocking. [...] His skin, white despite the faint flush from yesterday's hunting trip, literally sparkled, like thousands of tiny diamonds were embedded in the surface" (*T* 228).

[6] "It's so not my genre [...]. Erotica is not something I read. I don't even read traditional romance [...]. It's too smutty. There's a reason my books have a lot of innocence. That's the sort of world I live in" (Cochrane, "Stephenie Meyer").

Yet it is not only on the grounds of his 'addiction' to blood that Edward prevents Bella's attempts to seduce him, as he very pointedly emphasizes:

> 'There's something that I want to do before I'm not human anymore.' [...] My hands were slightly shaky as I unlocked my arms from around his neck. My fingers slid down his neck to the collar of his shirt. The trembling didn't help as I tried to hurry to undo the buttons before he stopped me. [...]
>
> 'I'm not saying no,' he reassured me. 'I'm just saying not tonight. [...] I swear to you, we will try. After you marry me.'
>
> I shook my head, and laughed glumly. 'You make me feel like a villain in a melodrama – twirling my mustache while I try to steal some poor girl's virtue.' [...]
>
> 'How many people in this room have a soul? A shot at heaven, or whatever there is after this life?'
>
> 'Two,' I answered immediately, my voice fierce.
>
> 'All right. Maybe that's true. Now, there's a world full of dissension about this [...].
>
> If it's too late for me ... Well, I'll be damned – no pun intended – if I'll let them keep you out, too.' (*E* 392-403)

In this passage, Edward reveals the moral concept of *Twilight*: sexual relations before marriage might deprive Bella of her soul and lead her to damnation. Meyer has Edward skilfully switch from one topic – having sex with Bella before marriage – to an entirely different one: the question whether a vampire would be allowed to enter into heaven. In Edward's reflections, both are equally detrimental to the young woman's salvation. Sexual relations before marriage are portrayed as dangerous and potentially fatal, both to Bella's body and her soul. However, the danger to the human body seems to be a pretext, as Edward's physical strength and possible lack of self-restraint objectively remain the same no matter if wedding vows have been exchanged. The fact that Edward no longer fears any danger of accidentally killing her *after* the wedding illustrates that his concerns are not physical, but in fact moral: "I swear to you, we will try. *After* you marry me" (emphasis added). The morning after the wedding night appears to prove that the physical threat in vampiric sexuality suggested by Edward has been exaggerated, as Bella merely discovers a few bruises, but cannot remember any pain (*BD* 81-82).

Edward never uses the word 'God' to justify why he refuses to give in to Bella's sexual curiosity: "I'll be damned [...] if I'll let *them* keep you out, too" (*E* 403; emphasis added). Who 'they' are is never specified, yet the word hints at some higher power whose moral standards will eventually determine whether Bella can be 'saved'.

Meyer has been criticized for passing off evangelical propaganda and misogynistic gender stereotypes as romance to inexperienced teenagers (Vanderbeke 18). Edward is the male protector who keeps the curious teenage girl safe from temptation and takes responsibility for any sexual actions. Emily Hodgson Anderson tries to account for the popularity of the *Twilight* saga: "The appeal [of vampires] now is precisely because we are *not* sexually repressed [...]. Sex is everywhere. We're pretty desensitized. So these stories re-introduce anticipation, the almost infinite deferral of any type of sexual consummation" (qtd. in Barnett).

Sexuality in *Twilight* is expressed in a subtle way: in longing looks, open buttons of a shirt, and stealing kisses between classes. It is the unfulfilled desire which holds a certain degree of fascination for a young teenage audience who might feel intimidated by a sexually aggressive vampire, as well as for an adult female audience fed up with the objectification of women. As Wieland Freund argues:

> Eine Generation von Mädchen und Frauen zwischen 13 und 30, für die die Gleichberechtigung der Geschlechter so selbstverständlich ist wie die Hosen im Schrank, findet den idealen Schmachtfetzen ausgerechnet in einem patriarchalischen und körperfeindlichen Geist, weil ihr ein bisschen altmodische Verdrucкstheit allemal lieber ist als die allgegenwärtige, stumpfe und menschenverachtende Sexualisierung einer Gesellschaft, die Frauen nach wie vor zu Objekten degradiert.[7]

Bella is sexually initiated by Edward as Flora is by Varney, or Lucy by Dracula. Embodying the fantasy of a form of sexual liberty that is both acceptable in terms of the moral strictures of right-wing America and risk-free in terms of unwanted consequences, the vampire's bite is the

---

[7] "A generation of girls and women between 13 and 30, to whom equality of the sexes comes as naturally as a pair of trousers in the wardrobe, finds its ideal of romance in a patriarchal and somatophobic spirit, preferring a little old-fashioned inhibition to the omnipresent, dull and inhuman sexualization of a society still ready to degrade women to objects any time" (trans. SB).

only 'safe' way to satisfy sexual curiosity because it is not 'real' sex. It is with a great deal of irony that director Chris Weitz transforms the novels' moral conservativism into the blockbuster *New Moon*. In a parodistic scene, the werewolf Jacob climbs a balcony, offering a humorous foil to Edward, who sternly quotes from *Romeo and Juliet*. Meanwhile Edward wonders whether Jacob, who takes every opportunity to show off his bare chest, is too poor to buy a shirt. As Hodgson Anderson argues, *Twilight* is "a Peter Pan-like fantasy. You're fixed in this moment right between childhood and adulthood. You always can enjoy the drama and intensity of the adolescent experience. You never have to grow up. Plus, you get to stay up all night" (qtd. in Barnett).

II. The *Southern Vampire Mysteries* / The *Sookie Stackhouse* Novels

However, not all twenty-first-century vampires share the concept of Meyer's reactionary 'vegetarians'. Charlaine Harris' *Sookie Stackhouse* novels – the alternate, yet more popular title of *The Southern Vampire Mysteries* – published from 2001 to 2013, and the TV adaptation by Alan Ball, *True Blood*, produced from 2008 to 2014, decidedly set themselves apart from Meyer's desexualized vampires. Harris' vampires are highly sensual, positioned within a long tradition of the vampire as a projection screen of sexual desires and transgression of taboo (Senf 9). Despite its setting in the conservative 'bible belt' state of Louisiana, the series' marketing strategy depends largely on the link between vampirism and the heroine's sexual awakening.

In the small town of Bon Temps, the vampire is still a curiosity although the undead are no longer in hiding but have revealed their existence to the human population. This development has been encouraged by the Japanese invention of synthetic blood, the most prominent brand being TRUEBLOOD, which allows vampires to move among humans without having to kill for sustenance. In terms of political correctness, vampires now call themselves 'Undead Americans'. They have 'come out of the coffin', pay taxes, and demand civil rights. The plot of the first *Southern Vampire Mysteries* novel, *Dead Until Dark*, published four years before Meyer's *Twilight*, centres around cocktail waitress Sookie Stackhouse, who finds her world turned upside down by her new neighbour, the vampire Bill Compton. Sookie is still a virgin at age 25 because she has, at least the way she sees it, a "mental disability" (*DUD* 2) – she can read minds.[8] Her telepathy immediately discloses the sexual thoughts of the men she dates, which is why she normally loses interest within minutes. She falls in love with Bill because she cannot read the vampire's mind.[9] In *Dead Until Dark*, Sookie's inability to read Bill's intentions is an important aspect of Sookie's attraction to him: "And for a miracle I only heard what his body was saying, not those niggling things from minds that only foul up moments like this. His body was saying something very simple" (*DUD* 143).

Sexually explicit, although not pornographic, first-person narratives of Sookie's relationships are paired with a strong sense of irony and humour, as an example from Sookie's first sexual encounter with the vampire Eric illustrates:

> [Eric's] manhood (as my romance novels called it – in this case, the popular adjectives 'burgeoning' or 'throbbing' might also be applied) was a daunting prospect to a relatively inexperienced woman like me. I felt like a car that had only been operated by one driver ... a car its new prospective buyer was determined to take to the Daytona 500. (*DTW* 121)

Sookie's description mocks the artificial, stereotypical language of romance novels, yet at the same time, she is being self-ironic by comparing herself to a car taken to a particularly challenging motor race. Sookie's sexual curiosity overcomes the morally conservative framework of her small-town Louisiana childhood; she decides against discussing with Eric "the moral aspects of mating with someone you [do not] love" (*DTW* 121). However, her thoughts reveal how much she is still influenced by the limits of an obsolete female gender stereotype that does not concede to women any sexual desires of their own: "It was somehow

---

[8] Individual volumes will be abbreviated as follows: *Dead Until Dark* (*DUD*), *Dead to the World* (*DTW*), *Living Dead in Dallas* (*LDD*), *Dead Ever After* (*DEA*).

[9] Meyer later recycled this idea with inverted gender roles, hiding Bella's thoughts from telepathic Edward. *Twilight* thus provides the male protagonist with the strategic advantage over his enemies, telepathy, predestining him for an active role in battles and negotiations. The female protagonist is, even in her second life as a vampire, attributed with the passive skill of shielding, which casts her in the traditional female role as caregiver and preserver of the family.

degrading, craving someone so … so *voraciously* […] just because he was physically beautiful. I hadn't thought that was something women did" (*DTW* 119; emphasis in the original). Sookie feels guilty about her passions, a guilt imposed by social conventions of 'what women do'. Only when she realizes that society has been treating her like an outcast does she begin to discard its rules of propriety: "it was beautiful Eric, who desired me, who was hungry for me, in a world that often let me know it could do very well without me. […] Oh, to hell with thinking" (*DTW* 121). Entering into a sexual relationship, for Sookie, is never a decision to be made lightly, yet it is not the epic moral choice it is in *Twilight*. Although her first lover Bill remains her friend and neighbour throughout the whole series, Sookie has other significant relationships with Eric, the weretiger Quinn, and her boss, the shapeshifter Sam.

Those who oppose her lifestyle most are the representatives of organized religion. They occur in the novel as the fundamentalist members of the Fellowship of the Sun, an evangelical sect whose methods are reminiscent of those of the Ku Klux Klan. The Fellowship decide that vampires and everyone who consorts with them had best 'meet the sun', a euphemism for being burnt to final death. According to the Fellowship, relationships between humans and vampires are unnatural since they constitute 'necrophilia'; and they are against the will of God (*LDD* 154).

Sookie is portrayed as an open-minded, modern young woman who takes the side of the vampires against religious fundamentalists. Nevertheless, Eric suspects that Sookie's inability to cope with his being a vampire is, ultimately, the reason for the failure of their relationship:

'I began to wonder if in your heart you really despised what I am.'

[…] 'No, I do not despise what you are. I just want to live my human life. […] I loved you. And I felt flattered that you wanted us to be united in your world's eyes. But you're right when you say I never regarded our marriage as equal to a human church marriage.' (*DEA* 128)

Although Sookie and Eric's relationship in the novels results in a vampire marriage, even Sookie regards the vampires' rites as somehow inferior to the human ones, mirroring the chauvinism of white, straight, middle-class prejudices. In the novels, marriages between humans and vampires are illegal.[10] This kind of discrimination is not unheard of in US legislation, referring to segregation laws still in effect in the 1960s, prohibiting marriages between black and white.[11] Furthermore, fundamentalist discrimination against human-vampire-couples serves as a code for the hostility of religious conservatives against the homosexual community. 'Coming out of the coffin', the public self-disclosure of vampires, derives directly from the idiom 'coming out [of the closet]', which denotes the disclosure of homosexual orientation.

Regardless of the fact that Sookie lives with vampires for most of the series, the conclusion of the series in *Dead Ever After* depicts her as being in a very conventional relationship with Sam. In the final novel, Sookie frequently expresses her wish to have children of her own, which rules out any permanent relationship to a vampire.[12] In comparison to the preceding novels, Sookie performs a disproportionately high number of household and gardening chores and takes part in leisure activities stereotypically linked to an 'All-American Girl' or 'Girl Next Door',[13] such as square dance and barbecues. Sookie even describes her first sexual encounter with Sam as "fireworks and Fourth of July" (*DEA* 310). She elaborates: "The years of experience of my vampire lovers might have made them skillful, but there is so much to say for sheer heartfelt enthusiasm; and the heat of Sam, the warmth of him, it was like the sun was soaking into my body" (*DEA* 311). With this remark, Sookie reduces her former vampire lovers to their eroticism and the darkness they live in, whereas Sam is associated with 'heat' – the body of a vampire is cold – and 'the sun'. If a relationship with a vampire is to be seen as a code for sexual self-determination, this conclusion is a backlash to the common conservative myths that homosexuality is just a 'phase' and that the

---

[10] In *True Blood*, Vermont is the first US state to legalize these unions in the twelfth episode of the first season ("You'll Be the Death of Me").

[11] This subject is touched upon in the episode "Spellbound" of *True Blood*. The African-American, Creole woman Mavis has the child of a white man who kills both her and the baby. Mavis returns as a vengeful spirit who is finally appeased by the discovery of her burial place.

[12] "I looked at the diaper bags and adorable baby items. [...] I touched a tiny green-and-white-striped sleeper with a lamb on the chest. Something deep inside me shivered with longing" (*DEA* 38).

[13] For a detailed discussion of the concept of an "All-American Girl" or "Girl Next Door", see Cogan 65-66.

desire for sexual self-determination is an adolescent extravagancy which will be overcome once maturity is reached. Furthermore, Sookie's attempted kidnapping by her cousin Claude ultimately fails because his accomplices cannot deal with the revelation that he is homosexual.[14] One of the final images of Sookie in the novel is her walking down the aisle as Maid of Honour at her brother's – the 'reformed' womanizer's – wedding. Sookie's friend Tara is already married with twin daughters, Halleigh Bellefleur and the witch Amelia are pregnant. For the female characters, 'happily ever after' is in accordance with the conservative gender identities of the 1950s.

Harris' unwillingness to go through with the agenda of the first books in the series, promoting sexual liberation and the equality of all lifestyles and gender identities, sparked off a storm of protest in the internet community (Flood). Readers frequently complained of the heroine's lack of evolvement and independence, as the following commentary quoted in *The Guardian* illustrates: "if Charlaine Harris had written the *Harry Potter* series, the end of *Deathly Hallows* would have Harry sleeping in the cupboard under the stairs with the spiders and no magic. While Voldemort would move in across the street, taunt him daily, and dispense life advice" (Flood).

Thus Harris paves the way for Sookie's regression to the "identity as domesticated female", as Lauren Rocha argues for Bella in *Twilight* (153). Both Bella and Sookie share a poor image of themselves that Sookie only temporarily escapes. After thirteen books, she still regards her individuality as a 'disability', renounces her own supernatural abilities and longs for a 'normal', *i.e.* mainstream, life. The marketing strategy of the novels was largely based upon the eroticism of the vampire stock character and the sexual tension between the vampire and the evolving heroine who has to stand her ground against domineering males – a strategy fuelled by the TV adaptation *True Blood*. Before the show, Harris' novels had sold approximately two million copies, but sold 30 million more copies in 35 countries (Alter). It appears that the expectations raised by an eroticized marketing strategy and the

---

[14] The kidnappers engage in a quarrel about whether Claude is going to hell for his homosexuality, which creates enough of a distraction for Sookie to escape (Harris, *DEA* 324).

conventional ending of the final novel constitute an unbridgeable chasm between writer and audience.

III. *True Blood*

Sookie's relationships, particularly with Bill and Eric, are also the focus of the advertizing campaigns of *True Blood*; the vampires' eroticism is emphasized both in terms of iconography and slogans. The campaign for Season 2 shows Bill and Sookie in a sensual embrace, with Bill flashing his fangs and Sookie displaying fresh bite marks.[15] The advertizements use ambiguous taglines such as "It Hurts So Good", "Thou Shall Not Crave Thy Neighbour" and "Do Bad Things".[16] Furthermore, Alan Ball deliberately provoked conservative moral conceptions by means of a photo shooting that had the three major characters of *True Blood* pose nude, sprinkled with theatre blood (Grigoriadis). Ball, who adapted Harris' novels for the small screen, is blatant about his view on *Twilight*: "The idea of celibate vampires is ridiculous. To me, vampires are sex. I don't get a vampire story about abstinence. I'm 53. I don't care about high school students. I find them irritating and uninformed" (qtd. in Grigoriadis).

The concept of vampiric sexuality as depicted in *True Blood* becomes apparent in the character of Jessica Hambly, exclusively created for the television series. Jessica is forcibly turned into a vampire at age 17, when she is still a church-going virgin, regularly lectured by her evangelical father in fire and brimstone sermons. Jessica's role in the Season 3 advertising campaign[17] is highly symbolic: she is sitting at Sookie's feet in a lascivious position, dressed in blood red. From between her legs, a serpent rises towards the couple. Bill and Sookie are resting on a felled tree, with Sookie's other love interest, the vampire Eric, lurking in the background. Symbolically, the Biblical Tree of Knowledge has been felled. The idea that sexual curiosity is sin and death is dismissed. The

---

[15] See "True Blood – Extras: Archived Wallpapers". *True Blood: The Official Site*. HBO. Web. 26 Aug. 2013.

[16] The latter being also a line from the theme song of *True Blood*, Jace Everett's "Bad Things" (Sony BMG, 2005).

[17] See "True Blood – Extras: Archived Wallpapers". *True Blood: The Official Site*. HBO. Web. 26 Aug. 2013.

skulls all lie at the characters' feet, overgrown with grass, one of them adorned with a floral wreath. The cast is positioned in a clearing with blue water and lush vegetation, symbols of life instead of death, with shadows and desires being an integral part of life.

Jessica has her first sexual encounter with nerdy Hoyt Fortenberry in the episode "Time Bomb". To her dismay, Jessica realizes that her vampire healing abilities preserve the exact state of her body at the moment of death – which implies that her virginity keeps being restored every single time she has sexual intercourse. Jessica's perpetual virginity can be regarded as an ironic take on Meyer's 'chaste' vampires.

The self-righteousness of religious groups who claim the right to dictate their own moral sense of right and wrong to others, as to be seen in Christian fundamentalist campaigns against homosexual marriages, is translated into discrimination against human-vampire-couples. In the opening credits of *True Blood*, the camera captures the portal of a church, above which the words "God Hates Fangs" can be read. The *Westboro Baptist Church* in Kansas has reached a doubtful fame for their slogan "God Hates Fags"; according to the church's website this is "a profound theological statement, which the world needs to hear more than it needs oxygen, water and bread" ("Westboro Baptist Church Home Page"). In the episode "Never Let Me Go", Sookie's brother Jason, who is temporarily interested in the Fellowship's ideology, tells her that he is now a member of the *Marl*boro Baptist Church, with a cigarette commercial poster in the background. The 'theological message' is, in fact, no more profound than a cigarette commercial – both attract 'followers' with a simplified depiction of the world and promises of freedom, but ultimately prove to be destructive.

In a scene from "You Smell Like Dinner", Jessica and Hoyt are leaving the vampire bar *Fangtasia*, only to be greeted by a group of fundamentalist Christian protestors who insult them.

PROTESTOR: Fangbanger!

HOYT: Do you see that woman over there? Not that devil, that woman! Yes, she's got fangs, and you can bet your ass we're doing it all the time because we're in love, and there ain't a damn thing wrong with being in love. Now how can you do this, and still call yourself a Christian?

PROTESTOR: I am a Christian, goddammit!

> HOYT: And I am clearly more of a Christian than you 'cause I got love in my heart, and you got nothing but hate. (08:13)

The confrontation between Hoyt and the protestor is highly ironic – religious fundamentalists are trying to invade the privacy of people whose lifestyles and sexual preferences they disapprove of, justifying their protest with religious convictions. At the same time, the protestor disqualifies himself by defying principles of Christian charity, using insults and curses – "I am a Christian, goddammit!". Hoyt argues that there can never be anything 'wrong' with love, and that people who call themselves Christians should display a more tolerant attitude. However, Hoyt's idealism does not last.

When Jessica's relationship with Hoyt fails in "Spellbound", he sends her a cardboard box – vengefully labelled 'Monster' – with her personal belongings inside, which include a copy of Meyer's *Twilight* (13:00). Thus Hoyt symbolically discards the naïve drama of adolescent love.

Both Hoyt and Sookie realize that being with a vampire does not guarantee eternal happiness, but brings with it as many concerns as an ordinary, all-human relationship. Ultimately, Hoyt is unable to deal with Jessica's otherness, as becomes evident in his unnecessarily cruel bluntness in the scene of their breakup:

> HOYT: You don't deserve me, and I sure as hell don't deserve you. I deserve someone who's not gonna be a fucking virgin for all of eternity. I deserve someone I can have a normal life with. With kids. And daylight. And someone who's not gonna look at all the love that I have to offer and just say, 'Sorry, not good enough'. And someone who's not fucking dead! (34:26)

Similarly, for Sookie it becomes increasingly difficult to deal with the supernatural world. In the Season 6 premiere, she tells Eric that she has to rescind his invitation to her house because she wants her old life back ("Who Are You, Really?"). In the TV series, Sookie temporarily opts for a relationship with the werewolf Alcide Herveaux, yet Bill's warning at the end of Season 6 foreshadows that Alcide is not strong enough to protect her against the dangers to come.

The encounter with the 'Other' has the potential to bring out the best or worst in the people of Bon Temps. Attempts to achieve equal rights and social status for vampires by political means prove to be half-hearted, as a conversation between Bill and Nan Flannigan, spokeswoman of the political Vampire League, illustrates. Bill and Nan are invited to "The Festival of Tolerance", a ceremony and celebration of vampires – remarkably, there are merely three vampires present:

> BILL: Are we the only vampires here? [...] How can you have an event in honor of the living dead without any living dead? It's like having a civil rights protest without any black people.

> NAN: They're called African Americans, and maybe those protests wouldn't have turned into the bloodbaths they became if they hadn't been there. Ever consider that? (41:51)

Whereas many discriminating encounters between vampires and humans are irritating, but harmless – newly turned African-American vampire Tara is, for example, greeted enthusiastically by a former schoolmate: "Now you're a member of two minorities!" ("Somebody That I Used to Know", 34:22) –, the peaceful co-existence of humans and vampires is challenged by fundamentalist groups on both sides in Seasons 5 and 6. A hate group ironically wearing Obama plastic masks begin to hunt down members of the supernatural community, while an extremist vampire sect claims that God is in fact a female vampire and created humans as cattle to feed upon. The vampire cult around the goddess Lilith – in Jewish folklore the first wife of Adam, created from earth like him, who refuses to submit to him and becomes the mother of demons (Kvam, Schearing, and Ziegler 204) – becomes the ultimate religious 'Other', challenging Christianity's claims to both human and male superiority.

The situation escalates. Vampires are transported to secret camps where they are tortured during immoral medical experiments and eventually killed by exposure to sunlight. Furthermore, the only remaining TRUBLOOD factory is contaminated by a virus with the intent to extinguish all vampires who drink the synthetic blood.[18] Systematic genocide and biological warfare expose that the true extent of human cruelty is far more repugnant than anything fictional vampires could inflict on their victims. As Senf has shown for Yarbro and Scott,[19] *True Blood* thus "put[s] the vampire's violence into historical perspective and [...] reveals that ordinary human behavior is both frightening and cruel.

---

[18] In the TV series the spelling of the synthetic blood product is TRUBLOOD – as opposed to the spelling TRUEBLOOD that is used in the novels.

[19] Chelsea Quinn Yarbro's *Hôtel Transsylvania* from 1978 and Jody Scott's *I, Vampire* from 1984.

The vampire, an oppressed outsider who is frightened by this ordinary behavior, thus becomes less horrifying by comparison" (6). Vampires kill for food, yet humans kill for refusal of 'Otherness' and change.

Whereas a lack of curiosity breeds fear and hatred, curiosity may aid in the process of overcoming prejudice. With its potential to create knowledge, it reduces the fear of the unknown and facilitates change towards a more tolerant society. It is through Sookie's and Hoyt's curiosity to 'see the other side' in their relationships with vampires that they transcend the narrow-minded small town mainstream and begin to convince their friends that their lifestyles are not 'unnatural'. Like the early gay movement, 'Undead Americans' demand an end to discrimination. Thus, the changing image of vampirism becomes a powerful metaphor, representing all lifestyles and sexual orientations.

Homosexual characters are more present in *True Blood* than in the novels themselves: Sookie's best friend Tara, Eric's assistant Pam, Lafayette, the African-American cook at Merlotte's bar, whose Hispanic partner is provokingly named 'Jesus', and Reverend Steve Newlin, who has his coming out when he is turned into a vampire. Even characters who are introduced as explicitly heterosexual are occasionally involved in homoerotic scenes: Sookies brother Jason has a sexual fantasy about Sookie's house-guest Ben and, later, also the vampire Eric. Eric pretends to seduce the vampire Talbot in order to kill him, Sam and Bill share a shower scene.

Over the first six seasons of *True Blood*, conservative sexual morals and gender stereotypes were constantly called into question. In an especially prominent parody of early 1960s television, Sookie, dressed in a red wrap dress and pumps, waits for her 'husband' Eric to come home, with music of the era playing in the background. The conventional setup is disrupted when Bill enters the scene. Sookie turns from domesticated housewife to seductress and suggests a *ménage à trois*, as she is unable to choose between Bill and Eric. The demand of the vampire as male predator who controls and practically 'owns' the female victim are defied by Sookie's domineering role in the scene and her unconventional suggestion, "I propose the two of you, be mine" ("Let's Get Out Of Here", 22:13).

In the light of such tongue-in-cheek comments on conservative notions of happiness, domesticated women and the traditional nuclear family, the conclusion of the final season appears like a break in the show's previous agenda. Bill decides to kill himself because he feels Sookie would never be able to have a 'normal' life with a human husband and children as long as she is still emotionally attached to him: "We're born, we grow up, we learn and we have children, maybe we get to see our children's children, but then we pass on, and that is a life! If we stay together, I will be denying you the best parts of that. [...] I would hate for you to never know what it feels like to have children of your own" ("Thank You", 01:30).

Although she has already made her choice in favour of a life with Bill, he takes the decision from her, emotionally blackmailing her into assisting him in his suicide. Acting the part of a patriarch of the Old South, who holds authority over the women in his life, he marries off his progeny Jessica to Hoyt in a rushed wedding ceremony. It is evident that he does not trust her to find her own path in life without his male guidance. Bill's actions reveal moral double standards: in his view, it is acceptable for Hoyt to enter into a relationship that will not produce any children because, for a man, a family is obviously not essential for happiness. On the contrary, Sookie's choice to be with Bill, a vampire who will not be able to give her any children, is unacceptable for him; motherhood is essential to a fulfilled life for a woman, one of "the best parts of" her life. Never once does he even ask Sookie or Jessica about their expectations of their future – as the patriarch, he is convinced that he knows best. The only female character to be in a happy relationship with a vampire is Sookie's colleague Arlene, a middle-aged woman who has been married four times and has already given birth to two children.

Her final scene shows Sookie about four years after Bill's suicide, in the last stage of pregnancy, hosting a Thanksgiving dinner for her friends. Her husband, in the 'power seat' at the head of the table, is only shown from behind because, according to showrunner Brian Buckner, "the character was intended to be an everyman whose identity was irrelevant"; portrayed by "the man with the best arms from our stunt crew" (Knox). From a feminist point of view, that conclusion is rather bleak; it no longer matters whom Sookie marries, as long as she fulfills a woman's duty to the patriarchal society, *i.e.* contributing to its continuing existence by producing offspring and passing on a conservative world view to the next generation.

Reviews of the final episode illustrate that viewers seem to feel that the earlier open-mindedness of the show was ruined by the conservative ending; *Time Online* critic Melissa Locker sarcastically remarks, "Sookie is pregnant, and because this is the 1950s, that's all we need to see to know that she is happy". *TV.com* reviewer Lily Sparks observes: "The world of vampires on *True Blood* has often functioned as stand-in for the hidden culture of the LGBT community [...]. Bill [...] choosing to die muddied one of the best messages of the show". *True Blood* creator Alan Ball emphasized as early as in June 2009 that the subtext of a minority fighting for equal rights was not the only way of reading the vampire motif in the series (Shen). However, the issue of discrimination against minorities, whether it be the racial segregration laws of the past or the current debate on same-sex marriages, is alluded to by Andy Bellefleur in the wedding scene of Hoyt and Jessica, as their marriage is illegal: "The state of Louisiana and the United States of America may not recognize this union, but for my money, there ain't a doubt in my mind that God does. [...] Love is love, plain and simple" (35:37).

Acceptance of diversity is discussed explicitly in a conversation between Sookie and Reverend Daniels. Sookie is given a chance to surrender her supernatural powers and wonders whether her being different, her telepathy, being part fae, could have been a mistake in her creation. The Reverend's reply is unequivocal: no human being can be a mistake, yet it depends on free will how individuals choose to live their lives (42:20-43:16). Ultimately, Sookie accepts that being part fairy is her nature, integral to her individuality. This choice clearly distinguishes her from the character in the novels, who denies her fae part until the very end – she chooses to accept herself with every part of her being, a choice she might not have been able to reach without the vampires in her life. Sookie's brush with the last taboo of the show, final death, leads to her embracing life and realizing her potential, not merely accepting, but celebrating diversity both in herself and in others.

Meyer, Harris, and Ball alike use images of sexuality and sexual awakening; they all employ the Gothic stock character of the vampire as a code for difference. Both approaches generate commercial success with their respective target groups by maintaining the Gothic tradition of the vampire as a projection screen of sexual desires and the aesthetics of danger. The sexual curiosity of the heroine in *Twilight*, fuelled by the vampire's 'Otherness' and sensuality, is a temptation to be avoided, as it bears the danger of complete extinction; in *True Blood*, it is a chance worth taking: the inexperienced teenage self has to be extinguished in order to create room for the new awareness of the adult personality, who creates knowledge from experience – as the vampire has to die first in order to become immortal.

Works Cited

Aikin, Anna Letitia [later Barbauld]. "On the Pleasure Derived from Objects of Terror, with Sir Bertrand, a Fragment." *Miscellaneous Pieces in Prose.* John Aikin and Anna Letitia Barbauld. 3rd ed. London: J. Johnson, 1772. 117-137.

Aleiss, Angela. "Mormon Imagery Runs Deep in *Twilight.*" *The Salt Lake Tribune.* 24 Jun. 2010. Web. 17 Sept. 2010.

Alter, Alexandra. "How to Kill a Vampire (Series)." *The Wall Street Journal Online.* 2 May 2013. Web. 28 Aug. 2013.

Askew, Alice, and Claude. *Aylmer Vance: Ghost Seer.* 1914. London: Wordsworth, 2006.

Barnett, Robert A. "Why Do We Love Vampires?" *Village Entertainment.* 17 Sept. 2009. Web. 3 Jun. 2011.

Cochrane, Kira. "Stephenie Meyer on *Twilight*, Feminism, and True Love." *The Guardian Online.* 11 Mar. 2013. Web. 31 May 2014.

Cogan, Frances B. *All-American Girl: The Ideal of Real Womanhood in Mid-Nineteenth-Century America.* Athens, GA: University of Georgia Press, 1989.

Flood, Alison. "Charlaine Harris Threatened by Fans over Final Sookie Stackhouse Novel. Author of longrunning [sic] vampire saga – inspiration for TV's *True Blood* – becomes target of online vitriol for her choice of ending." *The Guardian Online.* 10 May 2013. Web. 28 Aug. 2013.

Freund, Wieland. "So küssen Mormonen." Rev. of *Breaking Dawn. Die Welt Online.* 24 Nov. 2009. Web. 5 Apr. 2011.

Grigoriadis, Vanessa. "The Joy of Vampire Sex: *True Blood* on Rolling Stone's Latest Cover." 17 Aug. 2010. Web. 13 Jul. 2011.

Harris, Charlaine. *Dead Until Dark.* New York: Ace, 2001.

---. *Living Dead in Dallas.* New York: Ace, 2002.

---. *Dead to the World.* New York: Ace, 2004.

---. *Dead Ever After.* New York: Ace, 2013.

Koopmann, Helmut, ed. *Mythos und Mythologie in der Literatur des 19. Jahrhunderts.* Frankfurt am Main: Vittorio Klostermann, 1979.

Knox, David. "True Blood Finale – What Was That?" Rev. of "Thank You." *TV Tonight.* 28 Aug. 2014. Web. 1 Sept. 2014.

Kwam, Kristen E., Linda S. Schearing, and Valarie H. Ziegler. *Eve and Adam. Jewish, Christian, and Muslim Readings on Genesis and Gender.* Bloomington, Indiana: The Indiana University Press, 1999.

Locker, Melissa, "*True Blood* Series Finale: All's Well That Ends." Rev. of "Thank You." *Time Online.* 25 Aug. 2014. Web. 14 Sept. 2014.

Mann, Bonnie. "Vampire Love: The Second Sex Negotiates the Twenty-First Century." *Twilight and Philosophy: Vampires, Vegetarians and the Pursuit of Immortality.* Eds. William Irwin et al. Hoboken, NJ: John Wiley and Sons, 131-146.

Meyer, Stephenie. *Twilight,* London: Atom, 2005.

---. *New Moon,* London: Atom, 2005.

---. *Eclipse,* London: Atom, 2007.

---. *Breaking Dawn,* London: Atom, 2008.

---. "Twilight: FAQ." *Stephenie Meyer: The Official Site.* Web. 30 Sept. 2010.

Nietzsche, Friedrich. *Die Geburt der Tragödie.* Frankfurt am Main: Insel, 2000.

Rocha, Lauren. "Bite Me: Twilight Stakes Feminism." *Bridgewater State University Undergraduate Review* 7.1 (2010): 148-153.

Senf, Carol A. *The Vampire in Nineteenth-Century Literature.* Bowling Green: Bowling Green University Press, 1988.

Shen, Maxine. "Flesh and Blood." *New York Post.* 23 Jun. 2009. Web. 14 Sept. 2014.

Sparks, Lily. "The Unfortunate End – *True Blood* Series Finale Review: No Thank You." Rev. of "Thank You." *TV.com.* 25 Aug. 2014. Web. 14 Sept. 2014.

"True Blood – Extras: Archived Wallpapers." *True Blood: The Official Site*. HBO. Web. 26 Aug. 2013.

True Blood Episodes:

"Let's Get out of Here." *True Blood – Season 4*. Episode 9. Writ. Brian Buckner. Dir. Romeo Tirone.Warner. 2012. DVD.

"Never Let Me Go." *True Blood – Season 2*. Episode 5. Writ. Nancy Oliver. Dir. John Dahl. Warner. 2010. DVD.

"Somebody That I Used to Know." *True Blood – Season 5*. Episode 8. Writ. Mark Hudis. Dir. Stephen Moyer. Warner. 2012. DVD.

"Spellbound." *True Blood – Season 4*. Episode 8. Writ. Alan Ball. Dir. Daniel Minahan. Warner. 2012. DVD.

"Time Bomb." *True Blood – Season 2*. Episode 8. Writ. Alexander Woo. Dir. John Dahl. Warner. 2010. DVD.

"Thank You." *True Blood – Season 7*. Episode 10. Writ. Brian Buckner. Dir. Scott Winant Warner. HBO. 24 Aug. 2014. TV.

"Who Are You, Really?" *True Blood – Season 6*. Episode 1. Writ. Raelle Tucker. Dir. Stephen Moyer. Warner. HBO. 16 Jun. 2013. TV.

"You Smell Like Dinner." *True Blood – Season 4*. Episode 2. Writ. Brian Buckner.Dir. Scott Winant. Warner. 2012. DVD.

Vanderbeke, Dirk. "The Vampire Strikes Back: On the History of a Nightwalker." *Fastitocalon – Studies in Fantasticism Ancient to Modern* 1.1 (2010): 3-19.

"Westboro Baptist Church Home Page." *Westboro Baptist Church*. Web. 27 Aug. 2013.

Anna Powell

Enchanted Objects: Steampunk Fetishes and Machinic Desire

"Steampunk is too fetishistic about objects" (Miéville 186)

I. Steampunk as Gothic Hybrid

Steampunk is a fantastic sub-cultural hybrid blending Speculative Fiction with Gothic, past with future. It can also incorporate other source components, such as Surrealism, into the mix. Steampunk may be set in an alternative Victorian/Edwardian England or the American Wild West. First used in a book title in 1995 by Paul di Filippo, and linked to the post-industrial dystopias of Cyberpunk, the eclectic fantasy world of Steampunk includes fiction, film, artefacts, web fora, music and fashion as well as an immersive social subculture. As microchip technology is miniaturized into imperceptibility, Steampunk valorizes the aethyr as a mysterious unseen force and imagines an alternate universe powered by steam or clockwork. Its anachronistic penchants include steam powered contraptions, especially flying machines, elaborate clockwork and analogue computers. Drawing on a retro science-fiction 'founded' by Jules Verne and H. G. Wells, contemporary authors include China Miéville, Ian R. MacLeod and Gail Carriger.

Though not all Steampunk is Gothically inclined, both cultures share penchants, practices, and historical roots in the Victorian Gothic revival. Their common relations include stylistic elaboration; neo-Victoriana; Mad Scientists; magic; and abject monsters like kraken, a kind of giant squid. Steampunks might share social events with Goths, such as the Whitby Goth festivals in North Yorkshire. Broadly compared to Goth, Steampunk is more secular and industrial, diurnal, politically more vocal and foregrounds self-reflexivity and deliberate pastiche. Its mood is playful and jolly rather than melancholy. There are stylistic crossovers – e.g. corsets – but these might be embellished by a pair of brass goggles rather than a silver crucifix. Steampunk has strong links with Maker-Culture's hands-on fashioning of recycled material and rejection of throwaway culture. A Venn diagram of subcultural relations would locate a significant number of converts from Gothic black to Steampunk brown in the overlap (Plinke). As well as evident divergences, Steampunk's brighter, more flamboyant take on neo-Victoriana retains a deeper ideological congruence with Goth. Significantly for my current argument, both draw on elements from fetish culture.

Fig. 1: Amy Elizabeth Smith photographed by Eric T. Paradigm

One specific difference is the adoption of character personae by many Steampunks, who regard themselves not as Victorian re-enactors but "re-imaginers" (Bodewell 103). Characters like the dirigible commander, explorer and engineer draw on retro-science-fiction. Other Steampunk types are overtly Gothic: the Mad Scientist; the Vampire or Zombie Hunter; the Decadent Dandy and the *Femme Fatale*. Unlike Goth, Steampunk tends to be a more literary than musical culture. Gatherings, featuring games, parades, balls and competitions, such as tea-duelling, have a hearty and outgoing ambience with gloom or morbidity in scant supply.

One distinctive marker of the subculture is the special object, carried, worn and often made by Steampunks themselves. These objects differ from Goth symbolic talismans with religious, or para-religious, significance (Powell 357-375). Steampunks might wear machinery in the form of jewellery, e.g. clockwork, or perhaps prosthetic body extensions, e.g. mechanical hands. Such temporary body modifications recall Emile Durkheim's tribal clans who "seek to give themselves the external aspect of their totem" (117). I set out to explore the function of special artefacts within Steampunk via the figure of the fetish, an "object of special devotion that evokes powerful, even mythic, emotions […] imbued with a kind of magical power" (Ward 164).

The fetish has three meanings: anthropological, psychoanalytical and political. I will, therefore, consider the use of artefacts as magical, erotic and consumer fetish. Intriguingly, early theorists of fetishism, Durkheim, Sigmund Freud and Karl Marx, were contemporaneous with the Victorian/Edwardian setting of the Steampunk imaginary world. This period, itself a hybrid of reactionary imperialism, repressed manners and radical ferment, is re-presented by the Steampunk use of 'modding', the creative modification of extant material. The Steampunk imaginary era elaborates historical fact – technologies, events, styles and manners – using parody and camp excess as moves in a self-reflective game. My methodology combines theory and practice and offers some sense of how Steampunks perceive themselves. Research draws on personal observation and conversation at events like Lincoln Asylum Victorian Steampunk Convention, email interviews and internet sources. I include the comments of designers and practitioners on their work. My initial focus is the Steampunk machine, operant on the cusp of science and magic in ways that recall anthropological fetishism.

II. Making Magic

"[M]aking is the religion of Steampunk" (Bodewell 103)

For Durkheim, sacredness is a potentially heterogeneous quality, as "there are religious phenomena which belong to no determined religion" (36); indeed, "anything can be sacred" in the right context (37). Compared to the Gothic plethora of Christian and pagan iconography Steampunk appears secular, yet elements of its mythology, such as the Mad Scientist, draw on metaphysical ideas. The Gothic uncanny, which brings non-human, familiar objects disturbingly to life, is paralleled by

Steampunk's notions of mysterious powers that science can harness. Both types of force operate a kind of neo-animism in which human investment lends supplementary powers to objects. Steampunk's own magical thinking is manifest in the intimate relations of animate machines and their makers.

In Steampunk, intangible forces are invoked by turning machinery inside out to reveal its secret workings, e.g. clockwork. In both fiction and practice, engines may be driven by steam, electricity or oil derivatives, which are central to Dieselpunk, a retro-futurist subculture that foregrounds diesel technologies, art-deco and neo-noir. These ostensible fuels are, however, avatars for more elemental forces. This idea seems shaped by Frankenstein's Galvanism, which uses lightning to "infuse a spark of being into the life-less thing" (Shelley 38). *Frankenstein* is a seminal Steampunk inspiration via early horror film adaptations that "glorified machines with big switches and chaotic electrical discharges" (Hendley). The archaic term aether/yr has particular Steampunk resonance and draws on both Victorian scientists and Albert Einstein's modified "new aether" in his theory of general relativity from 1920. As well as using the term to signify the internet's transference of thought waves, Steampunks also deploy it more scientifically to mean Tesla's version of electromagnetic energy. Aether is frequently referenced in Steampunk fiction and is central to Ian R. MacLeod's novel *The Light Ages*, published in 2004, as the driving force behind the industrial revolution.

Some Steampunk perceptions of unseen forces draw on the hybrid relations of science and magic at the Victorian *fin de siècle*, as seen in the "Metaphysics" thread of the internet forum Brass Goggles and in "spirit collectors and ghost hunting gear" postings. The Victorian integration of science/electricity and spiritualism/occultism imbued these new concepts with "qualities that verge upon this spectral realm – hence the use of terms like 'Vibrations,' 'Animal Magnetism,' 'Electric Fluid' and 'Flux Condenser' in the spiritualist and magical literature of the era" (Postrophe). This notion of a ubiquitous, elemental, power *in potentia* recalls the *mana* of tribal cultures as referenced by Durkheim (218-219).

Durkheim's comparison of magic with religion asserts the former as "more elementary" because "seeking technical and utilitarian ends, it does not waste its time in pure speculation" (42). Rather than invoking the Gothic supernatural, the occult powers of Steampunk devices enhance the laws of physics. According to inventor Professor Brasspounder, Steampunk science combines a nostalgic "Jules Verne world view in which science appears powerful, somewhat mysterious and with dark overtones" with "a what-if alternative world, where ideas that fell by the wayside – such as the æther – are given the opportunity to flourish anew" (Brasspounder). For Brasspounder, "mysterious, but nevertheless material forces" offer to Steampunk "an effective alternative to Magick for a fantasy world-view that, as its clockwork suggests, is firmly rooted in the material universe".

Fig. 2: Wimshurst Machine by Professor Erasmus Brasspounder

Yet for other Steampunks, like Torrent, "things that exist in physics are just done better by magic". When Steampunk technology uses magic, "steel is stronger, black powder is more explosive, lifting balloons are more efficient. So magic becomes an intensifier and an enabler for the steam tech" (Torrent). Many devices, then, whether traditional, scientific or psychic, invoke and deploy special powers by which the creator imbues the machine with life.

III. Steampunk Animism

In Durkheim's account, the animist ascribes "souls [...] analogous to his own" to explain the "phenomena of the physical world" (53). Yet, the degree of sacredness varies considerably, some objects being regarded as "nothing exceptional" (Durkheim 37). The owner of a magical fetish manipulates it to get an intended result (Durkheim 38). Steampunks frequently express a desire to "find the spirit in the machine again" (New Orangutang) as an antidote to the perceived alienation of modern technology. Dr Simeon Marsh, an artisan who sells customized "Steampunk, neo-Gothic and urban survival creations", wants to "take today's technology and give it a soul by using materials such as brass and wood" (Marsh). He seeks to re-animate the inherent life of objects by "using discarded items and giving them life and soul" (Marsh). In both fiction and practice, then, some degree of animism is operant as Steampunk attributes consciousness to inanimate objects without a religious content.

Freud's theory of the uncanny from 1919 was a response to Otto Jentsch's 1906 paper on animism, and both referenced E.T.A. Hoffmann's Gothic tale "The Sand-Man" from 1815, in which a young man desires an automaton. Contemporary Steampunk forms of machinic animism recall Jentsch's uncanny rather than Freud's as they reinterpret non-living devices in "anthropomorphic terms, in a poetic or fantastic way" (Jentsch 13-14). Early twentieth-century theorists, including Freud, regarded animism negatively as a regressive tendency involving narcissistic fantasy. They aligned it to the "mentality of the primitive who, like an infant, cannot distinguish the animate and the inanimate" and they advocate that animistic desires be outgrown with the onset of normal adult development (Durkheim 53).

Yet, instead of denigrating animism as the phantasmatic repudiation of reality, it is possible to regard it more positively, as an attempt to recapture a vital connection with the environment. In *The Re-enchantment of the World*, cultural historian Morris Berman asserts that the denial of animism by a scientific world view has led to a condition of disenchantment. Berman's advocacy of a neo-animistic "participating consciousness" involves "a merger, or identification, with one's surroundings, and bespeaks a psychic wholeness that has long since passed" (16). For Berman, a participating consciousness thus seeks to bridge the experiential void of disenchantment.

Steampunk animism is closely linked to anthropomorphism. Whilst the former involves a numinous encounter with the natural world, the latter remakes the world in the human image. Steampunks' anthropomorphic tendencies are evoked in the oft-cited Catastrophone Orchestra's manifesto:

> Steampunk machines are real, breathing, coughing, struggling and rumbling parts of the world. They are not the airy intellectual fairies of algorithmic mathematics but the hulking manifestations of muscle and mind, the progeny of sweat, blood, tears, and delusions. The technology of Steampunk is natural; it moves, lives, ages, and even dies. (Onion 145)

The Mad Scientist of Gothic deploys mysterious forces for horrific ends, thus exemplifying the psychoanalytic view of animism as dangerously uncanny. Though Steampunk machines rarely produce terror, they might evoke a sublime awe and wonder in their admirers. Such expansive feelings recall Henri Bergson's concept of *élan vital*, or vital impulse, in his post-Darwinian *Creative Evolution* from 1911. Here, Bergson uses the 'age of steam' to speculate on the significance of machinery. He distinguishes mechanism, the soulless computation of parts added together, from the living machine driven by the intuitive energy of consciousness as "a machine which would triumph over mechanism" (Deleuze, *Bergsonism* 107; Bergson 278). Marsh celebrates the artisan as catalyzer of the hidden potential of raw materials who leaves a trace of risk or imagination on each piece. Metal brought to life in the Artisan's hands with colours and hues to delight the eye. Wood – once a living organism – is brought back to life, its colour and grain again adding beauty. Tool markings that enhance the look as well show processes used to create the item.

Steampunk Gothic is thus a contemporary artisanal reaction against an information technology perceived as soulless. In William Gibson and Bruce Sterling's seminal *The Difference Engine* from 1992, the artisanal Luddites are suppressed when the British Empire rule the world via the steam-driven difference engine. Steampunk culture, however, makes engineering into an artisanal craft as it challenges the sterile repetitiveness and built-in obsolescence of digital technology. As microchip electronics conceal production marks and hide inner workings, so Steampunk exposes them and makes them tangible. This artisanal ideal recalls the Victorian Arts and Crafts movement; the Asylum festival offers a Ruskin award for 2D art and a Rossetti prize for aesthetics. The producerly culture of Steampunk operates autopoetic fashioning of discarded materials to make new machines by hands-on methods. The modding – or, modification – of devices such as clocks to subvert the original use-value is also widespread. As Henry Jenkins comments, "Steampunks aren't just buying old stuff on Ebay; they are building the kinds of alternative technologies they are imagining; they are creating objects that have the functionality of contemporary technology but have the aesthetic beauty and craftsmanship we associate with the gilded age" (xv).

Steampunk machines thus appear driven by aesthetic rather than utilitarian rationales as they challenge capitalistic production in a period of economic decline by recycling and modding discarded found-objects from charity and junk shops. As Percival McGillicutty asserts, "as long as you have an imagination, you can be steampunk". For Cory Doctorow, "technology can be an artisanal, non-industrial practice", but "when you take humanity out of the technology, society starts to talk in a passive voice" and human agency declines (59). Margaret Magpie Killjoy claims that machines are alienated from their true purpose by industry. For Killjoy, "it's not the machines'" fault that they have been tied down in factories and been used to make the machinery of war or the machinery of social alienation"; she advocates destroying "not machines but industrialization" ("Technology" 50-51). Doctorow argues that vintage items that Steampunks consider "beautiful, quaint, and charming" should not be separated from the "harsh material conditions which made them possible, from the other cultures which were being suppressed in the name of extending the empire" (63). I will revisit some of these political issues in the light of consumer fetishism later. As the three types of Steampunk fetishism are mutually enhancing, I will give brief considera-tion to the erotic fetish.

IV. Erotic Fetishism

In the long-established wake of Gothic erotica, the production and consumption of Steampunk is a flourishing business. An Erotic Steampunk festival is held in Seattle and a plethora of novels and short stories with fetishism as a prominent feature appear online. So how has fetishism, which acts "like a magic charm that enables you to perform sexually" (Burnstein 263) been conceptualized by sexologists? For Richard von Krafft-Ebing, who first used the term to characterize sexual predilections, "fetishism concentrates the whole sexual interest in one part abstracted from the entire body" (35). Yet, its cultural operations are more extensive than body parts, as, being "complicated with purely aesthetic tastes", it can take on "an independent sensual value" (Krafft-Ebing 179). For Laplanche and Pontalis fetishism occurs "when the orgasm is subordinated absolutely to certain extrinsic conditions, which may even be sufficient in themselves to bring about sexual pleasure" (306).

So what did Freud intend by his use of the term fetishism, characterized as a perversion that "departs from reproduction in its aims and pursues the attainment of gratification independently" (*Introductory Lectures* 266)? For him, it extends or transgresses a limit "either to the part of the body concerned or to the sexual object chosen" (*Case Studies I* 83). As well as body parts, a fetish may be "an inanimate object" related to a desired person, such as fragments of clothing and underwear (Freud, *On Sexuality* 66). Freud characterizes fetishes as "unsuitable substitutes" for the "normal" sexual object and reproductive aim, leading to the "sexual overvaluation" of objects (*On Sexuality* 65). He sketches a continuum between perverse and "normal" overestimation, asserting that the fetish only becomes pathological when it "takes the place of the normal sexual aim" to become "the sole sexual object" (*On Sexuality* 65). It originates in childhood associations or unconscious "symbolic connection of thought" (*On Sexuality* 67). He mentions the foot as "a very primitive sexual symbol already found in myths" as well as fur associated with "the hair of the *mons veneris*" (*On Sexuality* 67). Freud aligns this substitution with the anthropological fetish, "in which savages believe that their gods are embodied" (*On Sexuality* 67). Psychoanalytically speaking, fetishism thus disavows – *Verleugnung* – the real, i.e. the fact that the mother lacks a penis (*On Sexuality* 353) and thus splits – *Spaltung* – the ego into two divergent tendencies, repression and idealization (*On Metapsychology* 150).

A celebratory view of the female fetishism denied by early sexologists repudiates Freud's "magisterial phallus" for a "multiplicity of pleasures, needs and contradictions" (McClintock 2). For McClintock, fetishes like leather, rubber, handcuffs, religious iconography are not phallic substitutes. Her emphasis is instead on their social resonance, since "fetishes involve the displacement onto impassioned objects of a host of social contradictions, they defy reduction to a single originary trauma or the psychopathology of the individual subject" (21). Though feminist-informed theory brings in wider social context for fetishism, much nevertheless remains limited to bondage and domination.

So what type of fetishistic scenarios are preferred by Steampunks? My research focused on female producers, consumers and commentators, who recalled the aesthetic-erotic pleasure and sensory stimulation of clothes, gadgets and other "inorganic objects" (Burnstein 267). For Kristina Wright, author of the "lush and fantastical world of women-centered stories", Steampunk erotica comprise "shiny brass and crushed velvet; mechanical inventions and romantic conventions; sexual fantasy and kinky fetish". Whilst "fetishizing the wardrobe, language, fantasy and rituals" of Steampunk, Wright's *Steamlust* series includes "alternate histories, second worlds, time travel and contemporary settings". J. Blackmore's collection *Like a Corset Undone* features a fairly typical array of lesbian Victoriana, whereas in Silvia Day's novella, *Iron Hard*, the scholarly narrator is aroused by the sight of the hero's mechanical arm.

It is a familiar cliché that Freud aligns weapons, both "*knives, daggers, lances, sabres* [emphasis in the original]" and firearms, "rifles, pistols and revolvers" with penises as fantasy formations (*Introductory Lectures* 30). Because of their "property of penetrating, and consequently of injuring" the body, he locates them in female anxiety dreams about sexual intercourse (130). Given the centrality of weaponry in Steampunk culture, guns feature as fetishes in an exaggeratedly Freudian way. In R. E. Bond's novella "The Skydancer", the heroine fires an overtly phallic pistol "shorter-barrelled [than the hero's] with a bulbous end over the handle" (73). When she holds "the wondrous, deadly thing" in her hand and fires, "the vibration spiked and the disc flared like a bright splash of lightning" so that "the contact of the trigger and the lightning splash went straight to [her] sex" (72). Ray Broadus Browne notes that the dichotomy of the sexual and the death fetish is artificial, as "the threat of castration with which the sexual fetish is closely and causally associated *is* the threat of death" (137; emphasis in the original). According to this theory, the erotic allure of Steampunk weaponry might bear a *frisson* of danger and threat despite this being disavowed or concealed.

For Steampunk maker von Plinke, fetishes include "guns, corsets, uniforms, boots, gloves, lace, velvet and straps" and notably "gadgets, some of which are prosthetic, and which may be working mechanical devices rather than just look like them". Steampunk fetishism features an element of self-parody, whereas Goth "fetish play" tends towards a more intense performance of S/M and bondage games (Weinstock 380). For von Plinke, water pistols and nerf guns offer an appealing way of "interacting playfully with other people." Her modded water pistol was consciously intended to evoke hybrid associations "with water and the sea through fish motifs (fish heads over the muzzles and fins along the sides), but at the same time to be slightly disturbing and emphasise the phallic associations of guns and fish" (Plinke). It was only when the gun – with its glossy black finish and gold decoration – was finished that she "realised it looked like rubber and had that kind of fetish aspect as well".

Fig. 3: Nerf Gun by Liliana von Plinke

A Steampunk gun, then, is a liminal object that is considerably more, and other, than a phallic substitute.

Steampunk guns are powered by magical substances. One fictional inventor (Nate) invents one using "liquefied Aetheric Ether" of which "a one ounce vial of the strange blue glowing liquid will power the gun for several thousand shots" (Smaggers). With wizards for ancestors, his skill as a technomancer is enhanced by an "innate magical talent" (Smaggers). Another writer deploys aether as a long-lasting "clean technology" fuel, "hazily amber in color", to power guns and other machines (Archibald Broce). Lord Nicholas Horsethorn built an Odic Force laser-gun by "putting a crystal in a sealed box, and then applying a "magical" method of extracting and using the energy produced [via] a set of Occult Symbols to concentrate the energy, amplify it with input from the operator's "Vital Energy" (Horsethorn). The creative conceptualization and concrete properties of such magical weaponry add a further metaphysical dimension to the erotic aura of Steampunk weapons.

As well as its magical Samaritan gun and prosthetic "hand of doom", the iconography of *Hellboy* (Del Toro) impacts on Steampunk fetishism in the "clockwork zombie" figure of Baron von Kroenen, whose gas mask hides the disfigurements of his masochistic surgical addiction. "Elder Goth" novelist Cherie Priest depicts her gas-powered zombies in *Boneshaker* with "much that is borrowed" from both fetish and Goth cultures (Priest 76). Masks combine rubber and leather fetishism with the potential *frisson* of autoerotic asphyxiation. William Gibson describes certain Steampunk bondage masks as "dark, spooky things: full head masks that you have to lace something back and they're made of horse hide and brass and repurposed industrial bits [...] formally fucked up and interesting things" (219). Alternately, Amelia Satchell Botham-Phelps evokes the romantic glamour of the Steampunk mask, which "shares the eroticism and mystery of the Venetian Masked Ball. Masks give "anonymity", although some "could be construed as passing over the boundary into fetish" (Botham-Phelps). So Steampunk objects function as fetishes in both magical and erotic senses. My next section develops their cultural implications via the socio-political landscape of Steampunk and the function of the consumer fetish within it.

V. Consumer Fetishism and the Politics of Steampunk

"A commodity appears, at first sight, a very trivial thing, and
easily understood. Its analysis shows that it is, in reality, a very
queer thing, abounding in metaphysical subtleties and theological
niceties" (Marx 163)

Browsing the internet, I found a "Victorian style steampunk capitalist
swine" for sale as a second-life avatar ("A Victorian"). Such an obviously
commercial, yet politically savvy item seems to embody the contradictory
nature of a Steampunk commerce that ranges from cheaply mass-
produced products to artists displaying their work at conventions in
exchange for Steampunk admiration as their main cultural capital. Some
merchants are also "middlemen", who sell recycled components such as
copper tubes and clock parts to artisans for modding into new devices.
Steampunk's reworking of the Victorian era raises questions for us in
contemporary society, itself neo-Victorian in many ways (Paul,
"Victorian Values").

Despite its ostensibly a-political veneer, Steampunk displays a broad
spectrum of contradictory and self-reflexive political perspectives,
including a contentiously neo-conservative imperialist nostalgia with
attendant fantasies that "continue the racist tradition of Orientalism"
(Killjoy, "Countering Victorientalism"). The subculture also encom-
passes a William Morris-style idealization of working-class artisans and
politics. Flynn MacCallister reflects that "the age of steam was built by
the working class"; yet, though nostalgic "for the old form of the unions",
she is "not fond of the modern version". For one socialist Steampunk,
some of his peers are "afraid of the realities of Victorian life, and use
steampunk as a form of escapism, a means of retreat rather than a
platform for activity, and even activism, which steampunk has so much
potential to be" (Wood).

Many Steampunks play at being 'toffs', often ironically. At the
Steampunk World's Fair in New Jersey, typical entertainment included
absinthe tasting, a tea party and a game of steam croquet. "During a
competition called the Dandy-Off, mock aristocrats traded insults to see
who could act the snobbiest" (Rose). Von Plinke notes that a mock-
military parade at Lincoln drew on the parodic British film *Carry on up
the Khyber*; yet the focus on Empire by some Steampunks remains
discomfiting, "because of the possibility of racism or racist associations

in a situation where most participants are white" (Plinke). Another commentator, however, regards Steampunk as non-discriminatory, as "anyone can be steampunk, no matter your size, shape, color, race, religious orientation, sexual orientation" (Rose).

The work of American Steampunk scholar Diana M. Pho critiques both Victorientalism and consumer fetishism. Pho considers how "various ideologies concerning the treatment of steampunk objects are embraced, rejected, and proliferated in a post-industrial, information economy and how steampunk's postmodern, mediatized identity serves both in conjunction with and in reaction against anti-consumerist stances". On the anarchist side are bloggers like Steampunk Emma Goldman and websites like the anachro-anarcho blog to celebrate Steampunk's subversive potential, as it "embraces the monstrous machine in neo-luddite fashion, and in its radical nature subverts the conventional morality, opinions and culture of the Victorian Era" (Sarat). For Christopher Andrews, the culture's anti-consumerist stance belongs to a continuum with the Occupy Wall Street movement.

Yet, Steampunk also exhibits consumer fetishism. Like Freud, Marx draws on anthropology to evoke the mystical allure of consumer objects, in "the whole mystery of commodities, all the magic and necromancy that surrounds the products of labour as long as they take the form of commodities" (169). For Marx, commodities operate on us as "something transcendent" and he references both tribal religious practices and séances to evoke their fetishistic power. A commodified table, for example, "evolves out of its wooden brain grotesque ideas, far more wonderful than if it were to begin dancing of its own free will" (164). The "mysterious character" of this transformation of objects into commodities originates neither in their use value or other "determining factors" of value (Marx 164).

For Marx, social relations thus assume "the fantastic form of a relation between things" (162) and the best analogy for this is "the mist-enveloped regions of the religious world" where phenomena "appear as independent beings endowed with life, and entering into relation both with one another and the human race" (165). Fetishism is likewise "inseparable from the production of commodities" (Marx 166). Value, rather than use, thus "converts every product into a social hieroglyphic" (Marx 167). Marx's identification of the "transcendent" allure of commodities is designed to demystify and expose "the peculiar social character of the labour that produces them" (165) as part of his revolutionary project. The secret of labour is "hidden under the apparent movements in the relative values of commodities" (Marx 168). Steampunks who sell out by buying mass-produced ready-mades rather than making their own have become "so used to capitalism, that is, having things done for them in exchange for money, which results in a lack of pride in appearance and attitude" (Wood).

One of the most vocal critics of Steampunk politics is the British novelist China Miéville. For him, the "reverence for the idea of creating as opposed to consuming" belongs to the surrealist tradition of bricolage via "magical objects" such as those produced by André Breton, Man Ray and Meret Oppenheim (181). The allures of these "enchanted objects" are, however, "Janus-faced" and can "become commodified in turn [in] an inevitable banalization" (Miéville 182). Miéville's Marxist-informed critique emphasizes that Steampunk's historical development is "absolutely related to relations of power in the last 12 years [...] not just neo-liberalism but neo-conservatism as well" (183). This "precise temporal overlap" between the rise of steampunk and neo-conservative reaction in both the UK and US might be viewed as sanctioning "a kind of propaganda of the rehabilitation of empire" (Miéville 185).

Specifically addressing the operations of consumerism, Miéville identifies a "ludicrous overinvestment" in Steampunk object fetishism which regards artisanal processes in isolation from political economy which becomes "abstracted out" (184). This kind of aestheticized abstraction enables reification and commercial exploitation, so that "once the culture industry really gets a hold of it, it becomes to a certain extent self-sustaining because as long as it's cool, people can make a buck on it" (Miéville 186). Miéville warns that unless a clear-headed economic and political critique is maintained, Steampunk is in danger of becoming "a subculture based on a certain set of delights in a particular aesthetically interpreted moment" (188).

VI. A Culture of Ambivalence

As befits both its Gothic and postmodern aspects, Steampunk object fetishism remains deeply ambivalent. Bloggers Parliament and Wake assert that Steampunk objects are more than merely "clever exercises in anachronism". For some, Steampunk "promises the progressive mobilization of ideas, a prime example of [the] 'ethical spectacle'", whereas to others its political potential is "deferred in favor of fulfilling artistic commercial aspirations" (Parliament and Wake). Diane Pho also admits confusion as to "whether the use of the Victorian aesthetic is a form of political appropriation by progressives, a form of socially conservative nostalgia for a problematic sociopolitical era or something else in between".

Within the complex dynamics of mass cultural fantasy, Parliament and Wake claim that "apparently escapist fantastical role-playing is actually protective against the malign influences of mass commercialism". Steampunk "worlds" remain "the inventions of their participants" and some might "imagine a world without shopping malls and a dominant automobile-petrochemical complex". Inevitably, though, the heterogeneity and size of the culture ensures "two (or more) intensely opposed points of view over even the most innocuous political positions" (Parliament and Wake). On the negative side the Steampunk aesthetic may be used to "market endless quantities of cheap plastic crap, and Steampunks themselves can be aggressively apolitical" and yet, for Parliament and Wake, even if "Steampunk is only an aesthetic, a style, a literary motif – we have to remember that aesthetics have power".

Other responses offer more partial advocacy of Steampunk's anti-consumerism. For Nick Ottens rejecting "the soullessness of mass produced consumer goods" is "not to say we all intend to fight the system, destroy the factories and dismantle consumerism altogether". Parliament and Wake themselves pessimistically note the "relentless efforts of retailers both independent and multinational to cash in on the appeal of Steampunk", exemplifying its reification by teen idol Justin Bieber's release of a Steampunk Christmas video in 2011 to cash in on the trend. So mutant Gothic fantasy grafts Victoriana onto contemporary concerns to produce new cultural hybrids, some of them disappointingly crass.

VII. Conclusion: From Fetish to Machine

So how far can the triple-headed figure of the fetish account for the objects of Steampunk culture? A useful tool to explore Steampunk signification in theory and practice, the triplicate fetish offers a mixture of progressive and reactionary conclusions. Yet, rather than fixing the Steampunk fetish under the aegis of the magical or 'primitive' repudiation of reality, or else the emblem of alienated production in late capitalism, another approach to conceptualizing Steampunk objects may be on offer to shift this negative paradigm.

A more expansive view of the Steampunk unconscious becomes visible through the prism of Deleuze and Guattari's work. They highlight two tendencies operant when fetishes are regarded solely as signifiers. The first finds "a problem of political power and economic and religious force inseparable from the fetish" (*Anti-Oedipus* 199). The second stems from psychoanalysis, which never says "Phallus-Oedipus-Castration more often than apropos the fetish" (Deleuze and Guattari, *Anti-Oedipus* 199). Rather than either of these signification-based approaches, Deleuze and Guattari use the figure of the machine to repudiate Freud's Oedipal ego in favour of a machinic libido by which desire might invest the social. For them, rather, it was "a mistake to have ever said *the id*. Everywhere *it* is machines" (*Anti-Oedipus* 1). In Deleuze and Guattari's critique of patriarchal capitalism, the machine can be used to figure new ways of conjoining human with non-human as machinic assemblage.

Fetishes, like symbols, are part-object "manifestations of desiring-machines" for Deleuze and Guattari (*Anti-Oedipus* 200). Rather than fixing fetishes as forms of representation, they seek to discover "the way these machines function" (*Anti-Oedipus* 200). Their critique gives part-objects a pivotal role in a new molecular machine of the unconscious where, "with every structure dislodged, every memory abolished, every organism set aside, every link undone, they function as raw partial objects, dispersed working parts of a machine that is itself dispersed. In short, partial objects are the molecular functions of the unconscious" (Deleuze and Guattari, *Anti-Oedipus* 356). Thus, libidinal components may work together in assemblage in an anti-Oedipal "desiring-production" because its molecular investments have entered the pre-personal regime "of partial objects, of singularities, of intensities, of gears and parts of machines of desire" (Deleuze and Guattari, *Anti-Oedipus* 358).

So how might we begin to reconfigure the psychological and cultural significance of Steampunk objects? Deleuze and Guattari's deployment of the book to model machinic assemblages might help to conceptualize Steampunk's literal machines as assemblages of part-objects. All machines, according to them, are crossed by "lines of articulation or segmentarity, strata and territories; but also lines of flight, movements of deterritorialisation and destratification" (*A Thousand Plateaus* 4). The machine is stretched in many, contradictory directions by the forces of majoritarian organization and minoritarian chaos. As Deleuze and Guattari suggest, magical transformations occur when "an intensive trait starts working for itself, a hallucinatory perception, synaesthesia, perverse mutation, or play of images shakes loose, challenges the hegemony of the signifier" (*A Thousand Plateaus* 16).

Steampunk machines are often non-productive and their recycling of discarded consumer items prefers libidinal expenditure to surplus-value. They are not inherently designed for corporate production and the top-down engineering of hegemony. It may be argued that minds in assemblage with such a machine experience a desire not entirely contained by the capitalist modes of signification. As transformational machines that produce not economic reification but aesthetic delight, they might be mobilized in this way because, "composed not of units but of dimensions, or rather directions in motion" they are compelled to change their nature as signs (Deleuze and Guattari, *A Thousand Plateaus* 23). From being a discrete unit in capitalist signifying systems to becoming an assemblage of shifting plateaus, such a machinic rhizome is always "in the middle" (Deleuze and Guattari, *A Thousand Plateaus* 24). By dint of having "neither beginning nor end" it continuously grows and "over-spills" its container as its living forces are magically set in motion (Deleuze and Guattari, *A Thousand Plateaus* 23).

Steampunk Gothic devices, powered by an aetheric blend of science and magic, are not distanced objects of aesthetic contemplation but incorporate us as components in their dynamic assemblage. Despite the reification of capitalist profiteering, historical amnesia and retro nostalgia, the magical machines of Steampunk are not reducible to these. These artisanal part-objects also offer creative play and the possibility of new thought. They both replicate and parody historical models and, by modding the unwanted detritus of capitalist production, create fresh hybrids. Sometimes they challenge the hegemonic reifications of corporate capitalism by exposing its hidden mechanisms and compelling its invisible forces to become manifest. In keeping with the Gothic milieu of their inception, the fetishes of Steampunk can be read as oscillators that both arrest the flows and act as the generators of desire. Moving towards "a radical change of regimes in the fetish" (Deleuze and Guattari, *Anti-Oedipus* 212), they might also have the potential to leave the signifying chain of representation via their mobilization of machinic desire.

Works Cited

"A Victorian Style Capitalist Swine." *Marketplace Second Life*. 33084323. Web. 31 August 2013.

Andrews, Christopher, and Lisa Rose. "Steampunk Power." *NJ.Com*. December 2012. Web. 12 September 2013.

Bergson, Henri. *Creative Evolution*. 1911. Trans. Arthur Mitchell. Lanham, MD: University Press of America, 1983.

Berman, Morris. *The Re-enchantment of the World*. New York: Cornell University Press, 1981.

Bibby, Michael, and Lauren Goodlad, eds. *Goth: Undead Subculture*. Durham, NC: Duke University Press, 2007. 357-375.

Bodewell, Jordan. "Steampunk: A Dinner in Three Courses." *Vintage Tomorrows*. Eds. James H. Carrott and Brian David Johnson. Sebastopol, CA: O'Reilly, 2013. 87-117.

Bond, R E. "Skydancer." Ed. J. Blackmore. *Like a Corset Undone*. Steampunk Library. Circlet Press. 2009. E-book, Web. 1 September 2013.

Botham-Phelps. Flight Lieutenant Amelia Satchell (Dr Janet Schofield). Message to Anna Powell. 1 Oct 2013. Email.

Brasspounder Professor Erasmus. Message to Anna Powell. 25 Sept 2013. Email.

Broce, Archibald. "Re: Aether, Magic, Machines." Brass Goggles. 29 April 2011. Email.

Browne, Broadus Ray, ed. *Objects of Special Devotion: Fetishism in Popular Culture*. Wisconsin: University of Wisconsin Popular Press, 1982.

Burnstein, Jessica. "Material Distinctions: An Interview with Valerie Steele." *Goth: Undead Subculture*. Eds. Michael Bibby and Lauren Goodlad. Durham, NC: Duke University Press, 2007. 257-277.

Carriger, Gail. *Soulless*. London: Orbit Books, 2009.

Carrott, James H., and Brian David Johnson, eds. *Vintage Tomorrows*. Sebastopol, CA: O'Reilly, 2013.

Day, Sylvia. "Iron Hard." *Sylviaday.com*. 6 August 2013. Web. 1 September 2013.

Deleuze, Gilles, and Félix Guattari. *A Thousand Plateaus: Capitalism and Schizophrenia*. Trans. Brian Massumi. London: Continuum, 2004.

---. *Anti-Oedipus: Capitalism and Schizophrenia*. Trans. Robert Hurley, Mark Seem, and Helen R. Lane. London: Athlone, 1984.

Deleuze, Gilles. *Bergsonism*. New York: Zone Books, 1988.

Di Fillippo, Paul. *The Steampunk Trilogy*. Philadelphia, PA: Running Press, 1995.

Doctorow, Cory. "Technology that Ships Broken." *Vintage Tomorrows*. Eds. James H. Carrott and Brian David Johnson. Sebastopol, CA: O'Reilly, 2013. 47-67.

Durkheim, Emile. *The Elementary Forms of the Religious Life*. Trans. Joseph Ward Swain. Release Date: November 13 2012. E-book.

Einstein, Albert. "Aether and Relativity." Address, University of Leiden. May 5 1920. Web. 3 June 2011.

Freud, Sigmund. "The Uncanny." 1919. Penguin Freud Library Vol 14: *Art and Literature*. Harmondsworth: Penguin, 1990.

---. *Case Studies 1: Dora and Little Hans*. Penguin Freud Library Vol 8. Harmondsworth: Penguin, 1990.

---. *Introductory Lectures on Psychoanalysis*. Trans. Joan Rivière. London: George Allen and Unwin, 1949.

---. *Three Essays on the Theory of Sexuality*. Penguin Freud Library Vol 7. Harmondsworth: Penguin, 1905.

Gamman, Lorraine, and Merja Makinen. *Female Fetishism: A New Look.* London: Lawrence and Wishart, 1994.

Gibson William and Bruce Sterling. *The Difference Engine.* New York: Bantam, 1992.

Gibson, William. "Punking Time in Key West." *Vintage Tomorrows.* Eds. James H. Carrott and Brian David Johnson. Sebastopol, CA: O'Reilly, 2013. 207-231.

Goldman, Steampunk Emma. "A Healthy Alternative to Fascism." *Anarcho-anarcho Blogspot.* 12 Dec 2011. Web. 31 August 2013.

Hellboy. Dir. Guillermo Del Toro. Perf. Ron Perlman, Selma Blair, John Hurt. 2004.

Hendley, Simon "Re: Steampunk Questionnaire." Message to Anna Powell. 24 Oct 2010. Email.

Hoffmann, E. T. A. "The Sandman." 1815. *Tales of Hoffmann.* Harmondsworth: Penguin, 1982. 85-127.

Horsethorn, Lord Nicholas. "Re: Aether, Magic, Machines." Brass Goggles. 24 April 2011. Email.

Jenkins, Henry. "Foreword." *Vintage Tomorrows.* Eds. James H. Carrott and Brian David Johnson. Sebastopol, CA: O'Reilly, 2013. vii-xvii.

Jentsch, Otto. "The Uncanny." 1906. Web. 4 March 2011.

Killjoy, Margaret Magpie. "Countering Victorientalism." *Steampunkmagazine.com.* March 2010. Web. 5 September 2013.

Krafft-Ebing, Richard von. *Psychopathia Sexualis: With Especial Reference to the Antipathic Sexual Instinct: A Medico-forensic Study.* Trans. Franklin S. Klaf. New York: Stein and Day, 1965.

Laplanche, Jean, and J. B. Pontalis. *The Language of Psychoanalysis.* London: Karnac, 1988.

MacCallister, Flynn. "Re: Steampunk Questionnaire." Brass Goggles.18 October 2010. Email.

MacLeod, Ian R. *The Light Ages.* London and Sidney: Simon and Schuster, 2004.

Marsh, Simeon. "Re: Steampunk Questionnaire." Message to Anna Powell. 20 April 2011. Email.

---. "Re: Steampunk Questionnaire." Message to Anna Powell. 30 Sept 2010. Email.

Marx Karl. *Capital*. Vol 1. A Critique of Political Economy. Trans. Ben Fowkes. Harmondsworth: Penguin, 1976.

McClintock, Anne. "The Return of Female Fetishism and the Fiction of the Phallus." *New Formations* 19. *Perversity*. Spring 1993. 1-21.

McGillicutty, Sir Percival Archibald, and Lisa Rose. "Steampunk Power." *NJ.Com*. Dec 2012. Web. 12 September 2013.

Miéville, China. "History has Sharp Edges." *Vintage Tomorrows*. Eds. James H. Carrott and Brian David Johnson. Sebastopol, CA: O'Reilly, 2013. 175-207.

---. *Perdido Street Station*. London: Palgrave Macmillan, 2000.

Onion, Rebecca. "Reclaiming the Machine: An Introductory Look at Steampunk in Everyday Practice." *Neo-Victorian Studies* 1:1. Autumn 2008. 138-163. Web. 30 March 2011.

Ottens, Nick. "Does Steampunk Matter if It isn't Revolutionary?" *Gatehouse Online Dieselpunk and Steampunk Magazine*. 9 Dec 2011. Web. 25 September 2013.

Parliament and Wake. "Why Steampunk (Still) Matters." *Parliamentandwake.com*. Web. 2 October. 2013.

Paul, Ronald. "Imperial Nostalgia: Victorian Values, History, and Teenage Fiction in Britain." Gothenburg University, 2009. Web. 1 June, 2014.

Pho, Diana M. "Objectified and Politicised: The Dynamics of Ideology and Consumerism in Steampunk Culture." *Academia.edu*. 126703. Web. 1 October 2013.

---. *Beyondvictoriana.com*. Web. 1 September 2013.

Plinke, Countess Liliana von. Message to Anna Powell. 18 September 2013. Email.

Postrophe, Professor. "Re: Aether, Magic, Machines." Brass Goggles. 24 April. 2011. Email.

Powell, Anna. "God's Own Medicine: Religion and Para Religion in UK Gothic Culture." *Goth: Undead Subculture*. Eds. Michael Bibby and Lauren Goodlad. Durham, NC: Duke University Press, 2007. 357-375.

Priest, Cherie. "A World-Destroying Death-Ray Should Look Like a World Destroying Death Ray." *Vintage Tomorrows*. Eds. James H. Carrott and Brian David Johnson. Sebastopol, CA: O'Reilly, 2013. 67-87.

---. *Boneshaker*. New York: Tor Books, 2009.

Sarat. "What is Steampunk?" *Airships, Anarchists and Anachronisms. Steampunkanarchist.Wordpress.com*. 27 March 2011. p. 1. Web. 30 August 2013.

Shelley, Mary. *Frankenstein*. 1818. Oxford: Oxford University Press, 1993.

Smaggers. "Re: Aether, Magic, Machines." Brass Goggles, 23 April. 2011. Email.

Torrent. "Re: Steampunk and Magic." Brass Goggles. 31 Aug 2007. Email.

Verne, Jules. *Twenty Thousand Leagues Under the Sea*. 1870. Harmondsworth: Penguin, 2007.

Vick, Diana. "Dressing Steampunk." *Squidoo.com*. Web. 9 September 2013.

Ward George B. "Guns and Game in the American West." *Objects of Special Devotion: Fetishism in Popular Culture*. Ed. Ray Broadus Browne. Wisconsin: University of Wisconsin Popular Press, 1982. 151-168.

Weinstock, Geoffrey Andrew. "Goth Fetishism." *Goth: Undead Subculture*. Eds. Michael Bibby and Lauren Goodlad. Durham, NC: Duke University Press, 2007. 375-398.

Wells, H. G. *The Time Machine*. 1895. Harmondsworth: Penguin, 2005.

Wood, Xander. Message to Anna Powell. 9 October 2013. Email.

Contributors

Dr Simone Broders studied English, Computational Linguistics and Italian at the University of Erlangen-Nürnberg and the University of Kent at Canterbury, UK, graduating from the former in February 2004. She obtained her doctorate in 2007 with a thesis on the role of history in Adam Thorpe's novels (published title: *'As if a building was being constructed' – Studien zur Rolle der Geschichte in den Romanen Adam Thorpes* [Münster: LIT, 2008]). She has been a member of the English Studies academic staff at Erlangen since 2007, teaching English and American literature. Her research interests lie in the contemporary novel and the literature of the 'Long' Eighteenth Century. She is currently working on her post-doctoral thesis ('Habilitation'), in which she will examine concepts of curiosity in British literature, with special emphasis on the eighteenth century.

Dr Kerstin Frank has been a lecturer in English literature and culture at the University of Heidelberg since 2008. She completed her doctoral thesis *Die Erneuerung des Romans im Zeichen postmoderner Realitäts-auffassung: Sinnstiftung und Sinnzerstörung in Christine Brooke-Roses Werk* (Trier: WVT, 2008) at the University of Würzburg in 2008 and is currently working on her post-doctoral thesis ('Habilitation') on fantastic and marvellous fiction in the eighteenth century.

Dr Susanne Gruss is a lecturer in English literature and culture at the University of Erlangen-Nürnberg. She has published a monograph on contemporary feminist writing (*The Pleasure of the Feminist Text: Reading Michèle Roberts and Angela Carter*), and written articles on film adaptation, questions of canonization, ecofeminism, Neo-Victorianism, and the Gothic conventions in *Harry Potter*. Her research interests include gender studies, film and media studies, contemporary literature, the intersection of legal discourses and literature, and Jacobean revenge tragedy.

Jeaneen Kish, M.A., is an Adjunct English Instructor at Westmoreland County Community College in Youngwood, PA, USA. She is also currently studying for her Ph.D. in Literature and Criticism at Indiana University of Pennsylvania. She earned her B.A. in English Literature in 1998 and her M.A. in English in 1999, both from Slippery Rock University of Pennsylvania. She has twelve years teaching experience as an adjunct at various colleges and universities in both Texas and Pennsylvania.

Dr Oliver Plaschka obtained his doctorate on pastoral motifs in early and mid twentieth-century fantastic literature (*Verlorene Arkadien: Das pastorale Motiv in der englischen und amerikanischen fantastischen Literatur – H.P. Lovecraft, James Branch Cabell, Mervyn Peake, William Gibson*) at the University of Heidelberg in 2009. His fields of interest also include science fiction and cyberpunk literature. He works as a translator and has published several novels in the fantastic genres.

Dr Anna Powell is Reader in Film and English Studies at Manchester Metropolitan University. Her interests include Film/Philosophy, Gothic affect in film and literature, experimental film and video. She has been researching and teaching Gothic Studies since the early 1990s. Her other research interest is Deleuze and she is the director of *A/V* web journal and a member of the editorial board of *Deleuze Studies*. Her books include *Deleuze and the Horror Film, Deleuze, Altered States and Film* and she co-authored *Teaching the Gothic* with Andrew Smith in 2006. She has also published a range of articles and chapters on Gothic aesthetics and affects in both the arts and popular culture using the technique of schizoanalysis.

Dr Ellen Redling has been a lecturer in English literature and culture at the University of Heidelberg since 2007. She completed her doctorate on Thackeray and Allegory in 2012. Much of her work so far has focused on literary, cultural, transgeneric and intermedial approaches regarding Victorianism, Neo-Victorianism, Romanticism and the Gothic as well as drama from the Renaissance to the present day. She is currently working on her post-doctoral thesis ('Habilitation'), which is entitled "New British

Drama of Ideas: Politics, Ethics and Aesthetics in British Big Issue Plays after 2000".

Prof. Erik Redling teaches American Studies at the Department of English and American Studies at the Martin Luther University Halle-Wittenberg. He completed his dissertation *"Speaking of Dialect": Translating Charles W. Chesnutt's Conjure Tales into Postmodern Systems of Signification* (Würzburg: Königshausen & Neumann, 2006) in 2003 and his post-doctoral thesis ('Habilitation'), *From Mimesis to Metaphor: Intermedial Translations in Jazz Poetry*, in 2009. His main areas of research include Edgar Allan Poe and the American Gothic, literary theory, cognitive theories, intermediality and translation, dialect literature, and Jazz poetry.

Dr Andreas Schardt completed his doctorate on *Gothic Pastoral: Terrible Idylls in Late Nineteenth- and Twentieth-century Literature* at the University of Heidelberg in 2012. He has taught courses on presentation skills and English literature at the Universities of Mannheim and Heidelberg. Among his further research interests are theories of genres and modes, dystopian fiction, contemporary drama and the reception of antiquity in the European literary tradition.

Dr Christian Schneider studied English Literature and Political Science at Ruprecht-Karls-Universität Heidelberg, where he now also teaches, and at the University of Wales Aberystwyth. In 2014, he published his doctoral thesis *Framing Fear: The Gothic Mode in Graphic Literature* (Trier: WVT), introducing a cognitive approach to the particular manifestations of the Gothic in the medium of comics. Besides his work on the Gothic and comics, his research interests include contemporary American fiction, the fantastic and cognitive literary studies.

Franziska Schneider, M.A., studied Scandinavian Studies and German Literature in Tübingen, Germany and Örebro, Sweden, and has been a lecturer in Scandinavian Studies at the University of Freiburg since 2013. She is currently working on her doctoral thesis, which deals with contemporary Scandinavian crime and horror literature, TV productions and films ("Crime Scene, do not cross: Raum, Angst und Transgression im aktuellen skandinavischen Kriminal- und Horrorroman sowie in aktuellen TV-Projekten und Filmen"). Her fields of research also include spatial theory, cognitive poetics and the Gothic.

Susan J. Tyburski, M.A., J.D., is an instructor in the Gender & Women's Studies department of the University of Denver, Colorado. She teaches a wide variety of courses exploring the intersections of law, literature and society, as well as gender studies, writing, critical thinking and communication. She also works as an Administrative Law Judge at Colorado State Personnel Board.

Index of Names